ACADEMIC ADVISING

AND THE FIRST COLLEGE YEAR

D1570306

editors
JENNIFER R. FOX
HOLLY E. MARTIN

Cite as:

Fox, J. R., & Martin, H. E. (Eds.). (2017). *Academic advising and the first college year.* Columbia, SC: University of South Carolina, National Resource Center for The First-Year Experience & Students in Transition and NACADA: The Global Community for Academic Advising.

ISBN: 978-1-942072-00-3

Published by:
National Resource Center for The First-Year Experience and Students in Transition
University of South Carolina
1728 College Street, Columbia, SC 29208
www.sc.edu/fye

The First-Year Experience® is a service mark of the University of South Carolina. A license may be granted upon written request to use the term "The First-Year Experience." This license is not transferable without written approval of the University of South Carolina.

Production Staff for the National Resource Center:
Project Manager: Tracy L. Skipper, Assistant Director for Publications
Design and Production: Allison Minsk, Graphic Artist

Library of Congress Cataloging-in-Publication Data

Names: Fox, Jennifer R., editor. | Martin, Holly E., 1952- editor.
Title: Academic advising and the first college year / Jennifer R. Fox and Holly
   E. Martin, editors.
Description: Columbia, SC : National Resource Center for The First-Year
   Experience & Students in Transition University of South Carolina, [2017]
Identifiers: LCCN 2016043557 | ISBN 9781942072003 (alk. paper)
Subjects: LCSH: Counseling in higher education--United States. | College
   student development programs--United States. | College freshmen--United
   States.
Classification: LCC LB2343 .A298 2017 | DDC 378.1/9--dc23

ABOUT THE SPONSORING ORGANIZATIONS

National Resource Center for The First-Year Experience and Students in Transition

The National Resource Center for The First-Year Experience and Students in Transition was born out of the success of University of South Carolina's much-honored University 101 course and a series of annual conferences focused on the freshman year experience. The momentum created by the educators attending these early conferences paved the way for the development of the National Resource Center, which was established at the University of South Carolina in 1986. As the National Resource Center broadened its focus to include other significant student transitions in higher education, it underwent several name changes, adopting the National Resource Center for The First-Year Experience and Students in Transition in 1998.

Today, the Center collaborates with its institutional partner, University 101 Programs, in pursuit of its mission to advance and support efforts to improve student learning and transitions into and through higher education. We achieve this mission by providing opportunities for the exchange of practical and scholarly information as well as the discussion of trends and issues in our field through convening conferences and other professional development events such as institutes, workshops, and online learning opportunities; publishing scholarly practice books, research reports, a peer-reviewed journal, electronic newsletters, and guides; generating, supporting, and disseminating research and scholarship; hosting visiting scholars; and maintaining several online channels for resource sharing and communication, including a dynamic website, listservs, and social media outlets.

The National Resource Center serves as the trusted expert, internationally recognized leader, and clearinghouse for scholarship, policy, and best practice for all postsecondary student transitions.

Institutional home. The National Resource Center is located at the University of South Carolina's (UofSC) flagship campus in Columbia. Chartered in 1801, UofSC Columbia's mission is twofold: to establish and maintain excellence in its student population, faculty, academic programs, living and learning environment, technological infrastructure, library resources, research and scholarship, public and private support and endowment; and to enhance the industrial, economic, and cultural potential of the state. The Columbia campus offers 311 degree programs through its 14 degree-granting colleges and schools. In fiscal year 2015, faculty generated $243 million in funding for research, outreach, and training programs. UofSC is one of only 32 public universities receiving both Research and Community Engagement designations from the Carnegie Foundation.

NACADA: The Global Community for Academic Advising

NACADA is an association of primary-role advisors, counselors, faculty members, administrators, and students working to enhance the educational development of students.

NACADA promotes and supports quality academic advising in institutions of higher education to enhance the educational development of students. NACADA provides a forum for discussion, debate, and the exchange of ideas pertaining to academic advising through numerous activities and publications. NACADA also serves as an advocate for effective academic advising by providing a Consulting and Speaker Service, an Awards Program, and funding for research related to academic advising.

NACADA evolved from the first National Conference on Academic Advising in 1977 and has over 13,000 members representing all 50 United States and 44 countries. Members represent higher education institutions across the spectrum of Carnegie classifications and include primary-role advisors/counselors, faculty, administrators, and students whose responsibilities include academic advising.

NACADA functions with volunteer leadership with support from the NACADA Executive Office. Members have full voting rights and elect the national board of directors as well as other leaders within the organization. NACADA is designated by the IRS as a 501(c)3 nonprofit educational association incorporated in Kansas.

ACKNOWLEDGMENTS

This book is a joint venture between NACADA: The Global Community for Academic Advising and the National Resource Center for The First-Year Experience and Students in Transition. *Academic Advising and the First College Year* is meant to be a resource for all who advise first-year students every day. It was created to update previous publications for those who advise first-year students. Much has changed in the field since the last publication for advising first-year students was published in 2007 (see Introduction), and many used their years of experience to contribute to this new publication.

We owe a great debt of gratitude to a number of individuals who contributed to the production of this text. We thank our colleagues who reviewed the book's outline and initial chapter drafts. Their feedback and suggestions truly shaped this volume. They include the following individuals:

Melinda Anderson, Virginia Commonwealth University

Danalee Brehman, Arizona State University

Maria Calkins, Becker College

Rebecca Cofer, Abraham Baldwin Agricultural College

Kyle Ellis, University of Mississippi

Shelly Gehrke, Emporia State University

Stephen O'Connell, University of Central Florida

Cynthia Pascal, Northern Virginia Community College

Rich Robbins, Bucknell University

Kyle Ross, Eastern Washington University

Marion Schwartz, Pennsylvania State University

Nora Scobie, University of Louisville

David Spight, University of Texas

Brenna Tonelli, Arizona State University

We also thank the authors for sharing their expertise in advising first-year students. Each was able to take an outline and turn it into a fully expanded chapter that will help advisors in their daily work and ultimately benefit students. The authors took reviewer suggestions and our content edits and spent a great deal of time crafting their work to create a cohesive whole that expands the literature on first-year advising.

We thank all those who worked hard on the production of this book, including Tracy Skipper, the editor at the National Resource Center for The First-Year Experience and Students in Transition. Tracy's thorough review of the chapters was key in shaping the work. We also thank everyone at the NACADA Executive Office for their support, especially Executive Director Charlie Nutt.

Finally, we could not have completed this book without the guidance and hard work of both Nancy Vesta, NACADA's copy editor, and Marsha A. Miller, the volume's managing editor. Both spent many hours talking through each page of this volume with us, and the book simply would not exist without them.

Jennifer R. Fox
Holly E. Martin
Editors

CONTENTS

Section I: Advising First-Year Students

Section II: Advising for Student Transitions

Section III: Advising for Student Engagement

Section IV: Strengthening First-Year Advising Practices

FIGURES

INTRODUCTION

Addressing Changes in Advising First-Year Students

Jennifer R. Fox and Holly E. Martin

The importance of excellence in advising first-year students has been recognized for many years (Gardner, 1986) and remains central to student academic success (Complete College America, 2016). During their first college year, most students are inundated with challenges that require them to learn and develop the skills needed to negotiate their new environment and discover a major that fits their talents and needs. Advisors of first-year students guide their transition, helping students develop the competencies necessary to negotiate their complex environment (King, 2007) and generate academic plans for timely graduation and appropriate career choices. Advisors help students learn to make the most of their college years, not merely by completing requirements toward a degree but also by growing intellectually and developing all aspects of their identity (Kincanon, 2009). As discussed throughout this volume, the increasing diversity of incoming students combined with heightened emphasis on timely college graduation makes quality first-year advising a crucial component for higher education.

In 1995, NACADA: The Global Community for Academic Advising (then the National Academic Advising Association) and the National Resource Center for The First-Year Experience and Students in Transition (National Resource Center) collaborated to publish a book for academic advisors of first-year students, *First-Year Academic Advising: Patterns in the Present, Pathways to the Future* (Upcraft & Kramer, 1995). In 2007, these two organizations published a new text to reflect the changed environment and theoretical landscape of advising students in their first college year, *Academic Advising: New Insights for Teaching and Learning in the First Year* (Hunter, McCalla-Wriggins, & White, 2007). Because of continued and rapid changes in higher education over the last 10 years, we present *Academic Advising and the First College Year* with academic advisors as the principal audience.

More than ever, first-year students need excellent advising. Since 2007, dramatic changes to the postsecondary environment as well as rapidly evolving profiles and needs of first-year students (Pryor, Hurtado, Saenz, Santos, & Korn, 2007) require reexamination of practice. For example, first-year students arrive on campus with wider differences in financial circumstances and academic preparation than their predecessors (Camera, 2016). In addition, a substantial number of first-year students deal with the transition to college while managing mental health challenges (American Psychological Association, 2013) or learning disabilities (Council for Learning Disabilities, 2010). Adult learners, military veterans, first in the family to attend, individuals from historically underrepresented groups, international students, and others with unique or nonmajority characteristics now make up a large percentage of current student groups.

Although not shown in the typical demographic profile, and therefore less evident to some, students today experience pressure to attend college and to finish with a credential in short order. Since 2009, U.S. policy makers have focused on increasing the number of college graduates (Obama, 2009), which has spurred organizations such as Complete College America (2015) to "work with states to significantly increase the number of Americans with quality career certificates or college degrees" (para. 1). Research into the factors that increase persistence was mandated by Congress (Ross et al., 2012) at the same time that Klepfer and Hull (2012) published their findings that "the strength of academic advising [is] a factor in persistence. College students who reported visiting with advisors frequently had a much greater likelihood of persisting than their peers who never did" (para. 17).

The need to persist and finish college within restricted time limits has raised the stakes for many students. As explained in chapter 1, state funding of educational institutions has dropped while costs have risen for various reasons (Woodhouse, 2015). As a result, students shoulder a greater burden than those in the past while their ability to secure federal student loans increasingly depends on swift progress toward a degree. In addition, the institutional definition of success, often measured by persistence within particular majors and graduation rates, and the student's definition of success, in terms of career and learning goals, may conflict. Wallace and Wallace (2016) explained, "When institutional circumstances interfere with students' success, advisors act as advocates, serving as mediators and facilitators who leverage their specialized knowledge and experience to help students remove obstacles in the path to success" (p. 98).

Advisors not only need to understand the precarious funding situation but also must recognize the specialized knowledge and experience necessary to advance students through their program of study. They must develop theory and practice based on recent research in academic advising, educational psychology, and other areas of higher education. For example, although referrals to tutoring and counseling remain essential, advisors must gain familiarity with ways to construct advising partnerships across institutional units and help students mitigate stereotype threat, strengthen a sense of belonging, and develop a growth mindset. Only with their own continued self-development can advisors guide students through stressors and setbacks that might otherwise derail their academic careers.

A number of excellent recent publications focus on assisting students and their families during the first year of college, such as *Navigating the First College Year: A Guide for Parents and Families* (Mullendore & Banahan, 2014) and *Academic Advising in the First Year of College: A Guide for Families* (Gordon, Levinson, & Kirkner, 2014). Furthermore, recent studies on theory and best practices for orientation programs, first-year seminars, and engagement practices have been published since 2007, but an updated publication on diverse first-year students, written specifically for academic advisors, that addresses the evolving issues in higher education, emerging theory, and recognized practice has been lacking. Both primary-role and faculty advisors must adjust to the many changes in higher education in the new millennium. The contributors to *Academic Advising and the First College Year* provide advisors some of the current information on demographics, theories, and best practices needed to support first-year students. They also direct advisors to updated resources for staying current with developments in the lives of first-year college students.

This book is organized into four interconnecting sections. The first focuses on the current state of first-year advising, including the emerging concerns of increasingly diverse students and the role of the advisor in this evolving high-stakes academic environment. The authors of the second section identify the challenges and situations of first-year transitions and present information on ways to advise students through them. The third section details means of encouraging students to engage in their educations via academic planning and advising, and the final section is directed toward those tools and support structures, including assessment, proven most important in delivering quality advising to first-year students. In each section the authors have kept both primary-role, faculty, and other advisors in mind and have highlighted new developments in first-year advising. In each chapter, Aiming for Excellence discussion questions and activities give advisors concrete ideas and strategies for expanding their knowledge and applying the readings to their advising practice.

Section I explains the rising importance of advising for first-year students and ways advisors support them through the application of appropriate theory. The first chapter examines the developing enrollment trends and constraints that modern circumstances put on students. It also focuses on the advising challenges associated with changes in the matriculating populations, stakeholder expectations for higher education, and mechanisms of financial support.

The second chapter follows up on the theme of change by offering summaries of the theories that explain the universal experiences of first-year college students. It focuses on advising theory applicable to the changing student body and accounts for recent research in advising, educational psychology, and higher education. The theories and practices proven most useful in supporting first-year students, especially the merits of proactive, developmental, and learning-centered advising, are articulated in depth.

The contributors of section II are concerned with transitions at the heart of the first-year student's experience and of critical importance for advisors to understand. Chapter 3 focuses on the adjustment to college life and describes the new theories and best practices advisors use to assist first-year students with transitioning and attendant challenges. By focusing on the experiences of students in two-year colleges, the authors of chapter 4 expound on the shared needs of most first-year students while featuring the unique demands associated with advising in two-year institutions.

To satisfy stakeholders, including parents and students, who have placed great importance on earning a college degree, proactive advising may prove most effective, especially for keeping underprepared first-year students on track for academic success. Proactive advising offers directed assistance with transition difficulties for both those who struggled in high school and those surprised that they are underprepared for their present academic situation in college. Chapter 5 offers details on proactive advising and other means of support that help advisors of at-risk and underprepared students assess and address student weaknesses.

In the absence of proactive advising, or even when it is employed, some students will not succeed in their first year of college. Chapter 6 explains the ways advisors can assist first-year students recovering from academic difficulty. It addresses the causes of struggles, including academic underpreparedness, by discussing a rich vein of new research and best practices coming out of educational psychology.

Chapter 7 goes into depth on advising the diverse populations of first-year students that have emerged in the last few decades. Advisors must recognize the specific challenges of students and the demographic profiles of their own institutions as well as those colleges that send or receive students. Advisors with skills to identify and address the multiple dimensions of student identity (e.g., disability, sexual orientation, first-generation status, social class) create the environment that welcomes and encourages diversity. Although impossible to address every type of circumstance advisors will encounter, chapter 7 provides resources and suggestions that help advisors develop the critical consciousness and cultural competency necessary to communicate and guide individuals at risk of feeling marginalized or unsupported.

Section III concentrates on heightening engagement of first-year students. A natural follow-up to the introduction on belonging broached in chapter 7, the discussion in chapter 8 presents both longstanding and emerging techniques for helping first-year students understand and engage in the advising process and in academic planning. Specifically, chapter 8 explains the theory behind and best practices for the learning-centered advising that encourages students to take ownership of their plans and create solid goals for their education. Advisors need to assist diverse first-year students in choosing majors that may lead to satisfying careers; however, because of current economic and political forces, students may feel compelled to choose a major early and stick with it despite growing disinterest in, or minimal talent for, the chosen discipline. This unfortunate situation calls for advisors to employ understanding and honed skills in motivating students to explore all options amid financial, parental, or societal pressures. Chapter 9 explains the signs of and remedies for ameliorating premature foreclosure on a major or career choice while advancing the student toward graduation.

Like those in the preceding sections, the authors of the two chapters in section IV wrote with the primary-role or faculty advisor in mind, but these closing discussions may also pique the interest of advising administrators, deans, and provosts. The section addresses the advising structures and assessment methods that support advisors of first-year students. Chapter 10 focuses primarily on proven and emerging tools and frameworks that advisors use to promote student learning, such as early-warning systems and partnerships. Ongoing evaluation of these tools and support systems keeps the changing needs of first-year students in the forefront of practice. Assessment practices have become more sophisticated and provide information useful to both advisors and supervisors in improving student support. Chapter 11 discusses the ways in which assessment of advising provides relevant information for meeting student needs.

Today's first-year students do not resemble those of the past. In addition, the academic environments, challenges, and pressures have also changed the milieu for students and advisors. Although advising theory and best practices have evolved to meet emerging challenges, advisors must continuously seek to support all first-year students in ways they need and deserve.

References

American Psychological Association. (2013). College students' mental health is a growing concern, survey finds. *The Monitor on Psychology, 44*(6). Retrieved from http://www.apa.org/monitor/2013/06/college-students.aspx

Camera, L. (2016, February 2). For today's college student, the data doesn't cut it. *U.S. News and World Report.* Retrieved from http://www.usnews.com/news/articles/2016-02-02/higher-education-data-doesnt-reflect-majority-of-students

Complete College America. (2015). *Our work.* Retrieved from http://completecollege.org//about-cca/

Complete College America. (2016). *Academic advising and GPS direct.* Retrieved from http://completecollege.org/academic-advising-and-gps-direct/

Council for Learning Disabilities. (2010). *College as a realistic option for students with learning disabilities.* Retrieved from http://www.council-for-learning-disabilities.org/college-as-a-realistic-option-for-students-with-learning-disabilities

Gardner, J. N. (1986). The freshman-year experience. *The Journal of the American Association of Collegiate Registrars and Admissions Officers, 61*(4), 261–274.

Gordon, V. N., Levinson, J., & Kirkner, T. (2014). *Academic advising in the first year of college: A guide for families.* Columbia, SC: University of South Carolina, National Resource Center for The First-Year Experience and Students in Transition.

Hunter, M. S., McCalla-Wriggins, B., & White, E. (Eds.). (2007). *Academic advising: New insights for teaching and learning in the first year* (Monograph No. 46). Columbia, SC: University of South Carolina, National Resource Center for The First-Year Experience and Students in Transition.

Kincanon, K. (2009). *Translating the transformative: Applying transformational and self-authorship pedagogy to advising undecided/exploring students.* Retrieved from http://www.nacada.ksu.edu/tabid/3318/articleType/ArticleView/articleId/647/article.aspx

King, N. (2007, June). *Setting the stage: Foundations of academic advising* [PowerPoint]. NACADA Summer Institute, Burlington, VT.

Klepfer, K., & Hull, J. (2012). *High school rigor and good advice: Setting up students to succeed (at a glance)*. Retrieved from http://www.centerforpubliceducation. org/Main-Menu/Staffingstudents/High-school-rigor-and-good-advice-Setting-up-students-to-succeed#sthash.zPqpn06s.dpuf

Mullendore, R., & Banahan, L. (2014). *Navigating the first college year: A guide for parents and families*. Columbia, SC: University of South Carolina, National Resource Center for The First-Year Experience and Students in Transition.

Obama, B. (2009, February 24). Address to the joint session of Congress [Transcript]. *The New York Times*. Retrieved from http://www.nytimes. com/2009/02/24/us/politics/24obama-text.html?pagewanted=all&_r=0

Pryor, J., Hurtado, S., Saenz, V. B., Santos, J. L., & Korn, W. S. (Eds.). (2007). *The American freshman—forty year trends*. Los Angeles, CA: Higher Education Research Institute. Retrieved from http://www.heri.ucla.edu/PDFs/pubs/ TFS/Trends/Monographs/TheAmericanFreshman40YearTrends.pdf

Ross, T., Kena, G., Rathbun, A., KewalRemani, A., Zhang, J., Kristapovich, P., & Manning, E. (2012, August). *Higher education: Gaps in access and persistence study* (NCES 2012-046). Retrieved from the National Center for Educational Statistics website: https://nces.ed.gov/pubs2012/2012046.pdf

Upcraft, M. L., & Kramer, G. L. (Eds.). (1995). *First-year academic advising: Patterns in the present, pathways to the future* (Monograph No. 18). Columbia, SC: University of South Carolina, National Resource Center for The Freshman Experience and Students in Transition. Retrieved from http://files.eric. ed.gov/fulltext/ED388142.pdf

Wallace, S., & Wallace, B. (2016). Defining student success. In T. J. Grites, M. A. Miller, & J. Givans Voller (Eds.), *Beyond foundations: Developing as a master advisor* (pp. 83–106). San Francisco, CA: Jossey-Bass.

Woodhouse, K. (2015, May 5). Who's to blame for rising tuition? *Inside Higher Ed*. Retrieved from https://www.insidehighered.com/news/2015/05/05/ report-says-administrative-bloat-construction-booms-not-largely-responsible-tuition

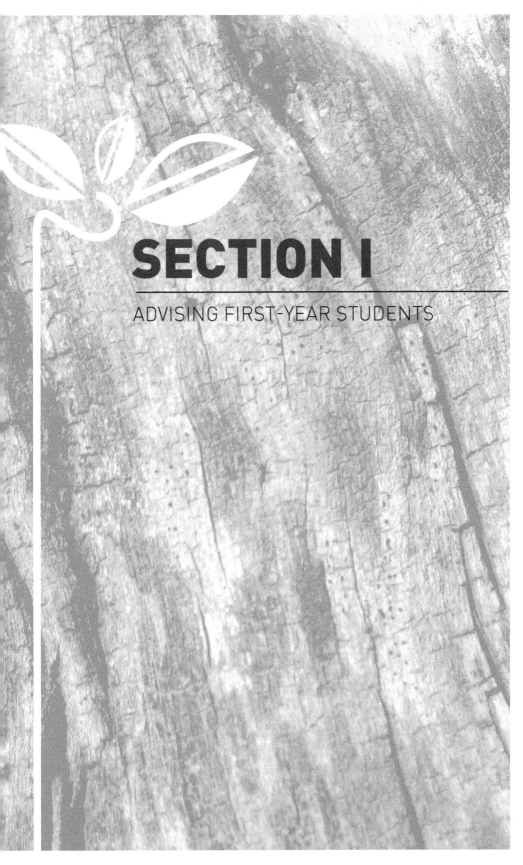

SECTION I

ADVISING FIRST-YEAR STUDENTS

CHAPTER 1

Emerging Concerns
Karen L. Archambault

In the not-so-distant past, first-year students were primarily White, middle- or upper-class 18-year-olds who sought separation from their families and made academic decisions based on their interests and passions rather than on future economic advantage; these times are long gone (Berrett, 2015; Levine & Dean, 2013). Instead, first-year college students from a variety of socioeconomic backgrounds, ethnicities, and ages look to higher education to enhance their career prospects as much (or more) than to cultivate the well-roundedness expected from the undergraduate experience; many also seek the fastest way to degree completion (Eagan et al., 2015). Whether seen as positive or negative, the motivations and matriculation patterns of first-year students today differ from those of their predecessors. In this chapter, I address external forces shaping students' access and transition to higher education, describe the changing demographic profile of the college-going population, and explain the shifting role of academic advisors in response to those changes.

Expanding Costs of Higher Education

The mid-20th century was characterized by a dramatic increase in college access and a commensurate expansion in the purpose of higher education. Millions who would not have gained entry in prior years sought and received financing for higher education (Fuller, 2014). At the beginning of the 21st century, both the intent and the funding of higher education shifted, a trend encouraged by the 2008 recession (Berrett, 2015; Selingo, 2015). Higher education as a necessary public good was increasingly viewed as a personal benefit at the same time that monies from county, state, and federal sources declined and the ratio of federal financial aid to college costs decreased (College Board, 2016; The Pew

Charitable Trusts, 2015). Simultaneously, the cost of higher education rose—in most cases outpacing the rate of inflation—such that the increasing financial burden now falls on students and their families (Douglas-Gabriel, 2015).

Shift of Funding Sources

Funding limitations, as well as the increased costs of education overall, have altered the manner in which families pay for college and affected the choices students make. This may be especially true of Pell Grant recipients. For example, more students attend less expensive colleges, rely on student loans, and choose programs based primarily upon economic benefit and likelihood of degree completion (Eagan et al., 2015). Practitioners may see these changes reflected in the characteristics of those who seek advising because the ability to attend a specific institution will be increasingly based upon funding and decreasingly on skill, ability, resilience, or drive. Although the total amount allocated for Pell Grants has increased, the real dollar value has declined (College Board, 2016; The Pew Charitable Trusts, 2015). When the Pell Grant Program was initiated in 1972, the yearly maximum of $452 per student covered approximately 90% of annual public university tuition on average (American Association of State Colleges & Universities, 1974; FinAid, 2016; Kingkade, 2012). By 2012, however, the grant met only 62% of the costs of an associate degree and 36% of the costs of a bachelor's degree from a public institution. Restrictions implemented in 2012 limited eligibility to 12 semesters (or the equivalent) and eliminated additional funding for summer Pell Grants (Federal Student Aid, n.d.). While aid availability and specific funding may change from year to year, grant aid, relative to tuition rates, will likely never return to the 1970s level (Mortenson, 2012).

According to an Institute for College Access and Success report on cumulative student debt (Reed & Cochrane, 2014), 7 of 10 students graduated in 2013 with loan debt of, on average, $28,400. Reversing the borrowing trend depends on doubling the maximum Pell Grant, increasing state dollars to support higher education, and students and families making better financial decisions (Reed & Cochrane, 2014). Despite some positive changes—including admission of tax information from a prior year to allow for earlier submission of federal financial aid applications (Baker, 2016) and a slight increase in Pell Grants—students will likely continue to depend on loans to attend college.

Effect on Educational Choices

These financial realities affect the matriculation choices of new college students and drive their motivation to progress efficiently through higher education, avoiding unnecessary time in college. As a result, families express a different expectation for the first college year than did their predecessors (Selingo, 2015). While some currently enrolled students may change their minds about majors or career paths multiple times, relatively few approach college as a time for discovery and indecision; furthermore, they may experience significant pressure from families to curtail exploration (Workman, 2015). For example, families expect advising goals to include plans for a career and academic advisors to encourage students to make educational decisions, at least in part, on the basis of projected salary outcomes and financial security (Workman, 2015).

In chapter 9, Leigh Shaffer and Jacqueline Zalewski discuss the concept of foreclosure in which individuals commit to plans despite a lack of understanding about themselves or their career and academic options. They present multiple examples, such as the confident student athlete seeking the easiest means of maintaining eligibility and the surest path to professional status as well as the student pursuing a nursing major despite lack of prerequisite academic skills. Advisors encourage foreclosed students to reflect on the bases for their decisions and to consider additional options rather than settling prematurely on a career or academic path.

As a response to the significant costs of college education and six-year graduation rates, which have hovered below 60% for decades, many colleges have implemented planned degree programs and support systems to improve completion rates and time to degree (Bailey, Smith Jaggars, & Jenkins, 2015; Complete College America, n.d.; National Center for Educational Statistics [NCES], 2014). Others have instituted credit-based strategies to ensure students remain on track to graduation. For example, students at North Carolina public postsecondary institutions face a tuition surcharge of 25% for each credit over a total of 140. Public institutions in Texas and Florida similarly penalize students for excess credits by charging out-of-state tuition when students exceed a certain threshold (Grove, 2007). Although punitive, these strategies encourage not only efficient use of state resources but also timely focus on degree completion (Grove, 2007). Personal financial realities and changes in state and federal policies have forced students and their families to think about the costs associated with time spent in college.

Changing Demographics of First-Year Students

Pursuit of college credentials, increasingly perceived as essential to financial and career success, contributes to changing enrollment patterns in higher education. As a result, first-year students no longer form homogenous on-campus groups of 18-year-olds, fresh from high school, with limited world experience;

instead, college cohorts include individuals who would not have sought higher education a few decades ago (Western Interstate Commission for Higher Education, 2013). Matriculants today include first-time college students from traditionally underrepresented racial and ethnic groups as well as adults (over 24 years), international students with limited knowledge of American culture, and military veterans using post-9/11 GI benefits to complete their college degrees (Hussar & Bailey, 2009; Institute of International Education, 2014; National Center for PTSD, n.d.b). In addition, an increasing number of students who present with physical, intellectual, and developmental disabilities may challenge the resources available at colleges and universities (Raue, Lewis, & Coopersmith, 2011).

Uniquely Skilled: Adults and Military Veterans

Adults comprised 41% of college students in 2012, and enrollment numbers increased by 35% in the prior decade. Furthermore, enrollment by students age 25 and older is expected to rise 20% by 2023, which exceeds the rate of increase for traditional-aged college students (NCES, 2015a). Adult students balancing school with other demands, including those related to family and work situations, present different needs from their traditional-aged counterparts, and they are motivated primarily by career advancement (Francois, 2014). First-time adult students may express concerns about the ability to maintain the pace and grades of classmates with more recent educational experience and may question their own academic aptitude (Minnesota Office of Higher Education, n.d.). In addition, more adult students than others attend part-time, which creates additional challenges for connecting and committing to their institutions (NCES, 2015c).

An increasing number of these college-going adults have recently served in the U. S. military. In 2013, up from 500,000 four years earlier, 1 million military veterans were enrolled in college, and by 2020, the number is projected to increase by 20% (National Center for PTSD, n.d.b). These veterans navigate not only new educational situations but also the complex veterans' benefits system, and some may confront challenges precipitated by their military experiences. For example, the core beliefs that many veterans carry off the battlefield, including respect for hierarchical authority and formal behavior, may make transitioning into a contemporary college campus particularly difficult (National Center for PTSD, n.d.a). In addition, although many demonstrate advanced academic skills, including the ability to connect with faculty members outside the classroom, relatively few veterans participate in internships or other experiential learning opportunities (National Center for PTSD, n.d.a). Finally, veterans may require additional support for unique physical and emotional disabilities unlike those of most civilian counterparts: musculoskeletal and hearing challenges, traumatic brain injuries, posttraumatic stress disorder, and depression. Furthermore, veterans may not seek assistance for these issues (National Center for PTSD, n.d.a).

Otherwise Prepared: International and Dual Enrollment Students

For the approximately 1.2 million students studying in the United States on academic and vocational visas, college enrollment presents opportunities for educational and career advancement unavailable or inaccessible in their home countries (Obst & Forster, n.d.; U.S. Immigration and Customs Enforcement, 2015). These nonnative students must resolve unique challenges, including those associated with visa requirements, cultural adjustments, and language barriers. International students studying in the humanities and liberal arts may feel particularly isolated as most international students study in colleges of business, engineering, math, and computer science (Obst & Forster, n.d.). Furthermore, international students may feel disappointed if their current credentials do not confer particular advantages or serve as preparation in specific academic areas at U.S. institutions.

Like high-achieving international students, some first-year native students bring with them college credits earned during high school, which may affect their expectations for the college experience. Secondary students may receive credit through Advanced Placement or International Baccalaureate tests as well as dual enrollment programs through which they receive both high school and college credits by completing college classes offered on campus, at satellite locations, or online. While the first collaborative partnership between high schools and colleges dates back to the early 20th century, dual enrollment has grown popular in recent years, increasing by 75% between 2002 and 2012 (ACT, 2015; Kleiner & Lewis, 2005; Kruger, 2000; Marken, Gray, Lewis, & Ralph, 2013). While many dual enrollment programs provide students with the opportunity to become immersed in a traditional college academic experience, more than 60% of high schools offer college credit solely on the secondary school campus (Marken et al., 2013). Although not first-time college credit earners, these high school students need much of the same support as those without previous college course work; furthermore, some of these credit earners erroneously believe that they fully understand the demands of the college curriculum.

Adversity Faced by First-Year Students

Although demographics of first-year students changed over the latter decades of the 20th century, current students, especially many of traditional age, experience the transition to college—much like those who have gone before—as a time of development and change. The characteristics students bring to campus shape the kinds of challenges they face and the ways they respond to them, which in turn, influences the likelihood of persistence beyond the first year and to graduation (Ballentine, 2010).

For some students, the transition to a new learning environment presents the greatest obstacle to overcome. Others need to develop self-management skills, such as those associated with waking up, getting to class, and completing assignments without parental guidance. For traditional students, issues related to their newfound independence and age-specific development may surface, and transfer students may seek to uncover and clarify goals. Veterans returning after military service may be rediscovering civilian life, and international students may require additional time and focus to understand the American culture and education system. Moreover, regardless of the academic strengths and accomplishments prior to college entry, first-year students may lack adequate preparation for the academic rigor of higher education (National Center for Public Policy and Higher Education, n.d.). Robbins et al. (2004) demonstrated that academic self-efficacy and motivation, more than involvement, academic skills, or academic goals, serve as strong predictors of high GPA. This finding suggests the need for advisors to support students in developing time management, decision-making, and problem-solving skills.

Social and Psychological Transition

For persistence, first-year students must establish commitment to the institution and gain an understanding of the academic requirements of higher education (Dalton & Crosby, 2014). To maneuver the intellectual part of this transition, students need to develop academic skills for use in the classroom. However, first-time students also face social and psychological transitions, which include becoming members of a new community, determining their position within that community, and navigating their own psychological needs. Advising can provide a connection between student and institution, creating a bridge to successful continuation at the institution for first-year students (Turner & Thompson, 2014) (see chapters 2 and 3).

Much like moving into a new neighborhood, students arrive on campus needing to learn new rules and standards for fitting into the environment because they must meet academic requirements and demonstrate self-efficacy (Krumrei-Mancuso, Newton, Kim, & Wilcox, 2013). Javeed (2013) suggested methods for advisors to teach self-management, including guidance for improving skills, assessing strategies and making adjustments, developing coping mechanisms to control emotions, and reinforcing self-image. Javeed also argued that students can learn task management by strategizing and focusing on engagement and enjoyment rather than dwelling on the perceived drudgery of assignment completion.

First-time students bring issues that complicate advising relationships, and sessions with students may require more time than those with students in years past; however, advisors who encourage and teach self-management push students to stay positive and focused. Effective advisors help students, including those with unique needs, develop skills for coping and support their transition.

Disability

Federal law, such as changes to the Individuals with Disabilities Education Act (IDEA), has created access to college for increasing numbers of students with disabilities. Wolanin and Steele (2004) reported that the number of students with disabilities completing high school increased by more than 17% from 1986 to 2001, and approximately 9% of those students enter higher education with need for support, tripling the percentage of 20th-century students requiring accommodations. The NCES (2015b) indicated that 11% of students in the 2011-2012 academic year reported a disability, and students over 24 years old, independent, and with veteran status made up a larger percentage of those with documented disabilities than independent students of similar age without military experience.

Despite their increased presence on campus, students with disabilities do not graduate at the same rate as their peers without a disability. Furthermore, despite allowances in the law for improved access, not everyone receives the services necessary for an effective transition (Brand & Valent, 2013). Advisors best advocate for students with disabilities by collaborating with them, their families, and support networks to access on- and off-campus resources that provide appropriate services. To help prepare students early for the transition to college, advisors may benefit from connections with K-12 educators.

Underpreparedness

College education is linked to lower unemployment and higher incomes (U.S. Department of Labor, Bureau of Labor Statistics, 2016). As a result, an increasing number of individuals are pursuing higher education (NCES, 2015a), including military veterans, those seeking access through community colleges, and those who in past decades would enter apprenticeships, the workforce, or the military. While many students matriculate fully prepared for the rigor of college-level academics, others lack the prerequisite skills and need significant support.

First-year students, especially those who identify as low-income, minority, or first-generation, may require developmental support (see chapter 5). Underprepared undergraduates are more likely than their peers to depart prior to achieving a credential (Complete College America, 2011), but studies demonstrate that a variety of methods can improve the likelihood of persistence among underprepared students, including interaction between students and faculty members; cocurricular involvement; and development of goals, motivation, and focus (Barbatis, 2010; Martin, Galentino, & Townsend, 2014). These students benefit from proactive approaches by advisors and technological tools, such as early-alert systems.

Evolving Role of Advisors

Because student experiences and needs do not fully resemble those of the past, the role of the advisor has also changed. Long-time advisors tell stories of receiving a course catalog on the first day of work and being sent to meet with students. While still found at some institutions, this practice offers less effective training than it did when student needs and goals reflected a more homogeneous population. Advisors must demonstrate a wide range of skills and knowledge to assist new arrivals to the academy, and they need to ask different questions of the diverse students today than their predecessors posed to advisees in previous generations.

Cuseo (2016) suggested questioning students about external obligations ("Will you have family responsibilities this term?") and about confidence level ("What are you most excited or enthused about now?" "What are you most concerned or worried about now?"). Advisors can discern student values with inquiries, such as "What does living a 'good life' mean to you?" and "How do you define success?" As early as the first encounter, advisors can probe into student expectations of the advising relationship to clarify student goals, interests, support systems, and experiences.

While learning about students and helping them explore, advisors should remain cognizant that, due to rising college costs, interested persons may not condone prolonged indecision. Advisors must also understand the ways in which acculturation challenges faced by international students and native students who identify as other—whether because of race, ethnicity, or prior life experience—shape students' experience of and success in postsecondary education (Archambault, 2015; DiMaria, 2015).

In any case, effective advising connects first-year students to the institution, supports their development, and assists in establishing a sense of institutional belonging (O'Keeffe, 2013). Students require regular and extensive contact with advisors invested in holistic advisee development and who use all available tools to support student growth (Filson & Whittington, 2013). These tools include early-warning systems and retention software that offer assistance to advisors of specific at-risk students. They also provide data support for the advising unit (see chapter 10).

In addition, the continued development of interpersonal skills encourages advisors to move beyond tolerance of the student to embrace all forms of diversity. Advisors recognize that students' many identities (e.g., race/ethnicity, gender, sexual orientation, religion, and socioeconomic status) intersect and that students' challenges change throughout their college years, often as a result of their backgrounds or particular circumstances (Archambault, 2016). Finally, although successful advising is predicated on practitioner knowledge, student perceptions of advisor knowledge affect satisfaction with the advising (Thompson & Prieto, 2013).

AIMING FOR **EXCELLENCE**

The following discussion questions and activities give advisors concrete ideas and strategies for expanding their knowledge and applying the information shared in this chapter to their practice:

- Meet with representatives from the admissions and financial aid offices to understand students' academic and financial profiles and to collaborate on ways to support high-need students.

- Collaborate with on-campus support units, such as the offices of disability support or veterans services, to understand the specific needs of student cohorts.

- Start a departmental or campus book club to discuss literature relevant to first-year students that you advise, particularly those whose demographics reflect a changing campus population.

Summary

For advisors, the changing environment of higher education brings significant pressures to everyday work. In advising first-year students, practitioners must recognize the forces beyond their direct control: Student demographics change and challenge conventional thinking; the fiscal situation of higher education remains volatile; students present with divergent needs. Advisors combat the effects of these emerging concerns to assist first-time college students in defining and reaching their educational goals.

As the remainder of this book reveals, the necessary skill set and knowledge base of effective advisors have expanded in recent years. Advisors serve as resource hubs for students in need of academic, financial, developmental, and psychological support. Therefore, their knowledge about all the available assets in multifaceted areas must remain current if they are to refer students appropriately.

The concerns presented by first-year students give advisors opportunities for growth, and advisors who embrace these experiences will not only advance professionally but will also facilitate the success of current and future students. This book serves as a starting point for the development of the advisor whose improved agency will manifest in their relationships with and outcomes for first-year students.

References

ACT. (2015, December 1). *Using dual enrollment to improve the educational outcomes of high school students.* Retrieved from http://www.act.org/content/act/en/research/using-dual-enrollment.html

American Association of State Colleges & Universities. (1974). *Tuition, room and board survey 1974-75.* Retrieved from ERIC database. (ED097852)

Archambault, K. L. (2015). Developing self-knowledge as a first step toward cultural competence. In P. Folsom, F. Yoder, & J. E. Joslin (Eds.), *The new advisor guidebook: Mastering the art of advising through the first year and beyond* (2nd ed., pp. 185–201). San Francisco, CA: Jossey-Bass.

Archambault, K. L. (2016). Knowing and reaching our students. In T. Grites, J. Givans Voller, & M. A. Miller (Eds.), *Beyond foundations: Becoming a master academic advisor* (pp. 107–122). San Francisco, CA: Jossey-Bass.

Bailey, T., Smith Jaggars, S., & Jenkins, D. (2015). *What we know about guided pathways.* New York, NY: Columbia University, Teachers College, Community College Research Center.

Baker, J. (2016, February 18). *Early FAFSA electronic Announcement #2—Preparing for 2017-2018 early FAFSA and prior-prior year* [Announcement]. Retrieved from http://ifap.ed.gov/eannouncements/021816EarlyFAFSAEA2andPriorPriorYear.html

Ballentine, H. M. (2010). *The relationship between wellness and academic success in first-year college students* (Doctoral dissertation, Virginia Polytechnic Institute and State University). Retrieved from http://scholar.lib.vt.edu/theses/available/etd-05012010-212110/unrestricted/Ballentine_HM_D_2010.pdf

Barbatis, P. (2010). Underprepared, ethnically diverse community college students: Factors contributing to persistence. *Journal of Developmental Education, 33*(3), 14–18, 20, 22, 24.

Berrett, D. (2015, January 26). The day the purpose of college changed. *The Chronicle of Higher Education.* Retrieved from http://chronicle.com/article/The-Day-the-Purpose-of-College/151359/

Brand, B., & Valent, A. (2013). *Improving college and career readiness for students with disabilities.* Retrieved from http://www.ccrscenter.org/sites/default/files/Improving%20College%20and%20Career%20Readiness%20for%20Students%20with%20Disabilities.pdf

College Board. (2016). *Trends in higher education: Maximum and average Pell grants over time.* Retrieved from http://trends.collegeboard.org/student-aid/figures-tables/maximum-and-average-pell-grants-over-time

Complete College America. (n.d.). *Guided pathways to success: Boosting college completion.* Retrieved from http://www.completecollege.org/docs/GPS%20BOOKLET%2006-14%20FINAL.pdf

Complete College America. (2011). *Time is the enemy.* Retrieved from http://www.completecollege.org/docs/Time_Is_the_Enemy.pdf

Cuseo, J. (2016). *How I use the advisee information card.* Retrieved from http://www.nacada.ksu.edu/Resources/Clearinghouse/View-Articles/Creating-a-new-student-intake-form.aspx

Dalton, J., & Crosby, P. C. (2014). The power of personal coaching: Helping first-year students to connect and commit in college. *Journal of College and Character, 15*(2), 59–66. doi: http://dx.doi.org/10.1515/jcc-2014-0010

DiMaria, F. (2015, September 14). Shifting from advising to mentoring for first-year students. *The Hispanic Outlook in Higher Education, 25*(19), 10–12.

Douglas-Gabriel, G. (2015, January 5). Students now pay more of their public university tuition than state governments. *The Washington Post.* Retrieved from https://www.washingtonpost.com/news/get-there/wp/2015/01/05/students-cover-more-of-their-public-university-tuition-now-than-state-governments/

Eagan, K., Stolzenberg, E. B., Ramirez, J. J., Aragon, M. C., Suchard, M. R., & Rios-Aguilar, C. (2015). *The American freshman: National norms fall 2015*. Retrieved from the Higher Education Research Institute website: http://www.heri.ucla.edu/monographs/TheAmericanFreshman2015.pdf

Federal Student Aid. (n.d.). *Federal Pell grants*. Retrieved from https://studentaid.ed.gov/sa/types/grants-scholarships/pell

Filson, C., & Whittington, M. S. (2013). Engaging undergraduate students through academic advising. *NACTA Journal, 57*(4), 10–17.

FinAid. (2016). *Pell grant historical figures*. Retrieved from http://www.finaid.org/educators/pellgrant.phtml

Francois, E. J. (2014). Motivational orientations of non-traditional adult students to enroll in a degree-seeking program. *New Horizons in Adult Education & Human Resource Development, 26*(2), 19–35.

Fuller, M. B. (2014). A history of financial aid to students. *Journal of Student Financial Aid, 44*(1), 42–68. Retrieved from http://publications.nasfaa.org/cgi/viewcontent.cgi?article=1078&context=jsfa

Grove, J. (2007). *Focus on state policies limiting excess undergraduate credit hours* (The SREB Focus Series, No. 07S05). Retrieved from the Southern Regional Education Board website: http://publications.sreb.org/2007/07S05_Credit_Hours.pdf

Hussar, W. J., & Bailey, T. M. (2009). *Projections of education statistics to 2018* (NCES 2009-062). Retrieved from National Center for Education Statistics website: http://nces.ed.gov/pubs2009/2009062.pdf

Institute of International Education. (2014). *Open doors report: Fast facts*. Retrieved from http://www.iie.org/~/media/Files/Corporate/Open-Doors/Fast-Facts/Fast-Facts-2014.pdf

Javeed, S. (2013, June). "How am I doing?" Self-management and resiliency as keys to student motivation. *Academic Advising Today, 36*(2). Retrieved from https://www.nacada.ksu.edu/Resources/Academic-Advising-Today/View-Articles/-%E2%80%9CHow-am-I-doing%E2%80%9D-Self-management-and-Resiliency-as-Keys-to-Student-Motivation.aspx

Kingkade, T. (2012, August 29). Pell grants cover smallest portion of college costs in history as GOP calls for cuts. *Huffington Post*. Retrieved from http://www.huffingtonpost.com/2012/08/27/pell-grants-college-costs_n_1835081.html

Kleiner, B., & Lewis, L. (2005). *Dual enrollment of high school students at postsecondary institutions: 2002–03*. Washington, DC: National Center for Education Statistics.

Kruger, L. (2000). *An analysis of the costs and savings of the concurrent enrollment program at Salt Lake Community College* (Doctoral dissertation, Brigham Young University). Retrieved from http://files.eric.ed.gov/fulltext/ED457947.pdf

Krumrei-Mancuso, E., Newton, F. B., Kim, E., & Wilcox, D. (2013). Psychosocial factors predicting first-year college student success. *Journal of College Student Development, 54*(3), 247–266.

Levine, A., & Dean, D. R. (2013). Five ways today's students are radically changing our colleges. *Trusteeship Magazine, 21*(6). Retrieved from http://agb.org/trusteeship/2013/11/5-ways-todays-students-are-radically-changing-our-colleges

Marken, S., Gray, L., Lewis, L., & Ralph, J. (2013). *Dual enrollment programs and courses for high school students at postsecondary institutions: 2010-2011.* Washington, DC: National Center for Education Statistics.

Martin, K., Galentino, R., & Townsend, L. (2014). Community college student success: The role of motivation and self-empowerment. *Community College Review, 42*(3), 221–241.

Minnesota Office of Higher Education. (n.d.). *Common concerns for adult students.* Retrieved from http://www.ohe.state.mn.us/mPg.cfm?pageID=673

Mortenson, T. G. (2012). *State funding: A race to the bottom.* Retrieved from http://www.acenet.edu/the-presidency/columns-and-features/Pages/state-funding-a-race-to-the-bottom.aspx

National Center for Education Statistics. (2014). *Table 326.10. Graduation rate from first institution attended for first-time, full-time bachelor's degree-seeking students at 4-year postsecondary institutions, by race/ethnicity, time to completion, sex, control of institution, and acceptance rate: Selected cohort entry years, 1996 through 2007.* Retrieved from https://nces.ed.gov/programs/digest/d14/tables/dt14_326.10.asp

National Center for Education Statistics. (2015a). *Digest of education statistics, 2013, chapter 3.* Retrieved from http://nces.ed.gov/programs/digest/d13/ch_3.asp

National Center for Education Statistics. (2015b). *Fast facts: Students with disabilities* (NCES 2015-011). Retrieved from https://nces.ed.gov/programs/digest/d13/tables/dt13_303.40.asp?referer=report

National Center for Education Statistics. (2015c). *Table 303.40. Total fall enrollment in degree-granting postsecondary institutions, by attendance status, sex, and age: Selected years, 1970 through 2023* (NCES 2015-011). Retrieved from http://nces.ed.gov/programs/digest/d13/ch_3.asp?referer=report

National Center for PTSD. (n.d.a). *What are common adjustment experiences?* Retrieved from http://www.mentalhealth.va.gov/studentveteran/adjustment. asp#sthash.xvDyZdQI.dpbs

National Center for PTSD. (n.d.b). *Who are today's student veterans?* Retrieved from http://www.mentalhealth.va.gov/studentveteran/studentvets.asp#sthash.3tcCk2A4.dpbs

National Center for Public Policy and Higher Education. (n.d.). *Beyond the rhetoric: Driving college readiness through coherent state policy.* Retrieved from http://www.highereducation.org/reports/college_readiness/gap.shtml

Obst, D., & Forster, J. (n.d.). *Perceptions of European higher education in third countries* (Country Report: USA). Retrieved from the Institute of International Education website: http://www.iie.org/~/media/Files/Corporate/Publications/International-Students-in-the-US.pdf?la=en

O'Keeffe, P. (2013). A sense of belonging: Improving student retention. *College Student Journal, 47*(4), 605–613.

The Pew Charitable Trusts. (2015). *Federal and state funding of higher education: A changing landscape.* Retrieved from http://www.pewtrusts.org/~/media/assets/2015/06/federal_state_funding_higher_education_final.pdf

Raue, K., Lewis, L., & Coopersmith, J. (2011). *Students with disabilities at degree-granting postsecondary institutions* (NCES 2011-018). Retrieved from the National Center for Education Statistics website: http://nces.ed.gov/pubs2011/2011018.pdf

Reed, M., & Cochrane, D. (2014). *Student debt and the class of 2013.* The Institute for College Access & Success (9th Annual Report). Retrieved from http://ticas.org/sites/default/files/legacy/fckfiles/pub/classof2013.pdf

Robbins, S. B., Lauver, K., Le, H., Davis, D., Langley, R., & Carlstrom, A. (2004). Do psychosocial and study skill factors predict college outcomes? A meta-analysis. *Psychological Bulletin, 130*(2), 261–288. Retrieved from http://ww.mrmont.com/teachers/self-Predictorsofsuccess2.pdf

Selingo, J. J. (2015, February 2). What's the purpose of college: A job or an education? *The Washington Post.* Retrieved from https://www.washingtonpost.com/news/grade-point/wp/2015/02/02/whats-the-purpose-of-college-a-job-or-an-education/

Thompson, L. R., & Prieto, L. C. (2013). Improving retention among college students: Investigating the utilization of virtualized advising. *Academy of Educational Leadership Journal, 17*(4), 13–26.

Turner, P., & Thompson, E. (2014). College retention initiatives meeting the needs of millennial freshman students. *College Student Journal, 48*(1), 94–104.

U.S. Department of Labor, Bureau of Labor Statistics. (2016). *Earnings and unemployment rates by educational attainment.* Retrieved from http://www.bls.gov/emp/ep_chart_001.htm

U.S. Immigration and Customs Enforcement. (2015). *Student and exchange visitor information system: SEVIS by the numbers general summary, quarterly review, November 2015.* Retrieved from https://www.ice.gov/sites/default/files/documents/Report/2015/sevis-bythenumbers-dec15.pdf

Western Interstate Commission for Higher Education. (2013, April). Demography as destiny: Policy considerations in enrollment management. *Policy Insights.* Retrieved from http://www.wiche.edu/info/publications/PI-knocking2013.pdf

Wolanin, T. R., & Steele, P. E. (2004). *Higher education opportunities for students with disabilities: A primer for policymakers.* Washington, DC: Institute for Higher Education Policy. Retrieved from http://files.eric.ed.gov/fulltext/ED485430.pdf

Workman, J. L. (2015). Parental influence on exploratory students' college choice, major, and career decision making. *College Student Journal, 49*(1), 23–30.

CHAPTER 2

The Role of the Academic Advisor in the First Year

Joanne Damminger and Melissa Rakes

The transition to college can be overwhelming for many students who know little about maneuvering complex higher education systems or who lack experience connecting thoughts about their education to future career goals. They may also feel lost as they separate from their previous environments. Although they may not consider the multiple dimensions of a successful college transition, students show up with expectations for graduation. To negotiate this transition, first-year students need encouragement to get involved and support to feel connected to the institution (Bigger, 2005; McClenney & Arnsparger, 2012; Tinto, 1993).

Academic advisors assist new students in successful transitions and help them recognize and accept responsibility as active participants in their educational journeys. Specifically, through partnership with advisees (Wallace, 2007), advisors assist students in "making intentional connections, creating coherence out of the disparate parts of the curriculum, reflecting on the similarities and differences among ways of knowing and how they complement each other" (Lowenstein, 2013, p. 256).

In this chapter, we define first-year advising and explain it as an important element for student success. We describe advisors' and students' responsibilities in the advising process and highlight various approaches proven effective for helping first-year students create educational plans.

Defining First-Year Advising

Advising as a student-centered process facilitates goal setting and planning by first-year undergraduates so they can identify and achieve their educational objectives (McClenney & Arnsparger, 2012). Effective advisors build trusting relationships with advisees, which they leverage when coconstructing road maps for an educational journey that culminates in a degree or credential.

Despite the acknowledged importance of advising for student success, developing an operational definition of academic advising is complicated by the numerous types of advising programs and the unique values, missions, goals, and program objectives of specific institutions in which they are based (Campbell, 2008; Habley, 1997). Several documents created by NACADA: The Global Community for Academic Advising (NACADA) benefit those defining advising, creating effective advising programs, and informing first-year advising practice. These documents, referred to as the *three pillars of advising*, need be integrated into practice as part of the toolbox of every first-year advisor (Folsom, 2015):

- *NACADA Statement of Core Values of Academic Advising* (NACADA, 2005; hereafter, NACADA Core Values),

- *Academic Advising Programs CAS Standards and Guidelines* (Council for the Advancement of Standards in Higher Education, 2015; hereafter, CAS Standards), and

- *NACADA Concept of Academic Advising* (NACADA, 2006; hereafter, NACADA Concept of Advising).

The NACADA Core Values articulate beliefs that influence and guide advising practice and serve as reminders of advisors' responsibilities to themselves as well as to their students, colleagues, society, and institutions (NACADA, 2005). The CAS Standards outline principles for devising advising programs and provide guidelines for assessing and improving advising practice (CAS, 2015). The NACADA Concept of Advising (Figure 2.1) affirms the perspective of advising as teaching and features three components: curriculum, pedagogy, and student learning outcomes (NACADA, 2006). Together these components provide a three-prong framework for understanding the integral connection of advising to the mission of teaching and learning in higher education.

According to the NACADA Concept of Advising, a "series of intentional interactions with a curriculum, pedagogy, and set of student learning outcomes" describe the advising process (NACADA, 2006, para. 11). The advising curriculum offers a set of informational concepts that advisees need to know, including ideals of advising and higher education in general. It also includes the procedures and processes specific to each institution.

Figure 2.1. Concept of Academic Advising by NACADA, 2006, NACADA Clearinghouse of Academic Advising Resources. Copyright 2006 NACADA. Used with permission.

The pedagogy of advising includes various methodologies or practices advisors can use to communicate information that students need to reach their goals (NACADA, 2006, para. 10). Approaches, such as advising as teaching as well as developmental, proactive, strengths-based, appreciative, and learning-centered advising, feature modalities that advisors employ to help individuals set and reach their aspirations. All these techniques encourage advisors to build professional relationships grounded in mutual respect, trust, and ethical principles (Drake, Jordan, & Miller, 2013).

Student learning outcomes articulate the skills, knowledge, and ideas an advisee will know, do, and value as a result of effective advising. These outcomes relate to learning and processes that lead to learning; they relate to specific advisee participation in the first and all subsequent years at an institution. When used effectively in advising sessions, the NACADA Concept of Advising helps students to understand and value advising as an integral part of learning and success (NACADA, 2006, para. 12).

Understanding the Challenges

Each year, millions of students attend college for the first time (Ifill et al., 2016). They enter institutions with eagerness and the belief they can succeed in college, but shortly into the term many confront unexpected academic rigor and upsetting culture shifts (McClenney & Arnsparger, 2012), and they may find the advisor to be the first representative of the institution capable of easing their transition (Drake, 2011). While students' preparedness and motivations for attending college differ, advisors recognize some typical characteristics of first-year students that require enhanced self-management skills: academic underpreparation and lack of clear educational and career goals. In addition, some of the challenges an advisor needs to address come from students who demonstrate little familiarity with diversity or may expect immediate responses to their needs (Currie et al., 2012; Gardenshire-Crooks, Collado, & Ray, 2006; Verrell & McCabe, 2015). The advisor needs to be ready to assist the first-year student not only with academic concerns but also with other transitional issues (see chapter 1).

Many first-year students are unprepared for college-level course work as typically determined through standardized tests, placement exams, or other measures. According to Sparks and Malkus (2013), more than 20% of incoming students at all institutions need remediation, and Bailey (2009) reported that 60% of all first-year community college students nationwide were enrolled in at least one developmental course. Advisors explain the importance of developmental requirements for academic success and provide specific reassurance to those reticent to accept remediation (see chapters 4 and 5). Advisors must provide this attentiveness because of the wide variety of preparation among incoming students.

Goal setting is a necessary and often underestimated developmental skill for college success (Congos, 2006). First-year students may enter college without clearly defined goals for their education or career (Gardenshire-Crooks et al., 2006), and students who articulate major and career goals may not have invested sufficient consideration into their decisions. Opinions of family, friends, and favored media personalities may unduly influence a traditional-aged college student who has never engaged in a mature self-evaluation of abilities, values, or interests. Recent high school graduates may also lack knowledge of the labor market (Shaffer & Zalewski, 2011) (see chapter 9). However, despite these shortcomings, students who make an early well-informed decision about academic and career goals likely understand the purpose and interrelationships of their course work, and this awareness increases their motivation and persistence (Jenkins & Cho, 2012). For this reason, students need robust guidance to select majors and successfully develop and execute plans to complete programs (Rosenbaum, Deil-Amen, & Person, 2006).

Students' abilities to expand their comfort zones are also vital to their success (Harding, 2013). First-year students may interact more readily with others from different racial or ethnic backgrounds than their upper-division counterparts, especially on residential campuses (Locks, Hurtado, Bowman, & Oseguera, 2008), but unaccustomed to the diversity of a college campus, they may not recognize the opportunities afforded by an inclusive campus. Although the range of nationalities, races, religions, sexual orientations, and ages of their peers may initially surprise those from a homogeneous background, students can consider different perspectives and explore their own beliefs in an atmosphere that welcomes diversity. Therefore, an accepting environment, as developed by leaders in the institution, will enhance both academic and interpersonal learning experiences (Light, 2001).

Even as they learn expectations and develop competencies, students anticipate immediacy in their interactions with the institution and staff (Oblinger & Oblinger, 2005). With social media and text messaging among the most prevalent forms of communication in the United States (Newport, 2014), students assume that e-mail and calls will be returned quickly, and they want 24/7 access to answers and advisor availability on short notice. Advisors must clearly outline standard response times so that first-year students understand communication time lines; they also must communicate any changes to these time frames, such as e-mailing students when deadlines change or using auto response explaining longer than normal response times. As student population characteristics and technology preferences for communications shift over time, advisors must stay abreast of first-year student traits and behaviors.

Beginning With the End in Mind

The first college year may prove the most crucial advising period for both advisors and students. In early advising encounters, students begin to develop meaningful connections to the institution and identify support systems that assist them in making a successful transition. Most important, effective academic advising contributes to students' personal and academic growth (Light, 2001), resulting in significant learning that provides a solid foundation for their college experience.

Clearly stated learning outcomes for academic advising identify concepts students are expected to know and the time frame in which they should demonstrate this knowledge (Martin, 2007). Learning outcomes can be classified into cognitive, behavioral, and affective (Robbins & Zarges, 2011):

- *Cognitive learning.* What should students *know* as a result of academic advising? In what ways should students think differently because of advising?

- *Behavioral learning.* What skills should students perform or *do* as a result of academic advising?

- *Affective learning.* What should students *value* and appreciate as result of academic advising?

Advising learning outcomes may reflect specific institution, program, or student population objectives, but some outcomes prove particularly valuable for all first-year students. Sample learning outcomes for first-year advising are listed in Figure 2.2.

Cognitive Learning Outcomes: What should student know as a result of advising?

- Identify graduation requirements.

- Define key college policies, procedures, and dates.

- Describe college rules and expectations (e.g., academic standing and code of conduct).

Behavioral Learning Outcomes: What should student do as a result of advising?

- Use institution's educational technology tools (e.g., self-service system and learning management software).

- Examine ways educational goal aligns with career goal.

- Select appropriate courses to achieve educational goal.

- Use college resources to achieve goals.

Affective Learning Outcomes: What should student value as a result of advising?

- Explain how personal and professional development opportunities (e.g., clubs, leadership roles, internships, civic engagement) help one reach intended goals.

- Value the role of academic advising in helping to achieve educational and professional goals.

Figure 2.2. Examples of advising learning outcomes. Adapted from "Assessment of Academic Advising: A Summary of the Process," by R. Robbins and K. M. Zarges, 2011, *NACADA Clearinghouse on Academic Advising Resources.* Copyright 2011 by NACADA. Used with permission.

Advisors need to map learning outcomes so they can share the expectations with other advisors and students. Maps include the information to learn, where it is obtained, when it needs to be demonstrated, and how it will be measured (Aiken-Wisniewski et al., 2010). (See chapter 11 for an example of a student learning outcome map.) Even after sharing a comprehensive learning outcomes map, advisors must convey information multiple times before the student can proficiently demonstrate the outcome. Just as a mathematics teacher would not teach the Pythagorean theorem once and then expect students to apply the concept successfully in a test, advisors should not expect students to exhibit the learning outcomes after one advising interaction.

Advisor Skills and Characteristics for Effective First-Year Advising

Strong academic advising programs support student development and learning outcomes, such as engagement, persistence, and completion (CAS, 2015). Therefore, academic advisors must develop the appropriate skills to help students achieve the identified learning outcomes. Specifically, they need to demonstrate proficiency in three major areas of advising: informational, conceptual, and relational (Habley, 1994). These components relate to the information relayed to students, the ideas that form the foundation of practice, and the delivery of advising.

Informational Skills

Acting as ambassadors for the institution, academic advisors provide accurate and timely information that first-year students must know to navigate their new environment (Yoder & Joslin, 2015). The specific information needed depends on the institution and the related mission and culture, as well as policies, procedures, regulations, programs of study, curriculum requirements, resources, and guidelines for referral to other departments (Habley, 1994). Perhaps most important, the type of necessary information provided depends on advisors' understanding of college students in general and the characteristics of the student body of the institution, including those in special population groups (Folsom, Joslin, & Yoder, 2005; Kolls, 2015; McClellan, 2007) (see chapters 1 and 7). In all cases, advisors abide by ethical standards and provisions of privacy, such as those outlined in the Family Educational Rights and Privacy Act (known as FERPA) as well as state and institution-specific laws (Damminger, 2015; Rust, 2013).

Conceptual Skills

The conceptual component of academic advising includes the major tenets practitioners must understand to make sense of the purposes, theories, and responsibilities of advising. Nutt (2003) explained the conceptual component of advising as consisting of the theories and major constructs that undergird practice. The conceptual component includes comprehending the major approaches to advising and discerning when to employ each in advising situations. Advisors who have mastered the conceptual nature of effective advising can help students connect the components of their college experience, including academic pursuits, career planning, and degree completion (Folsom et al., 2005; Yoder & Joslin, 2015).

Relational Skills

The relational component of advising refers to the effective interpersonal and communication skills that facilitate professional relationships with advisees (Nutt, 2003). Relational skills for effective advising include positive verbal and nonverbal communications, reflective and attentive listening, effective use of silence, and statement clarification as well as rephrasing, open questioning, and communicating mutual respect, warmth, and caring (Jordan, 2015).

While some advisors naturally and intuitively build relationships and communicate care, others need to learn these behaviors. Although practitioners with strengths in the informational or conceptual advising components may find mastering relational skills the most difficult, advisors can learn such skills by observing these behaviors in role models (Yoder & Joslin, 2015). Through relational skills, advisors establish rapport and build advisor–advisee relationships sustained throughout students' college tenure.

The characteristics required for advising first-year students include those needed by advisors of all students; however, advisors of first-year students may use a few attributes to a greater extent than advisors of more advanced students. For example, because they interact with students without previous college advising experience, advisors for first-year students, whether faculty members or primary-role advisors, must prioritize establishing a welcoming and comfortable environment that communicates their accessibility and willingness to support advisees.

Effective faculty, peer, and primary-role advisors communicate verbally and through body language that they care about students and their success. Academic advising may offer "perhaps the only opportunity for all students to develop a personal, consistent relationship with someone in the institution who cares about them" (Drake, 2011, p. 10). Skills associated with these relational advising components closely resemble counseling techniques, such as active listening, clarifying questions, culturally appropriate eye contact, and referrals that offer support or challenge as necessary to advance a student's learning (Jordan, 2015). Because advising connects students to the campus and conveys to them that someone cares about them (Kuh, Kinzie, Schuh, & Whitt, 2005), advisors must demonstrate student-centered, approachable, and engaging behaviors that build relationships. To accomplish rapport, advisors need to express empathy and support as they communicate to students the expectations for advising and address student inquiries. For example, an advisor of a first-year student may spend time expressing gladness that the student came for advising, explaining the topics they will discuss, and encouraging the student to ask questions and return anytime concerns arise.

In addition to the superior relational skills required to explain the value of academic advising and apply theories of development and transition, the advisor must possess extensive knowledge of the information first-year students need about the institution. Specifically, they need to describe policies and procedures, programs of study, sequences of courses, and support services. The success of the advising relationship depends on advisors providing accurate information. Advisors become the conduit students use to maintain their commitment to complete educational goals (Jordan, 2015).

Advisor Responsibilities and Preparation

Advisors must apply appropriate advising approaches, know the available resources, and understand career and student development theories. Advisors use this knowledge to share supportive resources within and beyond the institution, make accurate referrals, and follow up with students appropriately (Krumrei & Newton, 2009; Roundy, 1992).

Obtaining and Sharing Information

Advisors must prepare for each advising encounter, and before meeting students for the first time, they need to review the students' records for information on previous academic history, college readiness, major declaration (or not), outstanding enrollment requirements, and clues that indicate identification with a special population (Nutt, 2015). For students previously engaged in advising, some of this information should be documented. Many institutions implement an electronic system for maintaining files so that advisors and other educators can share information and perspectives easily and record discussions about student goals and progress (see chapter 10).

By law and best practice, advisors assure confidentiality of shared information and continue building trust. Advisors establish a reputation of reliability by their responsiveness, consistency, knowledge, effectiveness, advocacy, and care for advisees. They assess students' needs and provide information about transitions, developing effective study skills, performing well academically, and overcoming test or other anxieties. These characteristics and practices, important for all advisors, positively affect student participation and satisfaction with advising in the first year (Fox, 2008; Ohrablo, 2014).

In addition to interacting with students face-to-face, advisors must intentionally integrate technology to reach students (Endres & Tisinger, 2007). Students expect to communicate and receive advising information using technology, such as video chat systems, social media, text messaging, instant messaging, podcasts, and blogs (Johnson, 2015; Pellegrin, 2015). Therefore, advisors must stay current on emerging technology and consider ways these tools can support their practice (Steele, 2014) (see chapter 10).

For every advising interaction, the advisor needs to know the student's expectations and hopes for that meeting. To the extent possible, advisors ascertain the reason for student-scheduled appointments, research the answer to potential questions, and prepare informative materials in advance. Advisors structure interactions to achieve designated learning outcomes while also addressing needs that students share. They may request that the student return for advising sessions to discuss timely topics, such as academic progress, course substitutions, or graduation planning. In any case, advisors bear responsibility for communicating the goals of the meeting to the student (Nutt, 2015).

Setting Expectations and Looking Ahead

While establishing goals, advisors must recognize that some students do not know the reasons for advising nor do they present objectives they hope to accomplish during advising (Woolston & Ryan, 2015). New students, in particular, may view advising only as a mandatory requirement or a necessary step to register. They may not recognize the ways that advising can inform the decision making required in the early college years. Therefore, advisors must value academic advising, communicate the important role of it to students, and support a culture of advising at the institution (NACADA, 2005). Advisors need to help students understand all the ways advising can support learning and goal achievement (see chapter 4).

For example, students can explore their academic and career goals in collaboration with their advisor. Through self-assessment of interests, values, and skills, students investigate and affirm interest in academic programs and possible careers. While some institutions offer specialists for career exploration (e.g., a class or career development office), advisors who discuss exploratory outcomes with students encourage them to reflect upon the gained knowledge and experience that match their skills and interests. New students may not have engaged in this type of self-reflection, so advisors must be prepared to prompt students to think deeply and clearly (Gordon, 2006; Mahoney, 2006) (see chapter 9). To assist in this endeavor, advisors can compose open-ended questions to use as necessary, such as

- In what ways does this program of study complement your interests, values, and skills?
- How do your skills relate to those required for success in your major?
- What are your short- and long-term educational and career goals?
- How will _____ major help you reach your career goal?
- In addition to gaining the academic knowledge needed for a degree in this major, what other opportunities or experiences will help you prepare to enter this career?

These probing questions help advisors guide students' self-reflections such that they gain confidence and experience in making informed decisions. Students who gather key information through these open-ended questions also generate knowledge useful in directing their decisions on majors and creating effective educational plans, which include any cocurricular or extracurricular activities that enhance their experience (see chapters 3, 8, and 9).

Students who establish realistic career and major goals early in their academic experience can leverage specialized career services, if offered, most effectively, but prepared advisors often first assist students in connecting educational choices with future career aspirations. Therefore, advisors need familiarity with career exploration resources, regardless of the specialized services available, that can aid students in making career decisions. They may find online resources from vetted content providers, such as those associated with the U.S. Department of Labor, timely and useful:

- America's Career InfoNet provides videos that allow users to explore career clusters and specific careers.
- Career OneStop features resources to explore careers, find training, and search for jobs.
- MyNextMove offers career information and assessment tools.
- The Occupational Outlook Handbook provides a guide to career information.

- O*NET OnLine includes an occupation database that allows users to search, explore, and compare career options.

Although the titles and focus of these specific resources may change over time, advisors offer instrumental help for first-year students learning to make decisions and assume responsibility as active participants in their educational experience. However, as summarized by CAS (2015), "The ultimate responsibility for making decisions about educational plans and life goals should rest with the individual student" (p. 7).

First-Year Student Responsibilities and Preparation

Advisors and students act in partnership in the advising process, and both shoulder responsibilities for successful advising experiences (Wallace, 2007). Advisees should maintain regular communication with their advisors. They should initiate appointments, ask questions when they arise, report progress with action steps, and share obstacles (Nutt, 2015). However, all first-year students need guidance on how and when to schedule appointments as well as the preferred way to communicate with advisors.

As they take responsibility for their decisions and actions, advisees must develop knowledge about programs, resources, requirements, and activities. Advisors help students acquire this knowledge and identify tools to gain additional information (Johnson, 2015); however, to maximize the benefit of advising, students must prepare for individual advising sessions and readily engage in conversations about their goals (Wallace & Wallace, 2015). Therefore, first-year students need to learn the materials to bring to advising sessions, and some will need encouragement to keep an advising folder, notebook, or portfolio, where they save program information and record actions that need to be taken, progress on their objectives, and questions they need to ask.

An advising syllabus offers an effective way to communicate important information to advisees. Following the same format as an institutional syllabus for course content, the advising syllabus identifies the purpose of academic advising, establishes outcomes for it, outlines advisor and student expectations and responsibilities, and provides advisor contact information and other relevant resources (Trabant, 2006) (see chapter 8).

Students who actively accept their role in advising take responsibility for academic and career planning as early as their first year, and therefore, they can build a strong foundation for a successful college experience with the collaborative guidance of academic advisors. First-year students who participate in advising are taught to make intentional connections with the institution, and the experience engenders value for the tools for success that advising offers (Lowenstein, 2005). They learn to set specific goals, create a clear path to achievement, and progress through the steps to reach their ultimate educational goals (see chapter 8). Because of the opportunities that advising offers, the value of students' active involvement in first-year advising cannot be overestimated; advising can make a critical difference in students' success, persistence, retention, and completion.

Approaches for Advising First-Year Students

Advisors, like classroom teachers, must employ various approaches, or techniques, to meet the individual learning styles and needs of a diverse student population. Individual learners enter into advising partnerships and develop the tools necessary to take responsibility for their own academic, personal, and professional development (Drake et al., 2013). Therefore, advisors must have an operational mastery of different approaches to academic advising and consider ways these techniques support their personal advising practices (Williams, 2007). Advisors may find five approaches particularly effective with first-year students: developmental, proactive, strengths-based, appreciative, and advising as teaching.

Developmental Advising

Developmental advising is based on a consideration for the whole student, including academic, personal, and career aspects (Grites, 2013). An advisor using developmental advising asks appropriate questions to assess students' developmental stages and then assists them with current needs as part of helping them advance to the next developmental stage. Because students enter college at different maturation levels and with different experiences, an advisor must first assess the student, then learn his or her goals, and finally devise a plan with the advisee to meet those goals (O'Banion, 1972/2009). The advising questionnaire featured in chapter 3 provides an excellent tool for assessing a student's developmental needs.

Through this approach, students recognize the value of balancing commitments to their academics, personal lives, and extracurricular involvement. They also perceive challenges and make decisions to overcome them as they approach the next set of important decisions (see chapter 3). Developmental advising encourages students to make sense of their educational choices in relation to the curriculum as well as their career and life goals (Grites, 2013).

Developmental advising can help first-year students learn that the discomfort created by the transition to college is shared by others (see chapter 7), and companionship in this developmental stage can help them sense their own belonging to the new environment. Strayhorn (2012) explained that student identification with the institution creates a sense of belonging and contributes to the perceptions of a college education as a positive or negative experience. Walton (2007) showed that doubts about belonging in college were reduced when students received reassurance that other new students voiced similar uncertainties and that these feelings of uneasiness lessen over time.

As the most comprehensive and fundamental of approaches, developmental advising forms the basis from which many other advising approaches have evolved (Grites, 2013). When used successfully, developmental advising results in "a planned, strategic, intentional use of the curriculum and cocurriculum to maximize the opportunities and value of the undergraduate experience" (Grites, 2013, p. 56).

Effective developmental advising practice provides intentional and timely interactions that assist students in building the self-confidence they need for a successful first year. As students progress, build relationships, and connect to other students, staff, and activities at the institution, they increase the likelihood of persisting toward their educational goals (Astin, 1993).

Proactive Advising

Proactive advising is characterized by intentional and well-timed interactions with students to avert a critical condition or to respond to an emerging or anticipated problem. Through proactive advising, students learn to identify resources to resolve obstacles to success (Varney, 2013).

The proactive advisor does not wait for the first-year student to initiate contact; rather, the advisor reaches out frequently to the student. Some advisors make contact when the institution accepts the student, and others employ proactive advising selectively, such as with students who enroll with lower than average high school grades, known math anxiety, or other issues of underpreparedness as indicated by the need for developmental math or English (see chapter 5). During the first conversation with an underprepared student, the advisor might discuss tutoring, math and writing centers, and other supports known to promote student success. To engage the student further, the proactive advisor may encourage the student to sign a contract committing to a detailed time line for follow-up appointments (Varney, 2013).

Because the defining characteristic involves early communication, proactive advising reflects a combination of various advising approaches. The intrusive nature of it reflects prescriptive advising (Crookston, 1972/2009), in which students receive specific instructions for action, such as the course to take to rectify an academic conflict. However, the outreach aspect of proactive advising looks much like developmental advising, in which advisors meet students' needs at particular phases in their development (Grites, 2013). Proactive advising requires extensive advisor commitment, close monitoring of student progress, frequent student sessions that include assigned tasks, relevant referrals, and vigilant attention to uncovering stumbling blocks to student success (Spann, Spann, & Confer, 1995; Varney 2013).

Strengths-Based Advising

To recognize and remove challenges for students, many advising approaches were developed to address risk factors that prevent students from reaching their goals. However, strengths-based advising offers a unique shift away from a focus on deficiencies to an emphasis on student strengths (Schreiner & Anderson, 2005). As in the developmental approach, advisors ask open-ended questions; however, in the strengths-based practice, the advisor seeks to encourage student reflection on her or his own capacities for success. Questions the strengths-based advisor might ask include the following:

- What are some of your proudest accomplishments?
- Which strengths will help you succeed in college and your career?
- What are your biggest assets?
- What strengths will help you achieve your goal?
- Which subjects do you enjoy the most and come easiest to you?

Advisors use the responses to these questions to identify and affirm strengths as well as to increase students' awareness of their strengths and help them connect strengths to goals. Through this process of articulation and reflection, students learn to develop action plans to achieve their goals and overcome challenges (Schreiner & Anderson, 2005). Therefore, advisors help students recognize the strategies and skills that have worked well for them in the past and apply them in overcoming setbacks or addressing areas of weakness. Through this approach, advisors enhance students' confidence, motivation, sense of belonging, and resiliency (Schreiner & Anderson, 2005).

Appreciative Advising

Appreciative advising, first described and advocated by Bloom, Hutson, and He (2008), is based on both developmental advising and positive psychology. It emphasizes the collaborative relationship between advisor and student. In this model, advisors create a welcoming environment where students feel safe to engage in conversations aimed at maximizing their educational experiences and exceeding any self-limiting expectations. Appreciative advising may prove particularly useful with students nervous about new challenges and uncertain of their abilities. Appreciative advisors ask students to share information including role models, accomplishments, life-shaping events, and dream jobs as a means of connecting advisee strengths and skills to potential career goals. After creating specific goals, the advisor and student meet frequently to codesign a plan for success, eliminate obstacles, and push for excellence (Bloom et al., 2008).

As explained by Bloom et al. (2008), to effectively implement this approach, advisors use the six phases of appreciative advising: disarm, discover, dream, design, deliver, and don't settle. Initially, advisors disarm students by creating a positive first impression and establishing an environment conducive to sharing. Through open-ended questions, the advisor discovers a student's strengths, skills, and abilities. Next, the advisor encourages the student to share dreams for the future, which reveal links between strengths and goals. Together, the advisor and student design a plan and action steps to achieve the goals refined in the dream phase. The student delivers on the action steps with the advisor's continuous support and encouragement. To inspire students to achieve goals and not settle, the advisor challenges the student to raise self-expectations.

Advising as Teaching

The advising as teaching approach is based on a learner-centered philosophy (Lowenstein, 2005). The similarities between effective teaching and advising extend beyond establishment of learning outcomes. Like excellent teachers, excellent advisors develop positive relationships with students in which both parties share responsibility for the outcomes (Kramer, 2003). Advisors mirror quality teaching practices by sequencing topics to facilitate student learning, engaging students in active learning, assessing students' progress and providing feedback, making learning meaningful, encouraging career development, establishing high expectations to support growth, and connecting students with institutional resources (Kramer, 2003; Lowenstein, 2005). In addition, advisors act as teachers by helping students recognize interrelationships

AIMING FOR **EXCELLENCE**

The following discussion questions and activities give advisors concrete ideas and strategies for expanding their knowledge and applying the information shared in this chapter to their practice:

- Host a brown bag lunch for new and experienced faculty and primary-role advisors to discuss policies and procedures that could confuse new students. Brainstorm ways to better communicate and explain processes.

- Create an advisors' network and plan informal sessions in which advisors share experiences and discuss the rewards and challenges of advising first-year students.

- Create a liaison program between primary-role advisors, faculty advisors, and contacts within each program of study to ensure a consistent pipeline of accurate curricular, policy, and procedural information for timely sharing.

- Stay abreast of current research and literature on advising approaches, theories, and promising practices.

- Review the institutional learning outcomes for first-year advising with colleagues. Discuss student progress in demonstrating outcomes and consider ways the outcomes connect to other aspects of the first-year experience and future advising sessions.

across the educational experience and guiding them in reflection on the skills and knowledge developed throughout their interactions with the curriculum (Lowenstein, 2005).

Through the lens of advising as teaching, Drake (2013) analyzed research conducted by Delaney, Johnson, Johnson, and Treslan (2010) showing that sets of behaviors for effective teaching prove equally important for advisors. University students who participated in the study identified nine characteristics as essential for effective teaching: respectful, knowledgeable, approachable, engaging, communicative, organized, responsive, professional, and humorous (Delaney et al., 2010).

To demonstrate respect, the most valued characteristic emerging from the study by Delaney et al. (2010), advisors must know the attributes of new students and employ open-ended questions to identify a particular student's unique set of traits, opportunities, and challenges. Knowing as much as possible about the individual and responding accordingly demonstrates respect, responsiveness, professionalism, and engagement (Drake, 2013).

Advising as teaching is not the only learning-centered approach to advising. Learning-centered approaches, in general, focus on learning as a process that results from students' experiences. The techniques and tools that guide learning do not represent the defining feature of learning-centered advising; rather, any approach that features a learning-centered focus puts the student, not the advisor or a favored advising tool, center stage (Reynolds, 2013) (see chapter 8).

Summary

Successful advisors recognize the importance of first-year advising and implement effective advising practices grounded in sound advising theory. They understand the benefits of advising approaches to students and identify the best delivery to meet a student's needs. To fulfill their responsibilities to students, colleagues, and the institution, advisors demonstrate proficiency in informational, conceptual, and relational skills (NACADA, 2005, 2006). In the process, they teach students to take responsibility for their own education and guide their expectations for college. Effective advisors recognize that students present unique challenges and come from diverse backgrounds, so they seek to increase their own knowledge and strengthen their advising practices through ongoing professional development opportunities.

References

Aiken-Wisniewski, S., Campbell, S., Nutt, C., Robbins, R., Kirk-Kuwaye, M., & Higa, L. (2010). *Guide to assessment in academic advising* (Monograph No. 23). Manhattan, KS: National Academic Advising Association.

Astin, A. W. (1993). What matters in college? *Liberal Education, 79*(4), 4–13.

Bailey, T. (2009). Challenge and opportunity: Rethinking the role and function of developmental education in community college. *New Directions for Community Colleges, 2009*(145), 11–30.

Bigger, J. J. (2005). *Improving the odds for freshman success.* Retrieved from http://www.nacada.ksu.edu/Resources/Clearinghouse/ViewArticles/Advising-first-year-students.aspx

Bloom, J. L., Hutson, B. L., & He, Y. (2008). *The appreciative advising revolution.* Champaign, IL: Stipes.

Campbell, S. M. (2008). Vision, mission, goals, and program objectives for academic advising programs. In V. N. Gordon, W. R. Habley, & T. J. Grites (Eds.), *Academic advising: A comprehensive handbook* (2nd ed., pp. 229–241). San Francisco, CA: Jossey-Bass.

Congos, D. (2006, February 16). The indispensable importance of setting goals in college. *The Learning Center Exchange.* Retrieved from http://www.learningassistance.com/2006/february/indispensable.html

Council for the Advancement of Standards in Higher Education. (2015). *Academic advising programs.* Retrieved from http://standards.cas.edu/getpdf.cfm?PDF=E864D2C4-D655-8F74-2E647CDECD29B7D0

Crookston, B. B. (2009). A developmental view of academic advising as teaching. *NACADA Journal, 29*(1), 78–82. (Reprinted from *Journal of College Student Personnel, 13,* 1972, pp. 12–17)

Currie, L. K., Pisarik, C. T., Ginter, E. J., Glauser, A. S., Hayes, C., & Smit, J. C. (2012). Life skills as a predicator of academic success: An exploratory study. *Psychological Reports, 111*(1), 157–164.

Damminger, J. K. (2015). Ethical issues in advising. In P. Folsom, F. Yoder, & J. E. Joslin (Eds.), *The new advisor guidebook: Mastering the art of academic advising* (2nd ed., pp. 55–66). San Francisco, CA: Jossey-Bass.

Delaney, J. G., Johnson, A. N., Johnson, T. D., & Treslan, D. L. (2010). *Students' perceptions of effective teaching in higher education.* St. John, Newfoundland, Canada: Distance Education and Learning Technologies.

Drake, J. K. (2011). The role of academic advising in student retention and persistence. *About Campus, 16*(3), 8–12.

Drake, J. K. (2013). Advising as teaching and the advisor as teacher in theory and in practice. In J. K. Drake, P. Jordan, & M. A. Miller (Eds.), *Academic advising approaches: Strategies that teach students to make the most of college* (pp. 17–32). San Francisco, CA: Jossey-Bass.

Drake, J. K., Jordan, P., & Miller, M. A. (Eds.). (2013). *Academic advising approaches: Strategies that teach students to make the most of college.* San Francisco, CA: Jossey-Bass.

Endres, J., & Tisinger, D. (2007). *Digital distractions: College students in the 21st century.* Retrieved from http://www.nacada.ksu.edu/Resources/Clearinghouse/View-Articles/Advising-the-millenial-generation.aspx#sthash.afqnHhlY.dpuf

Folsom, P. (2015). Mastering the art of advising: Getting started. In P. Folsom, F. Yoder, & J. E. Joslin (Eds.), *The new advisor guidebook: Mastering the art of academic advising* (2nd ed., pp. 3–35). San Francisco, CA: Jossey-Bass.

Folsom, P., Joslin, J., & Yoder, F. (2005). *From advisor training to advisor development: Creating a blueprint for first-year advisors.* Retrieved from http://www.nacada. ksu.edu/Resources/Clearinghouse/View-Articles/Training-Blueprint-for-New-Advisors.aspx

Fox, R. (2008). Delivering one-to-one advising skills and competencies. In V. N. Gordon, W. R. Habley, & T. J. Grites (Eds.), *Academic advising: A comprehensive handbook* (2nd ed., pp. 342–355). San Francisco, CA: Jossey-Bass.

Gardenshire-Crooks, A., Collado, H., & Ray, B. (2006). *A whole 'nother world: Students navigating community college* (Opening Doors Project Report). Retrieved from the MDRC website: http://www.mdrc.org/sites/default/ files/OD_A_Whole%20_Nother_World_0.pdf

Gordon, V. N. (2006). *Career advising: An academic advisor's guide.* San Francisco, CA: Jossey-Bass.

Grites, T. J. (2013). Developmental academic advising. In J. K. Drake, P. Jordan, & M. A. Miller (Eds.), *Academic advising approaches: Strategies that teach students to make the most of college* (pp. 45–59). San Francisco, CA: Jossey-Bass.

Habley, W. R. (1994). Key concepts in academic advising. In *Summer Institute on Academic Advising session guide* (p. 10). NACADA: The Global Community for Academic Advising, Manhattan, KS.

Habley, W. R. (1997). Organizational models and institutional advising practices. *NACADA Journal, 17*(2), 39–44.

Harding, B. (2013, June). *Expanding your comfort zone: Working with rising potential students.* Presented at the NACADA Summer Institute, Jacksonville, FL. Abstract retrieved from http://www.nacada.ksu.edu/Portals/0/Events/ SummerInst/2013/AB-W1-AZ-Expand-B.pdf

Ifill, N., Radford, A. W., Wu, J., Cataldi, E. F., Wilson, D., & Hill, J. (2016, January). *Persistence and attainment of 2011-12 first-time postsecondary students after 3 years* (NCES 2016-401). Retrieved from the National Center for Education Statistics website: http://nces.ed.gov/pubs2016/2016401.pdf

Jenkins, D., & Cho, S. (2012). *Get with the program: Accelerating community college students' entry into and completion of programs of study* (CCRC Working Paper No. 32). Retrieved from the Community College Research Center website: http://ccrc.tc.columbia.edu/publications/get-with-the-program.html

Johnson, J. (2015). The new professional advisor: Building a solid informational advising component. In P. Folsom, F. Yoder, & J. E. Joslin. (Eds.), *The new advisor guidebook: Mastering the art of academic advising* (2nd ed., pp. 107–123). San Francisco, CA: Jossey-Bass.

Jordan, P. (2015). Effective communication skills. In P. Folsom, F. Yoder, & J. E. Joslin. (Eds.), *The new advisor guidebook: Mastering the art of academic advising.* (2nd ed., pp. 213–229). San Francisco, CA: Jossey-Bass.

Kolls, S. (2015). Informational component: Learning about advisees—putting together the puzzle. In P. Folsom, F. Yoder, & J. E. Joslin. (Eds.), *The new advisor guidebook: Mastering the art of academic advising* (2nd ed., pp. 177–184). San Francisco, CA: Jossey-Bass.

Kramer, G. (2003). Advising as teaching. In G. Kramer (Ed.), *Faculty advising examined* (pp. 1–22). Bolton, MA: Anker.

Krumrei, E. J., & Newton, F. B. (2009). *The puzzle of college students' success: Fitting the counseling and advising pieces together.* Retrieved from http://www.nacada.ksu.edu/Resources/Clearinghouse/View-Articles/How-counseling-and-advising-fit-together.aspx

Kuh, G., Kinzie, J., Schuh, J., & Whitt, E. (Eds.). (2005). *Student success in college: Creating conditions that matter.* San Francisco, CA: Jossey-Bass.

Light, R. L. (2001). *Making the most of college: Students speak their minds.* Cambridge, MA: Harvard University Press.

Locks, A. M., Hurtado, S., Bowman, N. A., & Oseguera, L. (2008). Extending notions of campus climate and diversity to students' transition to college. *The Review of Higher Education, 31*(3), 257–285.

Lowenstein, M. (2005). If advising is teaching, what do advisors teach? *NACADA Journal, 25*(2), 66–73.

Lowenstein, M. (2013). Envisioning the future. In J. K. Drake, P. Jordan, & M. A. Miller (Eds.), *Academic advising approaches: Strategies that teach students to make the most of college* (pp. 243–258). San Francisco, CA: Jossey-Bass.

Mahoney, E. (2006). Career advising competencies. In K. Hughey, D. Burton Nelson, J. Damminger, & B. McCalla-Wriggins (Eds.), *The handbook of career advising* (pp. 48–67). San Francisco, CA: Jossey-Bass.

Martin, H. (2007). *Constructing learning objectives for academic advising.* Retrieved from http://www.nacada.ksu.edu/Resources/Clearinghouse/View-Articles/Constructing-student-learning-outcomes.aspx

McClellan, J. L. (2007). *Content components for advisor training: Revisited.* Retrieved from http://www.nacada.ksu.edu/Resources/Clearinghouse/View-Articles/Advisor-Training-Components.aspx

McClenney, K. M., & Arnsparger, A. (2012). *Students speak: Are we listening? Starting right in the community college.* Austin, TX: Center for Community College Student Engagement.

NACADA: The Global Community for Academic Advising. (2005). *NACADA statement of core values of academic advising.* Retrieved from http://www.nacada.ksu.edu/Resources/Clearinghouse/View-Articles/Core-values-of-academic-advising.aspx

NACADA: The Global Community for Academic Advising. (2006). *NACADA concept of academic advising*. Retrieved from http://www.nacada.ksu.edu/Resources/Clearinghouse/View-Articles/Concept-of-Academic-Advising-a598.aspx

Newport, F. (2014, November 10). *The new era of communication among Americans*. Retrieved from http://www.gallup.com/poll/179288/new-era-communication-americans.aspx

Nutt, C. L. (2003). Creating advisor-training and development programs. In *Advisor training: Exemplary practices in the development of advisor skills* (Monograph No. 9, pp. 9–16). Manhattan, KS: National Academic Advising Association.

Nutt, C. L. (2015). One-to-one advising. In P. Folsom, F. Yoder, & J. E. Joslin (Eds.), *The new advisor guidebook: Mastering the art of academic advising* (2nd ed., pp. 251–264). San Francisco, CA: Jossey-Bass.

O'Banion, T. (2009). An academic advising model. *NACADA Journal, 29*(1), 83–89. (Reprinted from *Junior College Journal, 42,* 1972, pp. 62, 63, 66–69)

Oblinger, D., & Oblinger, J. L. (2005). Is it age or IT [*sic*]: First steps toward understanding the Net Generation. In D. Oblinger & J. L. Oblinger (Eds.), *Educating the Net generation*. Retrieved from https://net.educause.edu/ir/library/pdf/pub7101.pdf

Ohrablo, S. (2014). *Advising is more than a yes/no business: How to establish rapport and trust with your students*. Retrieved from http://www.nacada.ksu.edu/Resources/Clearinghouse/View-Articles/Advising-is-More-Than-a-YesNo-Business--How-to-Establish-Rapport-and-Trust-with-Your-Students.aspx

Pellegrin, J. (2015). Advising online. In P. Folsom, F. Yoder, & J. E. Joslin (Eds.), *The new advisor guidebook: Mastering the art of academic advising* (2nd ed., pp. 289–298). San Francisco, CA: Jossey-Bass.

Reynolds, M. M. (2013). Learning-centered advising. In J. K. Drake, P. Jordan, & M. A. Miller (Eds.), *Academic advising approaches: Strategies that teach students to make the most of college* (pp. 33–43). San Francisco, CA: Jossey-Bass.

Robbins, R., & Zarges, K. (2011). *Assessment of academic advising: A summary of the process*. Retrieved from http://www.nacada.ksu.edu/Resources/Clearinghouse/View-Articles/Assessment-of-academic-advising.aspx

Rosenbaum, J. E., Deil-Amen, R., & Person, A. E. (2006). *After admission: From college access to college success*. New York, NY: Russell Sage.

Roundy, J. (1992). Tips on making effective referrals in academic advising. *Academic Advising News, 14*(2). Retrieved from https://www.nacada.ksu.edu/Resources/Clearinghouse/View-Articles/Tips-on-making-effective-referrals.aspx

Rust, M. M. (2013). Legal issues in academic advising. In P. Folsom, F. Yoder, & J. E. Joslin (Eds.), *The new advisor guidebook: Mastering the art of academic advising* (2nd ed., pp. 159–176). San Francisco, CA: Jossey-Bass.

Schreiner, L. A., & Anderson, E. C. (2005). Strengths-based advising: A new lens for higher education. *NACADA Journal, 25*(2), 20–29.

Shaffer, L. S., & Zalewski, J. M. (2011). "It's what I have always wanted to do." Advising the foreclosure student. *NACADA Journal, 31*(2), 62–77.

Spann, N. G., Spann, M. G., Jr., & Confer, L. S. (1995). Advising underprepared first-year students. In M. L. Upcraft & G. L. Kramer (Eds.), *First-year academic advising: Patterns in the present, pathways to the future* (Monograph No. 18). Columbia, SC: University of South Carolina, National Resource Center for The Freshman Year Experience and Students in Transition and the National Academic Advising Association.

Sparks, D., & Malkus, N. (2013, January). First-year undergraduate remedial course taking: 1999–2000, 2003–04, 2007–08. *Statistics in brief.* Retrieved from http://nces.ed.gov/pubs2013/2013013.pdf

Steele, G. E. (2014). *Intentional use of technology for academic advising.* Retrieved from http://www.nacada.ksu.edu/Resources/Clearinghouse/View-Articles/Intentional-use-of-technology-for-academic-advising.aspx

Strayhorn, T. L. (2012). *College students' sense of belonging: A key to educational success for all students.* New York, NY: Routledge.

Tinto, V. (1993). *Leaving college: Rethinking the causes of student attrition* (2nd ed.). Chicago, IL: University of Chicago Press.

Trabant, T. D. (2006). *Advising Syllabus 101.* Retrieved from http://www.nacada.ksu.edu/Resources/Clearinghouse/View-Articles/Creating-an-Advising-Syllabus.aspx#sthash.a6CQJxJE.dpuf

Varney, J. (2013). Proactive advising. In J. K. Drake, P. Jordan, & M. A. Miller (Eds.), *Academic advising approaches: Strategies that teach students to make the most of college* (pp. 137–154). San Francisco, CA: Jossey-Bass.

Verrell, P. A., & McCabe, N. R. (2015). In their own words: Using self-assessment of college readiness to develop strategies for self-regulated learning. *College Teaching, 63*(4), 162–170.

Wallace, S. (2007). Teaching students to become responsible advisees. *Academic Advising Today, 30*(3), pp. 10, 22.

Wallace, S., & Wallace, B. (2015). The faculty advisor: Institutional and external information and knowledge. In P. Folsom, F. Yoder, & J. E. Joslin (Eds.), *The new advisor guidebook: Mastering the art of academic advising* (2nd ed., pp. 125–141). San Francisco, CA: Jossey-Bass.

Walton, G. M. (2007). A question of belonging: Race, social fit, and achievement. *Journal of Personality and Social Psychology, 92*(1), 82–96.

Williams, S. (2007). *From theory to practice: The application of theories of development to academic advising philosophy and practice.* Retrieved from http://www.nacada.ksu.edu/Resources/Clearinghouse/View-Articles/Applying-Theory-to-Advising-Practice.aspx

Woolston, D., & Ryan, R. (2015). Group advising. In P. Folsom, F. Yoder, & J. E. Joslin (Eds.), *The new advisor guidebook: Mastering the art of academic advising* (2nd ed., pp. 273–280). San Francisco, CA: Jossey-Bass.

Yoder, F., & Joslin, J. E. (2015). Advisor growth and development. In P. Folsom, F. Yoder, & J. E. Joslin (Eds.), *The new advisor guidebook: Mastering the art of academic advising* (2nd ed., pp. 301–315). San Francisco, CA: Jossey-Bass.

SECTION II

ADVISING FOR STUDENT TRANSITIONS

CHAPTER 3

Advising Students Through First-Year Transitions

Maura Reynolds

Whether they are confident and well prepared or have doubts about themselves and their academic potential, new students face adjustments as they make the transition to college. When they carefully structure sessions and activities with first-year students and walk alongside them as good company (Baxter Magolda, 2002), advisors can help students negotiate the challenges and opportunities of their new environment, set realistic expectations and goals, and make the most of their time in college.

Although the timing of advising interventions varies, establishing a relationship with first-year students, providing encouragement and support, and connecting them with professors and resources remain important goals of advising (Folsom, Yoder, & Joslin, 2015). This chapter features techniques, theories, and resources for establishing and developing a positive advisor–advisee relationship.

The First Post-enrollment Advising Session

Just as the first meeting of a class sets the tone for the rest of the term, so the first one-to-one advising session with newly enrolled students lays the groundwork for productive teamwork for the rest of the term and into the future. Advisors must overcome the temptation to turn the first meeting with students into an information session; instead, they must begin to establish a relationship with their advisees. Strategies for relationship building at this early stage include learning more about individual students and setting expectations.

Using a Questionnaire to Learn and to Teach

Before the first advising session, advisors can involve students actively by asking them to complete a short (paper or online) questionnaire (see Figure 3.1). The questionnaire encourages students to engage in reflection, self-assessment, and goal setting—skills needed throughout and after college. The instrument gives advisors insight into their advisees, suggests possible topics for future meetings, and creates a record that students and advisors can reference later.

---

1. What were your favorite classes in high school? What are your academic strengths?

2. What are your goals for your first year in college?

3. Are you considering fields of interest (or majors)? If you are, what are they? What attracts you to these area(s)?

4. What do you intend to accomplish in college?

5. What do you most eagerly anticipate in college?

6. What is your greatest academic concern?

7. What two academic skills will you work hardest to improve? Why are these skills important to you?

   ❑ Mathematics

   ❑ Studying

   ❑ Writing

   ❑ Reading

   ❑ Oral communication

   ❑ Time management

   ❑ Other _____

8. What activities outside the classroom interest you?

9. What brings out the best in you? How do you learn best?

10. Is there other information you would like your advisor to know?

Figure 3.1. Example of first-term advising questionnaire for new students.

To advise well, advisors must know their students, their goals, their preferred learning styles, their concerns, and their strengths (De Sousa, 2005, p. 2). Gathering such information before the first meeting establishes a foundation for the advising relationship (see chapter 7). When students share their greatest concerns, for example, advisors can suggest appropriate resources or schedule a follow-up meeting. Although the questionnaire items reveal important information, advisors may find the last question in Figure 3.1 especially valuable: "Is there other information you would like your advisor to know?" The students' responses may provide critical information not revealed elsewhere.

In addition to learning about student concerns, through use of this questionnaire (Figure 3.1) advisors demonstrate their interest in students' objectives and the adjustments they make to fit into the college environment. According to Schreiner, Hulme, Hetzel, and Lopez (2009), "Students who feel both challenged and supported by persons who matter to them … discover an environment that fosters the development of their intrinsic goals" (p. 573). To exert positive influence during the initial transition, effective advisors make time to learn about students new to the institution and lay the groundwork for lasting, trusting relationships (see chapters 1 and 7).

Whether they can offer only a few minutes for the first one-to-one session or enjoy the luxury of a longer appointment, advisors can accomplish much with students who prepared by completing an advising questionnaire. On one hand, if advisors ask these questions during the advising appointment, the student may feel interrogated rather than welcomed. On the other hand, students who complete the instrument before their first advising meeting can take time to respond thoughtfully, and advisors can focus their attention during the appointment on questions and comments that build on the students' responses. As Chickering (2006) pointed out, "[Students'] initial answers may not be very sophisticated. But the important thing is to raise the questions, *to start students thinking this way* from the beginning" (p. 11, emphasis added).

Advisors who cannot offer individual appointments may rely on published demographics and generalized strategies to learn about the students in their charge; however, Bonfiglio (2008) pointed out the shortcomings of this practice and suggested a more telling approach:

Examining lists of characteristics, reading articles and books, or attending workshops that describe how students think or what motivates them are poor substitutes for connecting with students as individuals. Even though it may not be feasible to enjoy a personal conversation with each and every student, it is essential that we take advantage of opportunities for one-on-one dialogue with students; proactively seek out chances to listen to, converse with, and get to know these individuals as the unique persons they are. (p. 32)

When advising is delivered in a group setting, responses to the questionnaire cannot be addressed individually. However, by asking students to complete such a questionnaire, advisors indicate their commitment to learning students' backgrounds and interests, which lays the foundation for future group or individual meetings (see chapter 7).

Setting Expectations

Before and during their first meeting, advisors can dispel the erroneous belief that advising focuses only on scheduling issues and course selection. Labeling the form *Advising Questionnaire* suggests that advising concerns more than scheduling.

Advisors should phrase their inquiries, whether on a questionnaire or in person, in a positive way to target students' strengths rather than their deficiencies (Schreiner et al., 2009). In response to students who want to improve all the skills listed on the questionnaire, advisors teach them to set priorities and target their efforts. To those who initially set goals in terms of a GPA, an understandable metric based on students' high expectations, advisors direct discussion to learning rather than reinforce a focus on grades alone, or they talk about the congruence and connection among students' favorite classes in high school, academic strengths, and goals.

To provide more information about advising, some practitioners give students an advising syllabus or refer them to a website that explains advisor and advisee responsibilities. While such information may help students understand their roles in the advising process, the description must convey a positive tone. Advisors should include the benefits, not just the responsibilities, of advising and suggest some occasions when students might want to meet with their advisor: for example, when celebrating an accomplishment, solving a problem, or talking about classes. Students who recognize advising as an appealing and helpful educational process may consult their advisors freely at times other than registration.

Early Term Advising

Contributing to Skill Development

As the term progresses, advisors focus on developing students' skills and connecting them to resources with just-in-time information. For example, advisors may recognize that first-year students are employing learning strategies used successfully in the past but now are achieving disappointing results. Students who relied primarily on memorization in high school may feel frustrated when faced with essay questions that require lateral thinking in college-level history and psychology classes or may struggle with problems that require application of concepts in new situations typical of college-level math and chemistry courses. Advisors who direct conversations toward learning strategies encourage students to consult their professors about the skills needed to be successful in their classes.

If time permits in an individual or group session, advisors can ask students to consult their syllabi and map out a weekly grid of the term, noting the tests, projects, quizzes, papers, and other assignments for all their classes. Some students can create this grid independently and bring it to the advising appointment; others may need hands-on instruction in creating the tool. First-year students with little or no experience using syllabi may focus on day-to-day work and fail to plan for larger assignments and tests as they organize their study time. Advisors can help students prepare by showing them ways to prioritize and determine an appropriate schedule that includes time to study for tests or prepare large assignments in addition to keeping abreast with daily work. Through such strategies, advisors can prompt students to organize their time effectively and break projects and test preparations into small, manageable tasks.

As students prepare for tests, advisors highlight effective learning techniques: summarizing in their own words the material they have read (rather than simply rereading notes or highlighting textbooks), studying with other students to quiz each other about class material, and distributing study over time rather than cramming immediately before the test. In a short 2013 *Scientific American Mind* article, Dunlosky, Rawson, Marsh, Nathan, and Willingham rated the effectiveness of a variety of study techniques.

Identifying Resources

Keeping a positive approach, advisors prompt students to consider obstacles as challenges rather than brick walls. Asking students to describe ways they have handled difficult situations in the past can fuel confidence in their ability to thrive. Athletics provide good examples for polishing skills and overcoming obstacles. For example, when learning to shoot free throws, basketball players must practice every day, not just the day before the game, and they consult with others about ways to handle both the ball and the pressure of the situation. Athletes learn that focusing their attention and showing determination (i.e., grit) in the face of difficulty can lead to successful mastery (Duckworth, 2013b). In contrast, athletes who spend too much effort using poor techniques in practice or ineffective strategies in competition will struggle to develop their skills. Determined athletes see obstacles as challenges to be overcome through effort, and they work with others to refine their skills. Determined students model these positive approaches as well.

New students often show understandable anxiety when they struggle in college academic or social settings and may verbalize doubts about whether they belong in college. Because students' academic and personal transitions to college can be undermined by a poor self-concept, advisors can anticipate these concerns by planning opportunities for new students to hear about the experiences of upper-level students who have overcome these issues.

In a recent study, entering first-generation students who listened to upper-level college students talk honestly about their adjustments and backgrounds used resources (e.g., professors' office hours) more frequently than those who did not hear students reflect on ways their backgrounds affected their adjustments. In addition, findings showed that the psychosocial outcomes (e.g., mental health metrics) for all students who attended the panel of upper-division students were better than those of the control group (Stephens, Hamedani, & Destin, 2014). Advisors who can organize such a panel of experienced students during the early weeks of the term may help new students understand that their concerns about belonging and succeeding are widely shared, can be overcome, and do not mean that they do not belong. In addition, after hearing panel participants talk about ways they used campus resources, new students may make use of these resources and strategies early in the term.

Offering Practical Encouragement

Advisors can inform students that research in brain science has shown that intelligence and the ability to learn are not fixed; these qualities can be improved with effort and strategies. For instance, research suggests the brain grows and changes, not just in infancy, but throughout the life span (Dweck, 2006, 2011). Advisors can coach students about ways to change their approach to difficulties by considering them challenges to be overcome rather than obstacles that block their path to success (Dweck, 2010). For additional ideas, advisors may also look to the University of Texas, which has adopted the online U.T. Mindset program as part of the orientation of all new students (Tough, 2014) or consult the resources included in the Aiming for Excellence ideas featured at the end of this chapter.

Although small interventions, such as organizing a panel of students and providing information about mindset and brain research, do not provide magic pills to alleviate all first-year challenges (Yeager & Walton, 2011), these approaches can encourage students to persist when they face challenges. In addition, because these strategies can be offered to groups of students, they are cost- and time-efficient. For those able to schedule individual meetings, these strategies, as well as those proposed by Walton (n.d., 2014), can be integrated throughout the term.

Connecting Students With Professors

No matter how welcoming and friendly professors may appear, many students will not speak with them. Some fear that professors will express disappointment in them for poor performance; others do not want to appear bothersome, perhaps feeling that their questions pale in importance to the work of professors; some see help-seeking behavior as a sign of weakness. In addition to the advice offered by upper-level peers, advisors provide specific suggestions about arranging meetings and talking with professors (Figure 3.2). Students may also benefit from coaching on crafting effective e-mails (see University of Nebraska–Lincoln, Office of Graduate Studies, 2016).

By posting suggestions shown in Figure 3.2 or providing them in a handout, advisors give students a clear path to follow when preparing to meet with professors. Because students need courage to talk with their instructors, advisors should follow up with an e-mail, phone call, or meeting to discuss the professor's suggestions.

Advising at Midterm

Whether or not colleges provide an interim grade report, advisors should contact students at midterm. Advisors can make these sessions more efficient and effective by asking students to complete another short questionnaire (Figure 3.3) before their meeting.

Like the initial instrument, the midterm questionnaire prompts students to reflect on their learning before meeting with advisors. It also references information students shared earlier—their goals and academic skill development—and asks them to assess their progress. Because nonacademic adjustments affect students' academic success and mastery, one question focuses on these concerns. If advisors feel incapable of addressing issues that come to light, they should be prepared to refer students to others with appropriate expertise.

While meeting with your professors will not substitute for attending class, keeping up with assignments, or studying regularly, these meetings can help you focus your efforts and connect with valuable resources. Whether your classes are going well or you would like to improve your learning, make meeting with your professors a priority.

- **Find a time to meet.** Check your class syllabus for the professor's office hours (times the professor sets aside to meet with students). To schedule a time to meet, talk with your professor before or after class, write a short note, or send a brief e-mail.

- **Prepare**. Before you meet with your professor, clarify your specific concerns or questions and be prepared to explain the ways you study and the study strategies you use. To avoid forgetting a question or getting off track, write down your questions or concerns. If you have questions about your performance on a paper, test, or assignment, carefully review the professor's comments and bring the materials to your meeting. If you are concerned that your class notes are inadequate, bring them for your professor to review.

- **Introduce yourself and your concern**. Be on time for your appointment. Introduce yourself, including your name, year in school, and the name of your class and summarize the reason for the visit. Describe the ways you study for the class, prepare for tests, or use writing strategies. Explain your reasoning so the professor can understand the way you think about the topic.

- **Summarize the professor's responses**. To ensure you understand your professor's responses to your questions and concerns, repeat them in your own words. Write down the professor's suggestions, and ask for clarification if your professor's responses do not clear up your confusion. The more specific you have been about your concerns, the more specific ideas your professor can provide. If your professor suggests getting a tutor or working with a learning or writing center, ask the professor to name two or three specific areas that you should address with the tutor first.

- **Wrap it up**. Thank your professor and (if necessary) ask to come back. Follow up on the professor's suggestions. Be sure to let the professor know how the ideas worked.

Figure 3.2. Making the most of meeting with faculty: Some ideas for students.

- What things are going well for you?

- What issues have emerged?

- How are you doing on reaching the goals you set at the beginning of the term?

- Do you have concerns about any of your classes? If you do, what are they?

- What about nonacademic parts of your life—meeting new people; keeping responsibilities and free time in balance; making time to eat, sleep, exercise, and so forth—are you doing as well as you would like?

- What is your favorite class this term? Why?

- What have you learned about yourself since you started college?

- Based on your experiences so far, what do you hope to do the same or differently for the rest of the term?

- How are you doing on improving the academic skills you targeted at the beginning of the term?

- Is there anything else that would be good for me to know?

Figure 3.3. Midterm advising questionnaire.

Checking Perception and Encouraging Reflection

At midterm, advisors remind new students to check the syllabi of their classes: How have midterm grades been determined and weighted? What percentages of final grades are yet to be determined for each class? What work remains? In addition to cumulative exams, many large projects and papers are submitted in the second half of the term, and advisors may need to coach students about organizing their time. Some students relied on extra credit work to improve their final grades in high school and are surprised and disappointed when this option is not offered in college. Advisors encourage students to develop a realistic plan to finish the term successfully, and they raise questions that prompt students to develop and implement it (see chapter 10).

Advisors can also ask students to predict their midterm grades. This exercise can help students assess their learning and verify that their perceptions comport with those of their instructors. Advisors can have fruitful conversations with students about their midterm predictions, their expectations about final grades, and the strategies they plan to use to earn the best possible final grades.

Just as in the beginning, at midterm advisors encourage students to reflect on their experiences and learning approaches rather than teach them generalized study skills (e.g., time management, test-taking strategies, note taking) (Figure 3.3). As Pizzolato (2008) stated, "When advising interactions are rooted in students' own experiences rather than in generic skill development exercises, students are more apt to use the resulting personally constructed strategies in new academic situations" (p. 23).

Making Effective Referrals

Regardless of their experience or counseling credential, advisors of all types may recognize that a student is struggling academically or personally (Jordan, 2015). Upon receiving formal (e.g., early alert) or informal notification from a professor about an academic concern, advisors may find that contacting students in a note or e-mail serves as a nonthreatening way to share the concern. Unlike a phone call or face-to-face meeting, the written correspondence gives students time to consider ways to respond appropriately. To encourage reluctant students to follow up with referrals, advisors remind students of their interest in them and willingness to help them reach their goals. As Jordan (2016) suggested, "Because of their level of personal commitment to students, advisors may have the greatest opportunity to participate in relationship with students, and as a result, may carry the influence necessary to inspire students to seek resources" (p. 29).

Testimonials from other students can be especially effective motivators for new students. If a panel of upper-division students talked with new students early in the term, advisors can remind discouraged students of the narratives they heard about transitioning to college academics. If the institution has a peer advisor program, advisors can arrange for students to hear directly from others who have experienced and overcome academic challenges.

When students' concerns interfere with their ability to reach their academic potential, advisors directly address the issues or suggest an appropriate referral. Advisors can handle personal concerns shared by their advisees using these approaches:

- An initial comment, "Tell me more …," sets the appropriate tone and agenda. Rather than trying to solve the students' problems, advisors encourage students to describe the problem and develop their own coping skills, including those that affect academic performance.

- Paraphrasing the student's words demonstrates that the advisor understands the situation, and if the advisor misunderstood it, the student can clarify. This approach communicates respect and helps students describe their situation accurately.

- Advisors should remind students of resources, but students should determine their next step. Whatever the decision, students must take ownership of it. To offer appropriate assistance for serious or life-threatening concerns, advisors must know and follow the institutional protocols for handling difficult or dangerous situations.

- Advisors should determine the limits of their time, energy, and professional expertise; they need to know professionals on and off campus who can help students with specific issues.

In a short article written for advisors, Krumrei and Newton (2009) discussed the ways counselors and advisors can work together to support student success. Although they may feel uncomfortable about a topic or confounded by a request, advisors can develop a repertoire to respond to areas they find difficult or troubling. Krumrei and Newton suggested phrases advisors can say to students who may benefit from mental health counseling:

- "College can be a stressful time. It seems like the problems you are facing right now might not go away on their own.... Folks at counseling services are trained to help students deal with such issues."

- "A counselor can help you learn skills and consider ways of looking at situations so that you will be more capable of solving problems on your own."

- "If you're not sure about counseling, you can make an appointment and discuss your reservations. Counselors will explain their practice and ways it may help with your situation."

Using Powerful Questions and Conversation Starters

By using questionnaires throughout the year, advisors encourage students to reflect on their academic progress, goals, and strategies. As Pizzolato (2008) explained, "Through questioning, advisors can help students better understand themselves, their strengths and weaknesses, and how to effectively make and act on decisions" (p. 23). The questions advisors ask and comments they make should encourage students' self-assessment, affirm the learning-based nature of advising, and enhance their competence to make independent decisions. Figure 3.4 features some examples that can be used throughout the academic year, from the first interaction to the last, but may prove particularly useful during stressful times such as at midterm.

- Let me make sure I understand your concern…

- I'm sorry you're having a difficult time.

- Sounds like you have many questions. Let's start with the one you are most concerned about.

- I'm concerned about you because…

- How important is this to you?

- How committed are you to reaching your goals?

- What are you willing to do (stop doing) to reach your goals?

- How will you know it is time to make a change?

- What can you do today and this week to help you reach your goal?

- I can suggest advantages and disadvantages, but the decision is yours.

- What a challenge! How do you think you might handle it?

- Can you break down these challenges into smaller tasks that are more manageable?

- Can I tell you my concerns about the plan as described?

- I can't fix this problem, but I can give you some ideas.

- How can you handle challenges differently next semester?

- What good outcome might result from handling [a difficulty] differently? What are reasons for not changing your strategy?

- What challenges have you faced and overcome in the past? Might some of those strategies work now?

- Have you spoken with your professor?

Figure 3.4. Powerful questions and conversation starters.

Because they realize that most first-year students need time to develop the skills necessary to take charge of their own learning and make mature decisions, advisors support their progress and prompt them with questions and comments to foster self-assessment and wise decision making. Chickering (1994) emphasized such an approach:

> Our relationships with students—the questions we raise, the perspectives we share, the resources we suggest, the short-term decisions and long-range plans we help them think through—all should aim to increase their capacity to take charge of their own existence (p. 50).

AIMING FOR **EXCELLENCE**

The following discussion questions and activities give advisors concrete ideas and strategies for expanding their knowledge and applying the information shared in this chapter to their advising practice:

- Identify your own intelligence mindset by looking at material presented by Dweck (2006, 2010, 2011). Based on your mindset, what do you think students notice about the verbal and nonverbal responses you share? What aspects of your mindset, if any, would you like to change? How would changing your mindset change the way you communicate with students about successes and failures?

- Learn more about fixed and growth mindsets, including the work of Dweck (2006, 2010, 2011) and research on brain science.

- Explore the concept of grit as explained by Duckworth (2013a, 2013b, 2016) in publications and videos found online. How might this information help advisors work with first-year students?

- See social belonging resources from Walton (n.d.). Choose some of his suggestions to use as a basis for a presentation or to inform research at your own institution.

- Host brown-bag lunches to discuss the research on mindset, grit, and social belonging. Encourage colleagues in attendance to identify strategies to approach first-year students, especially those who are struggling.

The Next Term: Reassessing and Goal Setting

After term grades are issued, students on the dean's list or on probation receive official notifications from the institution. However, advisors may want to contact those who worked consistently, even if they did not earn top grades in every course. Not only do short notes or e-mails affirm student effort, persistence (grit), and strategies, they also encourage continued focus and bolster motivation. Advisors can also congratulate those who earned high grades while emphasizing the hope that high grades indicate student enjoyment in classes. These approaches encourage students to keep the spotlight on personal growth and academic engagement, not solely on grades, and remind first-year students that advisors are committed to their long-term success.

At the beginning of the second term, advisors continue to build on the self-assessment and reflection skills fostered in the first term by raising questions that encourage goal setting and progress evaluation. Questions for this follow-up inquiry are listed in Figure 3.5. Advisors may also raise questions asked earlier in the year with the expectation that, after a term in college, responses may have changed or may be more mature and realistic.

Despite the importance of goal setting for first-year students, advisors may be the only people on campus who ask first-year students about their goals. By encouraging first-year students to focus on their goals, advisors help them

- What did you learn about yourself and college-level expectations last term?

- How can you apply newfound learning about yourself and college-level expectations in the upcoming term?

- What are your goals for the upcoming term?

- What kinds of support will you need to reach your goals?

- What academic resources do you plan to use in pursuing your goals?

- How will you hold yourself accountable for the decisions you are making now?

- How will you measure your progress in reaching your goals?

- How can your advisor help you reach your goals?

Figure 3.5. Example of a second-term advising questionnaire for new students.

handle difficult situations. Although they may not find every class exciting or every professor inspiring, when students are encouraged to focus on their goals, they may find purpose in their work and may remain motivated when faced with tedious, boring, or demanding course work (Yeager et al., 2014). When they raise questions asked earlier in the term (e.g., How committed are you to reaching your goals? What are you prepared to do [stop doing] to reach your goals?), advisors reenergize students to keep their goals in the forefront.

Summary

In an ideal world, advisors would enjoy abundant time for sessions with students, who thrive and enjoy limitless, easily accessible resources. In the real world, advisors must overcome resource limitations to empower students to make the most of college, especially during the initial transition to college. Not all students will experience a constructive and productive first year, but with advisor challenge and support, some will negotiate the transition successfully, gain important skills, and take increasing responsibility for their learning.

References

Baxter Magolda, M. B. (2002). Helping students make their way to adulthood: Good company for the journey. *About Campus, 6*(6), 2–9. doi:10.1002/abc.66

Bonfiglio, R. A. (2008). Bottom line: Shorthand or shortsightedness? *About Campus, 13*(3), 30–32. doi:10.1002/abc.256

Chickering, A. W. (1994). Empowering lifelong self-development. *NACADA Journal, 14*(2), 50–53. doi:http://dx.doi.org/10.12930/0271-9517-14.2.50

Chickering, A. W. (2006). Every student can learn—if.... *About Campus, 11*(2), 9–15. doi:10.1002/abc.161

De Sousa, D. J. (2005). *Promoting student success: What advisors can do* (Occasional Paper No. 11). Retrieved from the National Survey of Student Engagement at the Indiana University Center for Postsecondary Research website: http://nsse.indiana.edu/institute/documents/briefs/DEEP%20Practice%20Brief%2011%20What%20Advisors%20Can%20Do.pdf

Duckworth, A. L. (2013a, August 5). *Can perseverance be taught?* Retrieved from https://www.bigquestionsonline.com/content/can-perseverance-be-taught

Duckworth, A. L. (2013b). True grit. *Observer, 26*(4). Retrieved from http://www.psychologicalscience.org/index.php/publications/observer/2013/april-13/true-grit.html

Duckworth, A. L. (2016). *Grit: The power of passion and perseverance*. New York, NY: Scribner.

Dunlosky, J., Rawson, K. A., Marsh, E. J., Nathan, M. J., & Willingham, D. T. (2013). How we learn: What works, what doesn't. *Scientific American Mind, 24*(4), 46–53. doi:10.1038/scientificamericanmind0913-46

Dweck, C.S. (2006). *Mindset*. New York, NY: Random House.

Dweck, C. S. (2010). *Mindset* [Website]. Retrieved from Mindsetonline.com.

Dweck, C. S. (2011, November 7). *Brain research at Stanford: Mindsets* [Video file]. Retrieved from https://www.youtube.com/watch?v=WvIBG98wj0Q

Folsom, P., Yoder, F., & Joslin, J. E. (Eds.). (2015). *The new advisor guidebook: Mastering the art of academic advising* (2nd ed.). San Francisco, CA: Jossey-Bass.

Jordan, P. (2015). Effective communications skills. In P. Folsom, F. Yoder, & J. E. Joslin (Eds.), *The new advisor guidebook: Mastering the art of academic advising* (2nd ed., pp. 213–229). San Francisco, CA: Jossey-Bass.

Jordan, P. (2016). Theory as the foundation of advising. In T. J. Grites, J. Givans Voller, & M. A. Miller (Eds.), *Beyond foundations: Developing as a master academic advisor* (pp. 21–42). San Francisco, CA: Jossey-Bass.

Krumrei, E. J., & Newton, F. B. (2009). *The puzzle of college students' success: Fitting the counseling and advising pieces together*. Retrieved from http://www.nacada.ksu.edu/Resources/Clearinghouse/View-Articles/How-counseling-and-advising-fit-together.aspx

Pizzolato, J. E. (2008). Advisor, teacher, partner: Using the learning partnerships model to reshape academic advising. *About Campus, 13*(1), 18–25. doi: 10.1002/abc.243

Schreiner, L. A., Hulme, E., Hetzel, R., & Lopez, S. J. (2009). Positive psychology on campus. In S. J. Lopez & C. Snyder (Eds.), *Oxford handbook of positive psychology* (2nd ed., pp. 569–578). New York, NY: Oxford University Press.

Stephens, N. M., Hamedani, M. G., & Destin, M. (2014). Closing the social-class achievement gap: A difference-education intervention improves first-generation students' academic performance and all students' college transition. *Psychological Science, 25*(4), 943–953.

Tough, P. (2014, May 18). Who gets to graduate? *The New York Times Magazine, 26–33,* 41–42, 54. Retrieved from http://www.nytimes.com/2014/05/18/magazine/who-gets-to-graduate.html?_r=0

University of Nebraska–Lincoln, Office of Graduate Studies. (2016). *Five quick tips for writing effective e-mails*. Retrieved from http://www.unl.edu/gradstudies/current/news/five-quick-tips-writing-effective-e-mails

Walton, G. M. (n.d.). *Research*. Retrieved from http://gregorywalton-stanford. weebly.com/research.html

Walton, G. M. (2014). The new science of wise psychological interventions. *Current Directions in Psychological Science, 23*(1), 73–82. Retrieved from http://gregorywalton-stanford.weebly.com/uploads/4/9/4/4/49448111/ walton,_2014.pdf

Yeager, D. S., Henderson, H., Paunesku, D., Walton, G. M., D'Mello, S., Spitzer, B. J., & Duckworth, A. L. (2014). Boring but important: A self-transcendent purpose for learning fosters academic self-regulation. *Journal of Personality and Social Psychology, 107*(4), 559–580. Retrieved from https://p3.perts. net/static/documents/yeager_2014.pdf

Yeager, D. S., & Walton, G. M. (2011, April). Social-psychological interventions in education: They're not magic. *Review of Educational Research, 81,* 267–301. Retrieved from http://gregorywalton-stanford. weebly.com/uploads/4/9/4/4/49448111/yeagerwalton2011.pdf. doi: 10.3102/0034654311405999

CHAPTER 4

Unique Transitions at Two-Year Colleges

Tim Kirkner and Julie Levinson

The generalized profiles of students seeking a baccalaureate degree and the typical challenges they encounter during their first year may not substantially differ among those matriculating into two- and four-year institutions (American Association of Community Colleges [AACC], 2015); however, their characteristics and related transition experiences diverge in some meaningful ways. For example, two-year college students tend to enroll with a much broader range of short-term (e.g., personal enrichment or targeted job skills) and long-term (certificate, associate degree, or transfer) educational goals than their four-year counterparts (Wyner, Deane, Jenkins, & Fink, 2016). Furthermore, distinct factors affect the routes taken to a baccalaureate by students at the two-year college. Specifically, two-year college students may experience more difficulty achieving the same educational goals than those in four-year colleges and universities. In general, students enter two-year schools with substantial variations in enrollment intensity (i.e., full-time, part-time, nonsequential terms) (AACC, 2015), high rates of remedial placement (51.7%), and low levels of academic preparedness (Complete College America, 2016a). They also experience more uncertain completion outcomes than students who enter directly into a four-year institution (Hodara & Xu, 2014).

In addition, the statistics suggest that the term *two-year college* does not adequately reflect the reality that many students attend longer than two years. According to Complete College America (2013), 4% of students complete an associate degree within two years while 19% of students matriculating into four-year institutions complete their degrees in four years. Furthermore, data collected by the National Student Clearinghouse Research Center show that 26.1% of students who begin higher education at public two-year institutions graduate within six years, and 42.9% of these graduates had enrolled exclusively full-time to complete their degree within those six years (Juszkiewicz, 2015, p. 6).

Advisors who keep the statistical differences in mind can provide a meaningful, targeted, and tailored advising experience for the two-year college student. From students' first-term enrollment to the point of goal completion, transfer, or separation from the institution, advisors and administrators can enhance advising by adapting to the distinct characteristics of the two-year college student population. They must also determine the practices most suitable to serve the needs of the surrounding communities that often act as the employment and service pipeline for two-year college students. Moreover, they must seek innovative ways to deliver enhanced advising practices where student–advisor ratios are reported as high as 1,600:1 (Community College Research Center [CCRC], 2013, p. 21).

To help advisors understand and assist students enrolled in, coming from, or returning to two-year institutions, we provide descriptions of this broadly defined and unconventional student population. We specifically address the unique aspects of the first-year experience for these students and offer strategies for advising delivery in the two-year college.

Two-Year College Student Populations

In the United States, two-year colleges were established in the early 20th century to provide access to higher education to those populations previously denied it. Passage of the GI Bill in 1944 opened the doors even wider by continuing to break down financial barriers to a college education (AACC, 2016b). The basic goal—providing educational opportunity for all seeking it— remains the salient tenet of two-year colleges today. Offering both credit and noncredit courses that typically reflect the demands of the local workforce, the two-year college is designed to meet the needs of everyone in the community with little barrier for entry. In addition, two-year colleges serve as cultural centers that reflect the communities in which they are located (AACC, 2016b). To create a clear picture of the demographic and enrollment trends among two-year college students, the AACC website offers a wealth of statistics. In particular, the *DataPoints* archive presents interesting snapshots of topics, such as attendance, enrollment, and degree completion as well as costs and transfer outcomes that shape U.S. community colleges (AACC, 2014b).

The AACC (2014b) data illustrate that the diversity of the two-year college student extends beyond age, gender, and ethnicity to encompass other significant demographic variables, such as experiences with college, military service, and family responsibilities as well as funding sources, employment status, level of English proficiency, support needs, and educational aspirations. To further complicate any generalized picture of the two-year college student, the reasons for attendance have changed. Unlike those in the past, many eligible to enter a four-year college or university opt to begin their educations at the local two-year college to take advantage of affordability, quality of instruction, proximity to home, and partnerships with local schools or colleges (AACC, 2016c; McCullough, 2010).

At the time of this writing, 1,108 two-year colleges were operational in the United States, representing the education choice of 45% of all undergraduates nationwide (AACC, 2016a). The two-year college student reflects the makeup of the local community; therefore, advisors need to know the characteristics of the area populations known to attend the two-year college to learn or improve skills, earn a credential, or transfer to a four-year institution. Advisors may need to seek some of the pertinent data not gathered during intake processes or reported in the students' demographic profiles.

First-Generation Students

According to the AACC (2016b), first-generation college students made up approximately 45% of all undergraduates in 2014 and 36% of the U.S. two-year college population in 2011-2012. A significant portion of these students struggle to navigate the experience, which likely differs from that of peers whose parent(s) attended college (DeGiorgio, 2015, p. 1). For example, two-year college students report psychological struggles characterized by high levels of worry, guilt, and pressure to bring honor to their families as they seek to improve their own personal circumstances as well as those of future generations (Banks-Santilli, 2015).

As they interface with the first-generation population, advisors must first acknowledge the unique challenges faced by those with little tangible information from college-savvy parents. Advisors look for creative small- and large-scale approaches employed by two-year colleges to foster a sense of belonging and connection, important to all students but which may prove particularly critical to those first in their families to attend college (DeGiorgio, 2015; Tovar, 2013). By finding and directing first-generation students to support programs, such as TRIO or other grant-based mentoring initiatives, advisors help them persist and complete their educational goals (Salinitri, 2005). Some two-year colleges partner with local nonprofits to connect students with mentors and academic coaches outside the academy. Where large-scale support is lacking, advisors can communicate an inclusive and caring environment, valuable to all students, by placing "first-generation friendly" stickers on their office doors

(DeGiorgio, 2015, p. 15). Another useful strategy involves asking former first-generation faculty members to serve as informal advisors, resources, or mentors for students or as contributing board or committee members of advising units. Advisors can access or direct students to online resources targeted to first-generation students, such as those offered by the Loyola University of Chicago, Achieving College Excellence program (2016).

International Students

According to an AACC *DataPoints* report, "More than 146,500 international students enrolled at U.S. two-year colleges in 2012, comprising 1.2% of the total student body" (Wheeler, 2014, p. 1). Although some come with degrees or postsecondary education experience from their home countries, a large number will be directed into English-as-second-language courses to obtain the skills necessary to succeed in their chosen academic areas. Acquiring requisite language skills proves a lengthy and costly process for students eager to advance their life circumstances, but the push to accelerate prematurely into college-level courses can lead to poor performance. In addition to self- or family-induced pressures to progress quickly, those admitted on F-1 student visas are expected to carry a full course of study (U.S. Department of State, Bureau of Consular Affairs, 2015), which may lead to academic difficulty for those struggling with English or unfamiliar cultural expectations. In addition, international students pay more for course work at any U.S. institution, including two-year colleges, because most do not qualify for in-country or in-state tuition. Advisors help incoming students manage expectations and alleviate stressors.

On a practical level, advising international students attending the two-year college requires some basic knowledge of processes for obtaining and maintaining student visas, evaluating foreign credentials, securing health insurance, and seeking housing and financial support. Furthermore, many students experience additional "challenges as a result of language barriers, cultural differences, academic and financial difficulties, lack of social support, and alienation and discrimination" (Zhang, 2016, p. 1). The student may also be contending with demands from sponsors or relatives. Like their counterparts in four-year institutions, community college advisors need to employ cultural competency when advising a student whose evolving ideas or goals differ from those in the home country providing housing or other financial support.

Advisors can advocate for additional support for international students, such as seminars, multicultural centers, and handbooks that assist with adjustment issues or other matters distinct to international students, such as time management, social norms, homesickness, and culture shock. Advisors need to recognize the increased levels of stress and anxiety or the decreased levels of academic and social self-efficacy (Baier, 2005). International students may experience more acute homesickness as they struggle with missing family and friends, feeling lonely, making the adjustment to the new school and culture, and remembering life at home (Kegel, 2009). To learn more about strategies for cross-cultural advising, practitioners can strengthen their relationships with others who work closely with international students (Zhang, 2016). In advocating for interconnecting resources, Mamiseishvili (2012) argued that

> persistence of international students should not be viewed as the responsibility of only international student advisors on campus. Instead, it should become a joint responsibility of a broader campus community, including faculty, academic advisors, English language program staff, and student affairs professionals. (p. 15)

In addition to taking advantage of experts on campus, advisors can seek guidance available to support international students from organizations such as the AACC (2013).

The transition for international students, although not wholly unique, requires cultural competency based on acknowledgment of one's own personal history and knowledge of the varied population at the two-year college (Archambault, 2015) (see chapter 7). Most important, effective advisors of international students keep an open door, assert genuine friendliness, and celebrate cultural differences (Stürzl-Forrest, 2012).

Immigrant and Undocumented Students

Political debates over immigration policies have put a spotlight on the challenges faced by undocumented students enrolled in postsecondary education in the United States. Unique concerns facing this student population include barriers to continued education, exclusion from the legal workforce, discrimination, and limited access to financial aid (Gonzales, 2009, p. 4). Federal policies, such as the Development, Relief, and Education for Alien Minors (also known as the *DREAM*) Act and the Deferred Action for Childhood Arrivals (often referred to as *DACA*) program, offer pathways for many undocumented young persons to attend college and navigate the U. S. educational system (Perez, 2014), but they have been politically contentious. Advisors must stay abreast of federal policies as they develop. However, as of 2014, 18 states had enacted legislation to provide in-state tuition to undocumented students (National

Conference of State Legislators, 2014, para. 1). Taking advantage of these new opportunities, students without proof of citizenship or residency may break through the stigma of being undocumented and reassure family members wary of the U.S. education system.

To navigate the shifting legal landscape, advisors working in two-year colleges must stay informed of pertinent educational policies that impact local immigrant populations and understand the concerns of undocumented students. Mendoza (2015) suggested that educators establish a formal network of campus allies, similar to those providing LGBT safe zones, to send a message of inclusivity to students. Through this support structure, allies receive training to address misconceptions, raise awareness, and learn strategies to support undocumented students as they contend with compounding stressors such as first-generation status, lack of financial resources, legal matters related to their immigration status, and fear of deportation. Mendoza also recommended publishing a resource guide that specifically helps undocumented students succeed in college, "including admissions and financial aid guidelines and processes ... pertinent legislation ...," and most important, "a list of allies and departmental points of contact" for students and advisors alike (para. 8).

Students With Mental Health Issues

The two-year college offers a pathway to higher education for those whose mental health status may have restricted access to higher education in the past. Such students generally benefit from reasonable accommodations, such as taking courses at their own pace and working with personnel in a disability support office. However, many two-year colleges do not employ an adequate number of counseling professionals to handle the issues of those experiencing serious episodes of mental illness (Edwards, 2013). As a result, the support and understanding needed to keep a student on track during a given term may not be available at the levels necessary. Although shortages of mental health resources affect colleges of all sizes and offerings, students at two-year colleges have shown particular vulnerability for depression, anxiety disorders, and other mental health problems due to the number of outside stressors that characterize their situations (Chamberlin, 2012, p. 11).

A survey of two-year college counseling services conducted by the American College Counseling Association Community College Task Force validated concerns about advising students presenting with personal or mental health issues (Edwards, 2013). The common themes emerging from the study included underresourced and understaffed situations, role overload, mixed messages from administration, and challenges for making effective referrals to outside resources (Edwards, 2013, p. 3). Advisors with a realistic awareness of the themes and associated difficulties in providing adequate services manage their own expectations, as well as those of students, faculty members, and administrators, more effectively. They provide referrals to online, college, and community services, but they must know the scope of those services and explain to students the ways to access them.

Advisors may consider advocating for the formation of an on-campus support network by promoting programs that operate in the community, including groups associated with the National Alliance on Mental Illness, Active Minds, LGBTQIA concerns, and military veterans (Daniel & Davison, 2014). Some two-year colleges contract services with local mental health providers and form behavioral intervention teams to address student behaviors of concern proactively and prevent crises (National Behavioral Intervention Team Association, 2016).

Nontraditional Students

Although many people associate the label *nontraditional* with older students (over 24 years), age alone does not define this population. In 1996, Horn and Carroll offered a definition that focused on "choices and behavior that may increase students' risk of attrition" (p. 3) and encompassed variables other than age, such as delayed enrollment in postsecondary education, family responsibilities, and financial constraints as well as lack of a diploma earned from a recognized high school. Later, Furman (2011) offered a narrower definition, describing only students with delayed entry or reentry to college.

The nontraditional college population may be vulnerable for a host of reasons. For instance, many students will enroll in the midst of other life transitions, such as a divorce, change in job or career, pregnancy, recent birth of a child, or reduced childcare commitments as younger children enter school or older children leave home (Peters, Hyun, Taylor, & Varney, 2010). Advisors should initiate conversations with nontraditional students to determine their way of thinking, which may not have always included "higher education as a part of their development or life trajectory" (Peters et al., 2010, p. 1).

Unlike matriculating students experiencing major life transitions, some enroll in two-year colleges to advance or enrich their current circumstances. For example, the two-year college plays a special role in catering to the lifelong learner seeking continuing education credits. In addition, many two-year colleges offer special programs and incentives for students with specific goals. Some returning adults want to benefit from relatively low tuition to learn a new skill or stay active. Others wish to add to existing credentials, complete prerequisites, or meet employment requirements. Students with considerable life experience may readily grasp the ways to navigate the two-year college bureaucracy; however, a sizable portion of returning adults will seek out advising and other support services as their anxiety levels ebb and flow during the transition back to school. Advisors who actively seek to know their advisees will recognize the wide range of reasons students attend the two-year college, and they will readily appreciate the needs of the individuals they advise.

Advising in two-year colleges can be as complex as the varied student populations who need it. By taking the time to understand ways that issues may manifest for distinct populations, advisors can identify the most appropriate interventions. The NACADA Clearinghouse of Academic Advising Resources offers useful information on the populations attending college today.

Managing Student Expectations During Initial Enrollment

Some of the well-intentioned processes and programs in place to assist students with initial entry into advising may, in fact, undermine students' success from the start. Students must persist through enrollment, including intake, orientation, first-term advising, registration, and payment. Although advisors can play a vital role in minimizing confusion for students through direct intervention and advocacy efforts, greater effect may result from a critical examination of the enrollment process. Rather than helping solely as guides over obstacles, advisors may best assist two-year college students by advocating for systemic improvements that reduce the challenges.

Misinformation

From the first day, advisors must correct any misinformation in the promotions sometimes used to recruit students. While the allure of a quick entry and short path to a degree characterize the marketing strategies of many two-year colleges, such campaigns may lead prospective students to believe that they can complete the enrollment process in a few short steps. In theory, anyone can show up and be registered by day's end, but the reality for the typical student seldom resembles the brochure. Even with efforts to simplify the process for students, such as creating centralized one-stop or welcome centers, the easy steps typically require multiple days or visits to complete. In addition to negotiating personal logistics, such as work, childcare, and transportation, as well as obtaining necessary documents needed to complete the process, students may encounter other unanticipated obstacles to first-term enrollment.

Disillusionment results when enrollment processes are packaged as easy steps (Smith Jaggars & Fletcher, 2014) but important considerations that affect process, such as deadlines, fees, prior learning experiences, and prerequisites are overlooked. As a result, many students arrive on campus with unreasonable expectations and consumer attitudes, believing that anyone, regardless of educational history, can take any class, regardless of prerequisites, at the two-year college. Some come prepared to register and pay for the class of their choosing, regardless of their current skill level or educational history. Others expect to barter the costs, deadlines, and requirements. Such consumerist thinking is dispelled once the potential student learns that most two-year college courses require proficiency in English, reading, and some math.

Rolling deadlines create another area of misconception because credit and noncredit offerings begin and end at various times during the calendar year. Some mistakenly think that the entire intake and registration process can be accomplished after the start of classes because two-year colleges admit students throughout the year. In certain situations, students can register late or receive special permissions to circumvent requirements, leaving both students and advisors confused over the policies set in stone and those etched in clay. Intake policies and processes also depend on whether the two-year college emphasizes enrolling or retaining students. Knowing the college mission, keeping abreast of the active enrollment management strategy, and working collaboratively with other professionals across the college, advisors can offset the potential negative impacts that ill-conceived policies or promotions may have on students (Pollock, 2006).

In one common practice to combat misinformation, the college implements a gateway or welcome center, which offers a place where students get connected to the college by accessing basic information about policies. By serving as the repository of information, the welcome center frees time for advisors to focus on building good relationships with students. Some schools use an Internet space for welcoming students and websites with integrated onboarding tools, such as the Education Advisory Board (EAB) Navigate platform, to reach students with information. Other technology-mediated advising systems allow for creation of an individualized orientation process and delivery of customized information on demand (Kalamkarian & Karp, 2015). The approach to technology-mediated services, called *iPASS*, enables advisors to increase outreach and follow-up through tracking mechanisms and early-alert functions (Karp & Fletcher, 2015). (See chapter 10 for more on early-alert systems.)

Lack of Information

Even when provided a place to connect with information on policies, students may not know enough about specific procedures to seamlessly enroll, which typically involves applying for financial aid, completing placement testing, participating in new student orientation, advising, registering, paying, and obtaining a student ID. On paper, the steps appear straightforward, but to students without prior experience, the maneuvers seem quite complicated. The specific subtasks required to complete procedures defy simplistic explanations, and with minimal guidance from college personnel, students often flounder through the process.

Although they manage to make the application and complete registration, some students may make decisions about their first-term courses based on suboptimal information (Smith Jaggars & Fletcher, 2014). Advisors who meet with students before the term may improve the input used for decision making while also reviewing the entire enrollment process with students, redirecting them when necessary, and closing gaps in information or understanding. To optimize the delivery of key information at the institutional level, advisors also advocate for students through discussions on enrollment. Because they recognize and understand the ways the first (mis)steps on campus can affect a student's feelings about the college and persistence in higher education, advisors can offer administrators suggestions for improving the experience for students.

Advisors also intervene with placement testing or other assessments to counter inadequate information about requirements for classes. Hughes and Scott-Clayton (2011) explained that two-year colleges, most with open-door admissions policies, use placement assessments to reconcile the two, sometimes conflicting, aims of educating underprepared students while simultaneously maintaining institutional academic standards (p. 1). The placement process is designed primarily to measure proficiency in math, reading, and writing, as well as identify needs for remedial instruction in these areas, but it also creates problems for students and advisors.

After completing assessments, some students are placed into developmental courses to improve their chances of succeeding in college-level work, much to the consternation of some who hold elevated beliefs about their academic readiness. The disappointment stemming from being denied access to credit-bearing courses is compounded for students who had been directed to the testing center with little (or no) guidance about the purpose for, implications of, or necessary preparation for taking an assessment test. Furthermore, students may not completely understand the seriousness of the test until they receive the results and associated class recommendations. At this point, the advisor is placed on the frontline of the battle between the expectations stoked by the marketing campaign and the realities of the academic path leading to the student's educational goals. In recognition that early disappointments can be turned into realistic expectations, some promising practices have been developed to help students get on track early: checks on initial placements, bridge to success programs, early registration periods, and more recently, on-time registration policies (O'Banion & Wilson, 2013).

At a number of two-year colleges, leadership look to new ways for "removing the barriers of placements and long remedial sequences" (Complete College America, 2016b, para. 5), such as corequisite remediation as a successful practice for increasing completion rates of college-level course work. Some colleges use the high school transcript as an alternative to placement testing and as a proxy to assess students' academic skills and readiness for college-level work (Belfield & Crosta, 2012). While these alternatives show promise for improving student persistence, advisors may struggle to adjust promptly to quickly initiated reforms. To remain adaptable, advisors can regularly review websites and publications covering changes in student success practices, such as those sponsored by the Community College Research Center (CCRC), AACC, NACADA: The Global Community for Academic Advising, The Council for the Study of Community Colleges, Achieving the Dream, and Complete College America.

Too Much Information

Delivery mechanisms dictate the pace of information dissemination. With a captive audience, four-year schools devote days and often a week or more to orienting new students to the campus and shepherding them through advising and registration. Students not only receive orientation on academics but are also connected in social groups as they are directed, along with their floor mates or other related cohorts, to organized gatherings. Careful planning, coordination, and consideration go into creating a cohesive, mandatory experience before, during, and after the first day of instruction. In these forums at four-year institutions, information is metered out in a strategic manner and at a pace conducive to learning retention. The same cannot always be said for orientation programs at the two-year college (Bailey, Jenkins, & Smith Jaggars, 2015).

While research supports orientation as a successful way for both increasing use of student support services and improved retention of at-risk students, approaches to academic orientation vary widely (Center for Community College Student Engagement [CCCSE], 2012, p. 11). Two-year colleges may offer students an optional academic orientation or require it only for first-time, degree-seeking students (CCCSE, 2012, p. 12). This format appeals to students and college personnel who see mandatory participation as an obstruction in the road to a quick and flexible entry. In a convention that pits intent against realistic practice, administration may focus on efficient and effective advising only during peak enrollment periods when the ratio of students to advisors is highest. In the end, efforts to coordinate new student orientation activities, including academic orientation, often result in students experiencing information overload, misimpressions of the advising experience, and frustrating first encounters with advisors.

The primary purpose of initial advising interactions, to orient students to the academic side of college and offer guidance for their first term, translates to an emphasis on the basics: reviewing assessment results and placements; explaining the catalog, course offerings, general terminology, and requirements; and establishing an academic plan for the first term or year. In the absence of mandatory advising, the initial advising encounter may offer one of few opportunities for students to hear about many aspects of obtaining a credential or transferring to another institution.

To combat the problems associated with information overload found in some comprehensive orientation programs, many advising units effectively manage the new student advising experience through summer bridge programs, advising labs, convocations, and online modules. The CCRC (2013) highlighted several enhanced advising strategies that offer solutions to counter resource constraints and avoid overwhelming students with information. The report creators suggested that advisors take a developmental and integrated approach to advising (CCRC, 2013, p. 3) such that in early encounters the advisor emphasizes goal setting, relationship building, and continued use of advising services (CCRC, 2013, p. 2). They also recommended reformulating the process for accessing support services to feature a nonfragmented approach that also integrates career advising (CCRC, 2013, p. 4).

First-Year Persistence: Noncognitive Factors

Armed with the information they need, students may feel the shock of the first term. In the wake of intake processes and enrollment, some students struggle with their fit in the institution and may question whether they belong in college. The reality of life as a college student comes into clearer view after classes start, and this period of adjustment may present specific challenges for students at the two-year college. According to statistics compiled by ACT in 2011, the national first-to-second-year retention rate at public community colleges was 55.4%, and it was 73.3% at public four-year institutions (Tovar, 2013, p. 246). Because academic and social integration plays a significant role in first-year persistence, responsive advisors ensure students engage in experiences that encourage a sense of belonging and mattering to the institution (Tovar, 2013).

Perhaps the biggest challenge of all—helping students successfully navigate the first year at the two-year college—requires advisors who consistently encourage the first-year student to stay engaged, motivated, and focused in the face of increased expectations. Because a number of factors may lead to early academic difficulty and serve as predictors—separately or in combination—of student persistence, advisors must leverage more than a superficial understanding of student demographics. Specifically, in addition to the traditional academic, financial, and social support services offered at most two-year colleges, students need reassurance. Because noncognitive factors such as motivation levels, attitudes, values, and feelings factor into persistence, they are gaining greater recognition in the educational community (Markle & O'Banion, 2014).

To address the noncognitive aspects of student persistence during the initial, fragile period, timely interventions include "creating social relationships …, clarifying aspirations and enhancing commitment …, developing college know-how" (Karp, 2011, p. 6), and addressing conflicting demands of work, family, and college. To implement these initiatives, some two-year colleges have added personnel, such as mentors and academic coaches, to work in conjunction with and to boost support provided by advisors.

Advising Through Student Transitions

Despite institutional employment of identified programs and supplemental support staff, advisors may prove the most crucial in helping students improve educational outcomes during the first year; however, resource constraints and other factors that limit the intensive advising needed for many students may undermine the impact of advising. By understanding the most beneficial interactions and assessing the noncognitive factors early, such as through an intake questionnaire, advisors can intervene proactively and effectively (see chapter 3). However, two-year college advisors may feel challenged when making the case for integrating proactive and data-driven approaches into an established process created by other interests. For example, although student questionnaire completion can be forced through a registration hold, such an effective compliance tool may present barriers to enrollment perceived as contrary to the college or unit mission.

Like controversies caused by mandated and proactive advising, placement in developmental course work creates a point of conflict for advisors, advisees, and other institutional players. Nearly two thirds of students entering a two-year college require at least one remedial course in their first year (AACC, 2014a). Rather than viewing developmental courses as necessary to build skills for successful completion of college-level course work, many students, especially those hoping to transfer to a four-year school in the near future, see remedial placement as a costly and unnecessary obstacle to reaching their goals. Furthermore, advisors may need to spend significant effort helping overconfident students overcome feeling stigmatized by participation in developmental education. Advisors need to acknowledge students' feelings and help motivate them through the developmental sequences.

Although most do not exert a direct influence over institutional assessment and placement policies, advisors can collaborate with the faculty to advance ideas that help students. Advisors forge strong relationships by making classroom visits or inviting instructional faculty members to assist during peak advising periods. Some may explore opportunities for partnership through learning communities, such as pairing a study skills course with a remedial English or math course. By engaging with faculty members, advisors gain a deep understanding of the learning outcomes, benchmarks, and specific strategies for successful course completion.

To help advisors and students persist through the difficulties with developmental classes, two-year colleges are providing financial support (federal, private, or otherwise), and they are redesigning developmental education sequences. Some implement alternative approaches, such as coremediation, accelerated courses, self-directed learning labs, virtual tutoring, and integrated learning supports (Long & Boatman, 2013).

To take advantage of the latest developments to assist students, advisors need to stay informed of changes to assessment and placement processes, master knowledge of developmental sequences at the institutional level, and stay abreast of broader trends in remediation. They can advance their professional development by reviewing information provided by organizations, such as the National Association for Developmental Education and the National Center for Developmental Education. The result of professional development efforts includes more substantive interactions that enable the advisor to not only convey course sequences but also to educate students about the theory, purpose, and practice of developmental education.

AIMING FOR **EXCELLENCE**

The following discussion questions and activities give advisors concrete ideas and strategies for expanding their knowledge and applying the information shared in this chapter to their advising practice:

- Review the Center for Community College Student Engagement (2012) findings, compare them to the data collected by your institutional research office, and seek out additional information, such as retention and completion rates. Consider how these data may be helpful in understanding unique student populations as well as enrollment and completion patterns.

- Pursue professional development in topic areas particularly relevant to the two-year college populations, including issues pertaining to mental health, military veterans, and learning disabilities.

- Join or establish a national, regional, or statewide advising affinity group of two-year college advisors to discuss common struggles and share ideas, such as NACADA's Two-Year College Commission.

- Participate in enrollment management groups to learn about and advocate for students. Consider the experience of students undertaking the first-term enrollment steps, such as taking a placement test.

- Stay abreast of innovations within the two-year college sector. Browse topics covered by the League for Innovation in the Community College (http://www.league.org/) conference.

By creating guided pathways for students that promote a sense of productive persistence through key milestones and benchmarks, advisors critically address both cognitive and noncognitive factors with students (Silva & White, 2013). Promoting a mentality for success may especially benefit students with transfer goals. Because of the intensity of initial first-term advising activities, advisors may not address transfer planning immediately; however, helping students see the consequences of choices and actions in their early academic career may exert a significant positive influence on student persistence through a bachelor's degree. Advisors help students set a measured pace for transfer congruent with institutional, program, or advising benchmarks, which may specify completion of course work, but also include planning tasks such as meeting with a faculty advisor, declaring a major, selecting transfer destinations, researching transfer requirements, and undertaking other critical decisions and interactions.

Educating students about key milestones, helping them reach those milestones in a timely manner, and intervening when students lose sight of the goal or go off the path to it comprise key aspects of transfer advising (Wyner et al., 2016). However, to facilitate student transfer out of the two-year college, advisors need to look for opportunities to improve outcomes. Because 80% of new two-year college students aim to earn a bachelor's degree and only 33% transfer to a four-year college within six years (Wyner et al., 2016), students clearly need assistance to meet their educational objectives. With their knowledge of students, advisors can create an internal coalition or transfer champions team for improving transfer procedures, tightening relationships with recruiters and advisors at transfer destinations, and advocating for improvements to transfer policies (Wyner et al., 2016).

Summary

In addition to the knowledge and relational proficiency needed for all in the field, advisors in the two-year college must demonstrate competencies in confronting unique and evolving challenges. Advising in the two-year college may feel like climbing up an insurmountable mountain in which unpredictable winds of change and treacherous footing inhibit progress. Like all advisors of first-year students, those in two-year colleges will make the most advances by knowing the unique characteristics of their students, but more than their peers in other institutions, two-year college advisors also need to know and embrace the surrounding community that feeds the institution and provides opportunities for students.

Not in spite of, but because of students' unique and varied dreams and often challenging circumstances as well as the many obstacles they overcome, advising in a two-year setting is incredibly exciting work. With such a varied and diverse group of students and a broad range of duties and responsibilities, advisors in two-year institutions can easily stay engaged and professionally fulfilled while serving the ever-evolving two-year college community.

References

American Association of Community Colleges. (2013). *Profiles of U. S. community colleges: Guide for international students.* Retrieved from http://www.aacc.nche.edu/Resources/aaccprograms/international/Documents/profiles2013.pdf

American Association of Community Colleges. (2014a). *Data points: Remedial courses at community colleges.* Retrieved from http://www.aacc.nche.edu/Publications/datapoints/Documents/Remedial_04162014.pdf

American Association of Community Colleges. (2014b). *2014 Fact sheet.* Retrieved from http://www.aacc.nche.edu/AboutCC/Documents/Facts14_Data_R3.pdf

American Association of Community Colleges. (2015). *Data points: Who attends community college?* Retrieved from http://www.aacc.nche.edu/Publications/datapoints/Documents/WhoAttendsCC_1_MD.pdf

American Association of Community Colleges. (2016a). *Fast facts.* Retrieved from http://www.aacc.nche.edu/AboutCC/Pages/fastfactsfactsheet.aspx

American Association of Community Colleges. (2016b). *Significant historical events in the development of the public community college.* Retrieved from http://www.aacc.nche.edu/AboutCC/history/Pages/significantevents.aspx

American Association of Community Colleges. (2016c). Staying close to home. *Data Points, 4*(6). Retrieved from http://www.aacc.nche.edu/Publications/datapoints/Documents/DP_StayingHome.pdf

Archambault, K. L. (2015). Developing self-knowledge as a first step toward cultural competence. In P. Folsom, F. Yoder, & J. E. Joslin (Eds.), *The new advisor guidebook: Mastering the art of academic advising* (2nd ed., pp. 185–201). San Francisco, CA: Jossey-Bass.

Baier, S. (2005). *International students: Culture shock and adaptation to the U.S. culture* (Master's thesis, Eastern Michigan University). Retrieved from http://commons.emich.edu/cgi/viewcontent.cgi?article=1895&context=theses

Bailey, T. R., Jenkins, D., & Smith Jaggars, S. (2015). *Redesigning America's community colleges.* Cambridge, MA: Harvard University Press.

Banks-Santilli, L. (2015, June 3). Guilt is one of the biggest struggles first-generation college students face. *Washington Post.* Retrieved from https://www.washingtonpost.com/posteverything/wp/2015/06/03/guilt-is-one-of-the-biggest-struggles-first-generation-college-students-face/

Belfield, C., & Crosta, P. (2012). *Predicting success in college: The importance of placement tests and high school transcripts* (Working Paper No. 42). Retrieved from the Community College Research Center website: http://ccrc.tc.columbia.edu/media/k2/attachments/predicting-success-placement-tests-transcripts.pdf

Center for Community College Student Engagement. (2012). *A matter of degrees: Promising practices for community college student success (a first look).* Austin: The University of Texas at Austin, Community College Leadership Program.

Chamberlin, J. (2012, April). Mental health services remain scarce at community colleges. *APA Monitor on Psychology, 43*(4), 11. Retrieved from http://www.apa.org/monitor/2012/04/community-colleges.aspx

Community College Research Center. (2013, September). *Strategic advising.* Retrieved from http://ccrc.tc.columbia.edu/media/k2/attachments/designing-a-system-for-strategic-advising.pdf

Complete College America. (2013). *The game changers.* Retrieved from http://www.completecollege.org/gameChangers.html

Complete College America. (2016a). *Remedial education's role in perpetuating achievement gaps.* Retrieved from http://completecollege.org/the-game-changers/#clickBoxTan

Complete College America. (2016b). *The research behind corequisite remediation.* Retrieved from http://completecollege.org/the-research-behind-corequisite-remediation/

Daniel, S. K., & Davison, K. (2014). Community college student mental health: A comparative analysis. *Community College Review, 42*(4), 307–326.

DeGiorgio, E. (2015). *Understanding the uniqueness of the first-generation community college student: How much does it matter?* Retrieved from https://pdfs.semanticscholar.org/a122/7b8dc998722cc01d6eb8a3eb501f51c37965.pdf?_ga=1.11681332.1013312686.1481064645

Edwards, J. (2013). *2013 Community college task force survey results.* Retrieved from the American College Counseling Association website: http://www.collegecounseling.org/2013-community-college-task-force-survey-results

Furman, D. M. (2011). Nontraditional students: Is it time for a redefinition? *Franklin Business & Law Journal, 2,* 113–116.

Gonzales, R. G. (2009). *Young lives on hold: The college dreams of undocumented students.* Retrieved from the College Board website: https://secure-media.collegeboard.org/digitalServices/pdf/professionals/young-lives-on-hold-undocumented-students.pdf

Hodara, M., & Xu, D. (2014). *Does developmental education improve labor market outcomes? Evidence from two states* (Working Paper). Retrieved from the Center for Analysis of Postsecondary Education and Employment website: http://capseecenter.org/wp-content/uploads/2014/12/does-developmental-education-improve-labor-market-outcomes.pdf

Horn, L., & Carroll, C. D. (1996). *Nontraditional undergraduates: Trends in enrollment from 1986 to 1992 and persistence and attainment among 1989-90 beginning postsecondary students* (NCES 97-578). Retrieved from National Center for Education Statistics website: https://nces.ed.gov/pubs/web/97578.asp

Hughes, K. L., & Scott-Clayton, J. (2011, February). Assessing developmental assessment in community colleges. *CCRC Brief, 50,* 1–4. Retrieved from http://ccrc.tc.columbia.edu/media/k2/attachments/assessing-developmental-assessment-brief.pdf

Juszkiewicz, J. (2015). *Trends in community college enrollment and completion data.* Retrieved from the American Association of Community Colleges website: http://www.aacc.nche.edu/Publications/Reports/Documents/CCEnrollment_2015.pdf

Kalamkarian, H., & Karp, M. (2015). *Student attitudes toward technology-mediated advising systems* (Working Paper No. 82). Retrieved from Community College Research Center website: http://ccrc.tc.columbia.edu/media/k2/attachments/student-attitudes-toward-technology-mediated-advising-systems.pdf

Karp, M. (2011). *Toward a new understanding of non-academic student support: Four mechanisms encouraging positive student outcomes in the community college* (Working Paper No. 28). Retrieved from the Community College Research Center website: http://ccrc.tc.columbia.edu/media/k2/attachments/new-understanding-non-academic-support.pdf

Karp, M., & Fletcher, J. (2015, June). *Using technology to reform advising: Insights from colleges.* Retrieved from http://ccrc.tc.columbia.edu/media/k2/attachments/UsingTech-Insights-WEB.pdf

Kegel, K. (2009, March). *Homesickness in international college students.* Paper presented at the American Counseling Association annual conference and exposition, Charlotte, NC. Retrieved from https://www.counseling.org/resources/library/vistas/2009-V-Print/Article%207%20Kegel.pdf

Long, B. T., & Boatman, A. (2013). The role of remedial and developmental courses in access and persistence. In A. Jones & L. Perna (Eds.), *The state of college access and completion: Improving college success for students from underrepresented groups* (pp. 77–95). New York, NY: Routledge. Retrieved from http://scholar.harvard.edu/files/btl/files/long_boatman_2013_role_of_remediation_in_access_and_persistence_-_acsfa_routledge.pdf

Loyola University of Chicago, Achieving College Excellence. (2016). *First generation college student resources.* Retrieved from http://www.luc.edu/ace/resources/firstgenerationcollegestudentresources/

Mamiseishvili, K. (2012). International student persistence in U.S. postsecondary institutions. *Higher Education: The International Journal of Higher Education and Educational Planning, 64*(1), 1–17.

Markle, R., & O'Banion, T. (2014). Assessing affective factors to improve retention and completion. *Learning Abstracts 17*(11), 1–16. Retrieved from http://www.league.org/blog/post.cfm/assessing-affective-factors-to-improve-retention-and-completion

McCullough, A. K. (2010). *Factors that impact two-year college attendance and program enrollment among community college students* (Doctoral dissertation, The University of North Carolina at Chapel Hill). Retrieved from https://cdr.lib.unc.edu/indexablecontent/uuid:be35f207-598f-4566-800e-6fcfc157bd0d

Mendoza, S. (2015, September 15). Giving undocumented students safe harbor on campus. *Hispanic Outlook in Higher Education Magazine.* Retrieved from https://www.hispanicoutlook.com/featured-articles/2015/9/15/giving-undocumented-students-safe-harbor-on-campus?rq=Giving%20Undocumented

National Behavioral Intervention Team Association. (2016). *Behavioral intervention teams.* Retrieved from https://nabita.org/behavioral-intervention-teams/

National Conference of State Legislators. (2014, June 12). *Undocumented student tuition: State action.* Retrieved from http://www.ncsl.org/research/education/undocumented-student-tuition-state-action.aspx

O'Banion, T., & Wilson, C. (2013). The case for on-time registration [author proof]. *Leadership Abstracts, 26*(4), 1–5. Retrieved from http://www.3cmediasolutions.org/sites/default/files/OBanion_WilsonTheCaseForOn-TimeRegistration.pdf

Perez, Z. (2014, December 5). *Removing barriers to higher education for undocumented students.* Retrieved from https://www.americanprogress.org/issues/immigration/report/2014/12/05/101366/removing-barriers-to-higher-education-for-undocumented-students/

Peters, L., Hyun, M., Taylor, S., & Varney, J. (2010, September). Advising non-traditional students: Beyond class schedules and degree requirements. *Academic Advising Today, 33*(3). Retrieved from http://www.nacada.ksu.edu/Resources/Academic-Advising-Today/View-Articles/Advising-Non-Traditional-Students-Beyond-Class-Schedules-and-Degree-Requirements.aspx

Pollock, K. (2006). *Enrollment management in community college.* Retrieved from http://www4.aacrao.org/semsource/sem/indexd128-2.html?fa=view&id=3160

Salinitri, G. (2005). The effects of formal mentoring on the retention rates for first-year, low achieving students. *Canadian Journal of Education, 28*(4). Retrieved from http://www.csse-scee.ca/CJE/Articles/FullText/CJE28-4/CJE28-4-salinitri.pdf

Silva, E., & White, T. (2013). *Pathways to improvement: Using psychological strategies to help college students master developmental math.* Retrieved from http://www.carnegiefoundation.org/resources/publications/pathways-improvement-using-psychological-strategies-help-college-students-master-developmental-math/

Smith Jaggars, S., & Fletcher, J. (2014). *Redesigning the student intake and information provision processes at a large comprehensive community college* (Working Paper No. 72). Retrieved from Community College Research Center website: http://ccrc.tc.columbia.edu/media/k2/attachments/redesigning-student-intake-information-provision-processes.pdf

Stürzl-Forrest, S. (2012). *Helping first semester international undergraduates taxi to academic success.* Retrieved from http://www.nacada.ksu.edu/Resources/Clearinghouse/View-Articles/Advising-first-year-international-students.aspx

Tovar, E. (2013). *A conceptual model on the impact of mattering, sense of belonging, engagement/involvement, and socio-academic integrative experiences on community college students' intent to persist* (Doctoral dissertation, Claremont Graduate University). Retrieved from http://scholarship.claremont.edu/cgi/viewcontent.cgi?article=1083&context=cgu_etd

U.S. Department of State, Bureau of Consular Affairs. (2015). *U.S. Visas: Foreign students in public schools.* Retrieved from http://travel.state.gov/content/visas/en/study-exchange/student/foreign-students-in-public-schools.html

Wheeler, W. (2014). *Economic impact of international students.* Retrieved from http://www.aacc.nche.edu/Publications/datapoints/Documents/InterlImpact_03112014.pdf

Wyner, J., Deane, K. C., Jenkins, D., & Fink, J. (2016). *The transfer playbook: Essential practices for two- and four-year colleges.* Retrieved from http://ccrc.tc.columbia.edu/media/k2/attachments/transfer-playbook-essential-practices.pdf

Zhang, Y. (2016). An overlooked population in community college. *Community College Review, 44*(2), 153–170.

CHAPTER 5

Advising Academically Underprepared Students

Marsha A. Miller and Carita Harrell

The tectonic shift in student demographics (Staley & Trinkle, 2011) is associated with matriculation of students ill prepared to transition to college, persist, and graduate. According to ACT (2016), 38% of 2013 high school graduates who had completed the ACT met three of four college readiness benchmarks in English, math, reading, and science, with only 26% meeting readiness is all four areas (p. 5). Students who enter colleges and universities with inadequate academic skills are often considered at risk of attrition. Harding and Miller (2013) identified "academic background, poor prior performance, personal characteristics, and/or marginalized experiences" (p. 13) as metrics for assessing risk of attrition. For this chapter, we define underpreparedness as a key characteristic of at-risk students whose academic background or prior educational experiences (e.g., academic failure, poor preparation, low expectations) (King, 2004) make them academically vulnerable. Strategies discussed in this chapter are based upon a variety of theories and advising approaches deemed useful in supporting students whose academic skill sets need improvement to bolster their chances of reaching their goals.

The Academically Underprepared

Of the more than 1.9 million 2015 high school graduates completing the ACT, 86% reported the intention to pursue postsecondary education (ACT, 2015, p. 3). Although many college-bound students expressed high aspirations, approximately one quarter of them had completed the recommended years in four subjects: English, reading, mathematics, and science (ACT, 2015, p. 8). "Roughly half of all undergraduates and 70 percent of community college students take at least one remedial course and only a quarter of those students graduate within eight years" (CorePrinciples.org, 2015, para. 3). In addition, completion rates range from 21.9% for open (nonselective) admissions at two-year colleges to

62.4% for selective admissions at doctoral degree-granting universities (ACT, 2014, p. 7). These dismal success rates have prompted many within higher education, and especially those at two-year colleges, to seek research that better delineates the predictors of student persistence to graduation.

According to Ross et al. (2012), the students most likely to persist took pre-calculus and earned college-level credits in high school, completed college entrance exams, met with an advisor during their first year in college, came from homes that rank in the highest income quartile, and lived with a parent who holds a bachelor's degree (pp. xv, xvi). Their findings comport with those from Klepfer and Hull (2012), who identified three factors related to an increased chance of students completing a credential:

- high level of mathematics (increased likelihood of staying on track by 10 to 20%),

- successful completion of Advanced Placement/International Baccalaureate course (the more of these courses a student passed, the higher their persistence rate), and

- academic advising (which is associated with student persistence rates as high as 53%). (p. 2)

Only one of the success factors can be controlled after the student is admitted to college: academic advising.

Academically underprepared students hail from a variety of backgrounds, including historically underrepresented groups as defined by race and ethnicity, socioeconomic status, and first in family to attend college (Grimes & David, 1999). These findings are supported by a National Center for Education Statistics report illustrating that the rates of college enrollment among African American, Latina/o, and American Indian students lag behind their White counterparts by as much as 18% (Horn & Carroll, 2006). The disparities in college enrollment correspond to low secondary school graduation rates for these ethnic groups. Layton (2014) reported that "in many states, one third of students from low-income families did not graduate" from high school in 2012 (para. 6). Specifically, 69% of African Americans and 73% of Hispanic students graduated high school, while White and Asian students graduated at rates exceeding 85% (Layton, 2014, para. 6). Data collected over 20 years by the National Education Longitudinal Study on students of color enrolled in nonselective, open enrollment institutions show relatively low rates of retention and graduation. According to the same study, enrollment of underrepresented minorities in selective institutions, where student persistence outcomes are deemed more positive, has declined since 1992 (Melguizo, 2008).

Students from families of low socioeconomic status likely face financial challenges that place them at a disadvantage for success (Barton, 2004; Valencia, 2015). Explaining that stressed families—financially or otherwise—dedicate relatively less time and resources to children's learning activities than nonstressed families, Rothstein (2004) argued that "characteristics that define social class differences inevitably influence learning" (p. 43). Data suggest that African American children are three times more likely to live in poverty than White children and less likely to enroll in college or complete degrees (American Psychological Association, 2015, para. 4; Barker, 2011, para. 3). In 2005, African American college graduation rates were calculated at 42% of those who enroll initially ("Black Student College Graduation Rates," 2005-2006, para. 3).

Engle and Tinto (2008) found that 24% of the undergraduate population possessed two underpreparedness risk factors: low-income and first-generation status (p. 8). These students "were nearly four times more likely—26 to 7 percent—to leave higher education after the first year than students who had neither of these risk factors" (p. 11). These students were "less likely to be engaged in the academic and social experiences that foster success in college," such as studying in groups, interacting with faculty members and other students, participating in extracurricular activities, and using support services (p. 21).

Because low-income students are more likely to enter college underprepared with remediation needs (The Executive Office of the President, 2014), many campus efforts are directed to providing developmental education for them; however, legislators and constituents in groups, such as Complete College America, have debated the effectiveness of these measures. Some states (e.g., Florida and Connecticut) have scaled back or eliminated monies for such course work (Munsch et al., 2015). The continued debate compels advisors to adopt new strategies. Advisors cannot simply refer underprepared students to developmental classes; instead, they must employ a variety of theories, approaches, and strategies to teach underprepared students the ways of success.

By asking students to reflect upon their perceived knowledge about a subject and their ideas on ways to improve their performances (Conley, 2008), advisors coax underprepared students to pinpoint possible incongruence with course level. Advisors address contextual skills and awareness when they direct the underprepared student to potential financial aid sources and point out deadlines.

Personal management skills may prove especially important for underprepared students from low socioeconomic environments who must grapple with financial issues as they adjust to all other aspects of college life (Harackiewicz et al., 2013). Advisors must guard against assuming that all low-income students need substantial assistance and that all students from middle- or upper-income families have received adequate academic preparation for college success.

Theories That Connect Academic Advising, Academic Underpreparedness, and Student Development

Academic advisors should draw from a number of theories when advising underprepared students. For instance, underprepared students from low-income households often function at the lower levels of Maslow's (1954) hierarchy of needs (e.g., physiological or safety levels). These students may shoulder family and employment obligations that make full-time participation in the college experience unrealistic (Engle & Tinto, 2008).

In his description of challenges experienced by students on college campuses, Tinto (1993) noted two specific obstacles: isolation and incongruence. Isolation, or feeling disconnected from daily academic life, often results from students failing to integrate fully into the institution. According to research supported by the Center for Community College Student Engagement, student interaction with collegiate peers, including active and collaborative learning, predicts college completion (Price & Tovar, 2014).

Student engagement indicators include history of undertaking academic challenges, learning alongside peers, gaining experiences with faculty members, and interacting in campus environments (National Survey of Student Engagement [NSSE], 2015). Academic advisors know that underprepared students who participate in high-impact practices—learning communities, service-learning, research with faculty, internships or field experience, study abroad, and capstone experiences—demonstrate a greater likelihood of completing a degree (NSSE, 2015, p. 1). Therefore, advisors should query students concerning engagement indicators (e.g., ask them to summarize learning in a class) to determine the level of their engagement (NSSE, 2015). Despite the value of this information in assessing student risk, the engagement indicators offer no guidance for advising students with academic and social skills incongruent with those needed in a specific academic program or for life on campus.

Incongruence characterizes the student "at odds with the institution in terms of academic expectations, social norms, or financial costs" (Tinto, 1993, p. 186). Conley (2008) delineated four facets of college readiness that affect student success: academic content knowledge and skills, key cognitive strategies, academic behaviors, and contextual skills and awareness levels. In an explanation of the readiness lessons offered to improve content knowledge and skills, Conley pointed to practices in developmental courses that teach reasoning, problem-solving, and self-management skills.

By asking them to explain issues, defend a point of view, or critique a learning experience, advisors encourage students to exercise their reasoning abilities (Conley, 2008). Advisors can introduce problem-solving strategies, such as identifying key elements of an issue, and suggest strategies that help students address each element separately, and in this way, assist students in understanding and analyzing complicated situations (Malouff, n.d.). Self-management skills include proficiency to assess, monitor, and evaluate abilities to manage time, curb procrastination, use confidence strategies, handle distractions, and cope with stress (Trinity College Dublin, 2015). Academic advisors who prompt students to consider ways of thinking or teach stress management compel students to take charge of their academic experiences and increase resilience.

Astin's (1984/1999) theory of student involvement focuses on the importance of students' interaction with their environment. He outlined five factors of college student involvement: investment in physical and psychological energy, involvement along a continuum, measurable participation, learning and personal involvement proportional to the quantity and quality of student investment, and effective campus practices to increase engagement (p. 519). Advisors know the indicators of underpreparedness and determine whether students experience isolation on campus or engagement with others. More recently in a published interview, Astin ("Q & A with Alexander Astin," 2012) urged the academy to provide opportunity and support for students to reflect on their situations and goals. As a reflection strategy, journaling benefits advisees, as can job shadowing or visiting with individuals working in a field of interest. Through observation of the world of work, students connect classroom learning with their goals, which may confer particular advantage to students as they interact with persons in their social or family circles. To motivate them to acquire or improve proficiencies, advisors can share with students the skills employers want (Adams, 2014) and prompt advisees to build their career potential by creating a working portfolio of curricular and cocurricular experiences that illustrate mastery of these skills (Shaffer & Zalewski, 2011) (see chapters 8 and 9).

Many first-year college student programs offer the appropriate balance of challenge and support for students as first explained by Sanford (1962). The advisor uses Sanford's idea of balance to assist students deemed underprepared for one major but who demonstrate the academic skills needed for another, related major. For instance, a pre-med student with a keen desire to help children but who struggles in science classes may benefit from exploring majors that require fewer science courses or less stringent grade requirements and that lead to careers working with children.

Personal choices, including those related to institution and major, may contribute to the struggle of underprepared students. Without adequate support, underprepared and underinformed students may not consider all the facets of their decision and thus select institutions, programs, or courses that do not align with their interests or proficiency levels (Steele, 2013). Furthermore, ill-prepared students may lack the coping tools needed to overcome unintended setbacks. In fact, overly challenging environments "are toxic … and promote defensiveness and anxiety" (Northern Illinois University, n.d., p. 4). Academic advising offers "perhaps the only opportunity for all students to develop a personal, consistent relationship with someone in the institution who cares about them" (Drake, 2011, p. 10), and advisors provide both direct assistance and referrals to appropriate specialists.

Resilience in Retention, Persistence, and Graduation

Through Tinto's 1990s research, the importance of retention was infused into many campus discussions (see, e.g., Tinto, 1993). During the decades that followed, institutions created initiatives targeting first-year students (Bean, 2015). In some cases, these initiatives were the result of requirements (e.g., from the U. S. Department of Education) that colleges and universities measure and report retention (percentages) for each program of study (National Center for Education Statistics, 2015); that is, stakeholders took an interest in and tracked the percentages of first-time, full-time students who reenroll in college their sophomore year. At the dawn of the new millennium, many institutions expanded retention efforts to include strategies aimed at helping students persist to graduation (Castellanos & Jones, 2003). In the second decade of the 21st century, *persistence* was used to refer to the actions a student takes to stay in the higher education system from matriculation through degree completion (Berger & Lyon, 2005). Thus, the measure of student success on many campuses evolved from student retention to student persistence until graduation.

McGillin (2003) hypothesized that students who succeed are resilient "in the face of stress, despite the presence of pervasive factors that would put them at risk" (p. 47). In a Stockholm Resilience Centre publication, Moberg and Simonsen (n.d.) described resilience as the capacity of an individual to deal with change and "continue to develop" (p. 3). McGillin pointed out that both personal characteristics and environmental resources contribute to student resilience.

Specifically, institutions with little control over personal characteristics can manage environmental factors including those associated with students' connections to knowledgeable, supportive, and caring academic advisors who teach them self-efficacy skills.

Bandura (1986) defined self-efficacy as the belief in one's "capabilities to organize and execute courses of action required to attain designated types of performances" (p. 391). Advisors promote resilience when they teach students specific self-efficacy strategies, such as ways to approach faculty members and build an academic support network (see chapters 3 and 10) that bolster students' self-confidence and their ability to succeed. Through their relationship with students, "advisors are uniquely placed to help a student connect-the-dots ... and develop a sense of mastery as they begin to understand" the campus and the connections that they can leverage (McGillin, 2003, p. 51). Thus, advisors who help students connect with others across campus can serve as the "critical coach in learning, selecting, and implementing academic coping strategies" (McGillin, p. 52).

Student Goals Inform Advising Approaches and Strategies

While foundation directors and politicians may define success as graduation (e.g., Complete College America, 2016a; Obama, 2009), students tend to focus on short-term outcomes. Academic advisors who assist entering students in articulating long-term goals and short-term outcomes help them delineate a personal, operational definition of success. Research shows that advisors who help advisees identify goals and connect learning to achieving them encourage persistence (Caspar, 2014-2015). Advising strategies that help students determine long-term goals and apply skills toward achieving future outcomes may prove especially useful in community colleges, in which a relatively large percentage of first-time students require developmental courses (Complete College America, 2016b) (see chapter 4).

Cuseo (n.d.) recommended that advisors learn about students through the use of an intake form or questionnaire through which advisees answer questions in six general areas: personal background, future plans, abilities or aptitudes, interests, values, and advising expectations (para. 2). Responses to questionnaire items provide insight that advances advisor understanding and clarifies the support needed by all students, not just those who are underprepared (see chapters 3 and 11). They also help the advisors tailor advising approaches and strategies to student needs.

No one academic advising approach fits all situations, including those of underprepared students (see chapter 2). Therefore, advisors gain familiarity with various strategies and adapt them to help "students articulate and achieve their academic goals and career aspirations" (Drake, Jordan, & Miller, 2013, p. ix). Some students enter college focused on earning a degree, others seek a major that leads to profitable employment, while others focus on taking the courses necessary to achieve a particular outcome (e.g., establishing or retaining eligibility for insurance or a sport). A Pennsylvania State University study found that "80% of freshmen—even those who have declared a major—say they are uncertain about their major" (Simon, 2012, para 5); this statistic applied to all students, including the underprepared.

When applying developmental academic advising (Crookston, 1972/2009), practitioners understand underprepared students' motivations and can guide them in achieving academic competency and continuing individual growth. Grites (2013) noted that Crookston's initial treatise on college student development encouraged others to apply theories, including those by Astin (1984/1999), Conley (2008), and Tinto (1993), in advising practice.

In his explanation of developmental advising, O'Banion (1972/2009) took a slightly different approach than Crookston did and suggested that an effective advising process is initiated in steps: student exploration of life goals; the continued examination of vocational goals, program choice, course choice; and finally, the creation of course schedules. Cate (2013) postulated that the O'Banion steps may work better in another order for many students, including those underprepared for their chosen major. Because some students come to an advisor with the sole objective of choosing and scheduling courses, Cate suggested that advisors encourage students to consider course work that interests them before addressing program choice, vocational selections, and life goals. Cate also recommended use of the motivational interview advising approach, noting that it simultaneously challenges students to explore and overcome barriers to their goals. Through motivational interviewing, advisors consider specific factors that incentivize students to achieve rather than focus on their level of drive, and they help students identify issues affecting their academic progress and determine their willingness and ability to improve (Hughey & Pettay, 2013).

The appreciative advising approach is rooted in appreciative inquiry theory "focused on the cooperative search for the positive in every living system" (Bloom, Hutson, & He, 2013, pp. 83–84). Appreciative advising does not encourage a spotlight on underpreparedness or perceived obstacles; instead, practitioners ask "positive, open-ended questions that help students optimize their educational experiences and achieve their dreams, goals, and potentials" (Bloom et al., 2013, p. 83). Advisors guide students to discover, dream, design, and deliver as means of establishing and achieving their goals (Bloom et al., 2013).

Strength-based advising, as the name suggests, is predicated on establishing and using areas of proven ability rather than trying to correct potential weaknesses (see chapter 2). By encouraging students to delineate their strengths (e.g., through assessment instruments), advisors can motivate students to appreciate and seize upon their own talents. According to Louis (2008), the potential for increased self-confidence and self-efficacy through this approach gives students a "greater sense of control over their academic outcomes" (as cited in Louis, 2011, p. 205). Strengths-based advising, applicable to all students, may prove particularly relevant to those needing assistance in understanding the ways to use their skills to stay motivated and overcome challenges (Schreiner, 2013).

Hagen (forthcoming) referred to the narrative advising approach as "the most important way we have of creating, maintaining, defining, or changing" student identities. He explained that practitioners using this strategy encourage students to tell their stories and then listen carefully as the unique narrative unfolds. In response to those who think that storytelling seems an inadequate method for understanding, Hagen argued that narratives may provide the best means to understand students and be understood by them. Advisors who encourage sharing ensure that students are heard, and such validation contributes to student creation of their success identities. When students craft their stories, they share the "longing, imagination, interpretation, intentionality, and memory" that shape their college experiences (Hagen, forthcoming). Advisors who prompt students to envision the remaining chapters of their stories can guide them to the practices and resources that help them reach their desired endings (see chapter 8). Underprepared and other at-risk students may particularly benefit from envisioning success and learning the steps necessary to reach goals.

Proactively Connecting With Underprepared Students

Gardner (2001) identified factors that contribute to student success: orientation, first-year seminars, learning communities, service-learning, academic support services, health education, and the recruitment of upper-division students to serve as mentors who contribute to the success of first-year students (p. 6). Many academic advisors' responsibilities connect them directly with students via Gardner's student success factors (Carlstrom, 2013a, 2013b). Thus, advisors interact with students to notice and address potential roadblocks before they become insurmountable obstacles. Proactive advising strategies used during the first year support students, decrease attrition rates, and help students succeed (Glennen, 1975; McGrath & Burd, 2012).

Proactive advising has evolved as a vital tool for assisting academically underprepared students. Early-warning systems (i.e., computerized systems that alert advisors to students who miss class, fail a test, or display other nonproductive behaviors) offer information for timely advisor connections with students (see chapter 10). However, proactive advisors do not wait for alerts; instead, they reach out to students before they make poor decisions. They interact purposely and frequently to stay abreast of potential problems and offer preemptory solutions that include referrals (Varney, 2013). Some use a planning session (Cloud Community College, n.d., para. 1) to identify new student aspirations and abilities in the educational planning context (Miller & Murray, 2005). For example, based on discussions with advisees after the first round of exams, advisors can determine whether nonacademic responsibilities or adjustment concerns hinder a student's progress.

At institutions where academic advisors facilitate programs and services (e.g., teach, provide career advising, coordinate student internships), students receive directed, specific assistance to persist to graduation or other educational goals (Winston, Miller, Ender, & Grites, 1984). Advisors who take an active interest in their advisees and in first-year programs (e.g., teach sections of first-year courses) contribute to the overall undergraduate experience (Miller, 2013b), and those who collaborate to address current issues (e.g., serve on committees studying first-year issues) affect retention and success for academically underprepared students. The connections made in these advocacy efforts provide additional support for advisors (and others) helping underprepared first-year students successfully navigate college (King, 2007) and overcome any incongruence described by Tinto (1993).

Institutional Support of Underprepared Students

Students considered underprepared encounter challenges based on institutional characteristics. Institutions use different strategies for determining preparedness: Some rely on test scores to determine preparedness, others give more weight to high school transcripts, while others use data from predictive analytics to identify potential problems. However, the selected practices may not identify all students who need assistance or offer adequate information for provision of appropriate support to those identified as underprepared. To fill gaps in support, many institutions also invest in predictive analytics, peer advisors, and early-warning systems to assist first-year students.

Predictive Analytics

Toner (2015) believes that strategies for student success are best created through predictive analytics, which provide more than test scores and high school transcripts. Predictive analytics track new student data so advisors and other educators can look for patterns of first-year retention (Miller, 2013a). Profiles emerge when college personnel use the data to ask pertinent questions about student persistence: Who succeeds? Who does not? What characteristics do successful students share? What dissimilarities are found between those who reach their goals and those who do not? (Miller, 2013a)

Effective advisors know the entry-level courses considered high risk, such as those defined by a D/F/withdrawal rate higher than 30% (Missouri State University, n.d., para. 2). Predictive analytics tools (e.g., Degree Compass) detail "factors that measure how well each course might help the student progress through their program" (Austin Peay State University, n.d., para. 2) such that advisors can recommend courses that will increase the probability of students achieving their educational goals. In addition, advisors know the profile (i.e., test scores, background, and use pattern of support services) of students who succeeded in those courses. When emulating strategies used by previously successful students, new students—including the underprepared—increase their chances of success (Ellucian, n.d.).

Peer Advisors

Previously successful students can provide direct peer support. In 2012, as many as 65% of institutions responding to a NACADA-member survey reported use of peer advisors to support student learning and development (Koring & Zahorik, 2012, p. 11). Peer mentorship programs assist with retention as well as the overall college experience (Renn & Arnold, 2003). Mentoring for provision of emotional support, guidance, and connection as well as modeling of transitional skills may make students feel connected to campus life and capable of achieving their desired academic goals (Coles, 2011). Successful peer mentoring programs foster student loyalty, belonging, and support retention (Vianden & Barlow, 2015); they feature advisor commitment to the program, genuine care, mentee perception, and agreeable relationships (Shotton, OoSahwe, & Cintron,

2007). Peer mentoring, coupled with the resources available through primary-role or faculty advisors, may contribute to the success of students reaching their academic goals.

Early-Warning Systems

Institutions that provide supportive, structured tools (e.g., early-alert systems) assist advisors in identifying and connecting with students and prove critical for reaching the underprepared. By working with the faculty to enforce holds on services, such as registration, advisors provide the timely assistance shown to increase college retention. In addition to early-warning systems, advisors who collaborate with faculty instructors and department staff to organize resources streamline accessible support for students who need the most assistance.

Underprepared students may feel isolated and fail to admit that they need services (Tinto, 1993). Therefore, advisors cannot merely tell students about resources; instead, by hosting proactive workshops and offering summer bridge opportunities (e.g., upward-bound programs), advisors partner with those less prepared and mentor (or work with mentors) to offer assistance nonthreatening to self-esteem or cultural norms. "In some cultures, students are more accustomed to seeking help from peers than from the professor. This may be because the student feels self-conscious approaching an authority figure, because seeking extra assistance is viewed as inappropriate" (Carnegie Mellon, n.d., p. 15).

Gardner (2001) suggested that advisors can play an important role in student adjustment to college life and effectively help them meet personal and institutional goals. To support advisors, college and university administrators provide tools for identifying students who are underprepared, teach them strategies for success, and thereby fortify institutional sustainability. As part of the toolkit, campus leaders offer continuous training and professional development opportunities that encourage application of developmental theories in advising practice, whether face-to-face or through technology, to meet and assist students at their personal and academic levels (Givans Voller, 2012).

Providing a seamless support system for students from the beginning of their college experience to graduation may increase retention and persistence, especially for those who are underprepared. Gardner (2001) reported that interweaving orientation programs, mentoring, early-warning systems, and other forms of support early in the transition to college helps students master needed skills (p. 6). Furthermore, as underprepared students develop their competencies, they need leadership opportunities to mentor others (Colvin & Marinda, 2010). This cyclical process of peer mentoring requires thoughtful planning from dedicated people in multiple departments committed to creating a welcoming, affirming environment conducive to successful outcomes. The creation of a robust, stimulating, and safe learning environment remains the responsibility of higher education institutions and respective constituents.

AIMING FOR **EXCELLENCE**

The following discussion questions and activities give advisors concrete ideas and strategies for expanding their knowledge and applying the information shared in this chapter to their advising practice:

- Learn about the undergraduates considered academically underprepared at your institution. Meet with advising directors, institutional research personnel, or the registrar's office to determine who succeeds, who does not, and the reasons for these outcomes.

- Obtain the D/F/withdrawal rates for introductory courses. Who succeeds in those courses? Who does not? Query successful students to determine the strategies they find most helpful to their success.

- How do you define resilience? Which characteristics do you repeatedly see in resilient students? Discuss strategies to develop these characteristics in underprepared students with colleagues.

- Determine the intervention strategies discussed in the chapter that will most likely build resilience in advisees identified as underprepared.

- Implement one of the strategies discussed in this chapter with underprepared students. Document how well this strategy worked in helping students reach their educational goals.

- Expand your knowledge and use of advising approaches. Determine which of the advising approaches introduced in chapter 2 and discussed in this chapter you think would prove most beneficial to your underprepared advisees.

- Select a new advising approach and seek out others who use this approach to learn more about it. Create a plan to incorporate the approach and some of the strategies associated with it into your advising practice.

Summary

To meet the needs of all students and help them succeed, academic advisors must embrace several perspectives, especially in relating to advisees who fit the definition of underprepared or at risk. Effective advisors employ carefully selected tools (e.g., predictive analytics) to know and reach students. They also base their advising practice on theory and tailor their advising approaches to the needs of the individual, including those underprepared for college academics and life.

To connect with underprepared students, advisors must remain creative, collaborative, and intuitive. They must vary advising approaches and strategies to apply theory in effective student interactions. Only the full linkage from theory to practice makes the positive impact that helps students, including the underprepared, complete their goals.

References

ACT. (2014). *National collegiate retention and persistence to degree rates.* Retrieved from: http://www.act.org/content/dam/act/unsecured/documents/retain_2014.pdf

ACT. (2015). *The condition of college & career readiness 2015.* Retrieved from https://www.act.org/content/dam/act/unsecured/documents/CCCR15-NationalReadinessRpt.pdf

ACT. (2016). *The condition of college & career readiness 2016: National ACT.* Retrieved from https://www.act.org/content/dam/act/unsecured/documents/CCCR_National_2016.pdf

Adams, S. (2014, November 12). The 10 skills employers most want in 2015 graduates. *Forbes.* Retrieved from http://www.forbes.com/sites/susanadams/2014/11/12/the-10-skills-employers-most-want-in-2015-graduates/

American Psychological Association. (2015). *Education and socioeconomic status.* Retrieved from http://www.apa.org/pi/ses/resources/publications/factsheet-education.aspx

Astin, A. W. (1999). Student involvement: A developmental theory for higher education. *Journal of College Student Development, 40*(5), 518–529. (Reprinted from *Journal of College Student Personnel, 25,* 1984, pp. 297–308)

Austin Peay State University. (n.d.). *Degree Compass—What is it?* Retrieved from http://www.apsu.edu/information-technology/degree-compass-what

Bandura, A. (1986). *Social foundations of thought and action: A social cognitive theory.*

Englewood Cliffs, NJ: Prentice-Hall.

Barker, C. J. (2011, August 10). Black graduation rates on rise. *New York Amsterdam News.* Retrieved from http://amsterdamnews.com/news/2011/aug/10/black-graduation-rates-on-rise/

Barton, P. E. (2004). Why does the gap persist? *Educational Leadership, 62*(3), 8–13. Retrieved from http://www.ascd.org/publications/educational-leadership/nov04/vol62/num03/Why-Does-the-Gap-Persist%C2%A2.aspx

Bean, J. P. (2015). *College student retention: Defining student retention, a profile of successful institutions and students, theories of student departure.* Retrieved from http://education.stateuniversity.com/pages/1863/College-Student-Retention.html

Berger, J. B., & Lyon, S. C. (2005). Past to present: A historical look at retention. In A. Seidman (Ed.), *College student retention: Formula for student success* (pp. 1–29). Westport, CT: Praeger.

Black student college graduation rates remain low, but modest progress begins to show. (2005-2006, Winter). *The Journal of Blacks in Higher Education,* 88–96. Retrieved from http://www.jbhe.com/features/50_blackstudent_gradrates.html

Bloom, J. L., Hutson, B. L., & He, Y. (2013). Appreciative advising. In J. K. Drake, P. Jordan, & M. A. Miller (Eds.), *Academic advising approaches: Strategies that teach students to make the most of college* (pp. 83–99). San Francisco, CA: Jossey-Bass.

Carlstrom, A. H. (2013a). Job responsibilities: 2-year institutions. In A. H. Carlstrom & M. A. Miller (Eds.), *2011 NACADA National survey of academic advising* (Monograph No. 25). Retrieved from http://www.nacada.ksu.edu/Portals/0/Clearinghouse/M25/M25%20Chaper%2010%20Tables%202-23-16.pdf

Carlstrom, A. H. (2013b). Job responsibilities: 4-year institutions. In A. H. Carlstrom & M. A. Miller (Eds.), *2011 NACADA National survey of academic advising* (Monograph No. 25). Retrieved from http://www.nacada.ksu.edu/Portals/0/Clearinghouse/M25/M25%20Chapter%2011%20Tables%202-23-16.pdf

Carnegie Mellon. (n.d.). *Recognizing and addressing cultural variations in the classroom.* Retrieved from http://www.cmu.edu/teaching/resources/PublicationsArchives/InternalReports/culturalvariations.pdf

Caspar, E. (2014-2015). A path to college completion for disadvantaged students. *Focus, 31*(2), 24–29.

Castellanos, J., & Jones, L. (2003). *The majority in the minority.* Sterling, VA: Stylus.

Cate, P. (2013). So, I've been thinking ... O'Banion in reverse. In J. K. Drake, P. Jordan, & M. A. Miller (Eds.), *Academic advising approaches: Strategies that teach students to make the most of college* (pp. 61–63). San Francisco, CA: Jossey-Bass.

Cloud County Community College. (n.d.). *New student planning conference.* Retrieved from http://www.nacada.ksu.edu/portals/0/Clearinghouse/Links/documents/New-Student-Planning-Conference.pdf

Coles, A. (2011, Spring). The role of mentoring in college access and success. *Research to Practice Brief.* Retrieved from http://www.ihep.org/sites/default/files/uploads/docs/pubs/the_role_of_mentoring_in_access_and_success_final_spring_2011.pdf

Colvin, J., & Marinda, A. (2010). Roles, risks, and benefits of peer mentoring relationships in higher education. *Mentoring & Tutoring: Partnership in Learning, 18,* 121–134.

Complete College America. (2016a, May 10). *Complete College America and the alliance: Redefining how we measure success.* Retrieved from http://completecollege.org/complete-college-america-and-the-alliance-redefining-how-we-measure-success/

Complete College America. (2016b, February 12). *Remedial education's role in perpetuating achievement gaps.* Retrieved from http://completecollege.org/remedial-educations-role-in-perpetuating-achievement-gaps/

Conley, D. T. (2008). Rethinking college readiness. *New Directions for Higher Education, 2008*(144), 3–13. Retrieved from http://www.csub.edu/eap-riap/day1/Rethinking%20College%20Readiness.pdf

CorePrinciples.org. (2015). *National organizations and states endorse design principles to support student success and scale effective higher education practices* [press release]. Retrieved from http://www.core-principles.org/uploads/2/6/4/5/26458024/press_release.pdf

Crookston, B. B. (2009). A developmental view of academic advising as teaching. *NACADA Journal, 29*(1), 78–82. (Reprinted from *Journal of College Student Personnel, 13,* 1972, pp. 12–17)

Cuseo, J. (n.d.). *How I use the advisee information card.* Retrieved from http://www.nacada.ksu.edu/Resources/Clearinghouse/View-Articles/Creating-a-new-student-intake-form.aspx

Drake, J. K. (2011). The role of academic advising in student retention and persistence. *About Campus, 16*(3), 8–12. Retrieved from http://advising.arizona.edu/sites/default/files/jaynearticle%20(3).pdf

Drake, J. K., Jordan, P., & Miller, M. A. (Eds.). (2013). *Academic advising approaches: Strategies that teach students to make the most of college.* San Francisco, CA: Jossey-Bass.

Ellucian. (n.d.). *Retention and student success: Implementing strategies that make a difference.* Retrieved from http://www.ellucian.com/Insights/Retention-and-student-success--Implementing-strategies-that-make-a-difference/

Engle, J., & Tinto, V. (2008). *Moving beyond access: College success for low-income, first-generation students.* Washington, DC: The Pell Institute for the Study of Opportunity in Higher Education. Retrieved from http://files.eric.ed.gov/fulltext/ED504448.pdf

The Executive Office of the President. (2014, January). *Increasing college opportunity for low-income students: Promising models and a call to action.* Retrieved from https://www.whitehouse.gov/sites/default/files/docs/white_house_report_on_increasing_college_opportunity_for_low-income_students.pdf

Gardner, J. N. (2001). *Focusing on the first-year student* (AGB Priorities, No. 17). Washington, DC: Association of Governing Boards of Universities and Colleges.

Givans Voller, J. (2012). *Advisor training and development: Why it matters and how to get started.* Retrieved from http://www.nacada.ksu.edu/Resources/Clearinghouse/View-Articles/Advisor-training-and-development-Why-it-matters-and-how-to-get-started.aspx

Glennen, R. E. (1975). Intrusive college counseling. *College Student Journal 9*(1), 2–4.

Grimes, S. K., & David, K. C. (1999). Underprepared community college students: Implications of attitudinal and experiential differences. *Community College Review, 27*(2), 73–92.

Grites, T. J. (2013). Developmental academic advising. In J. K. Drake, P. Jordan, & M. A. Miller (Eds.), *Academic advising approaches: Strategies that teach students to make the most of college* (pp. 45–59). San Francisco, CA: Jossey-Bass.

Hagen, P. (forthcoming). *Aspects of narrative in academic advising.* Manhattan, KS: NACADA: The Global Community for Academic Advising.

Harackiewicz, J. M., Canning, E. A., Tibbetts, Y., Giffen, C. J., Blair, S. S., Rouse, D. I., & Hyde, J. S. (2013, November 4). Closing the social class achievement gap for first-generation students in undergraduate biology. *Journal of Educational Psychology, 106,* 375–389. doi: 10.1037/a0034679

Harding, B., & Miller, M. A. (2013). *Cultivating the potential in at-risk students* (NACADA Pocket Guide, No. 11). Manhattan, KS: NACADA: The Global Community for Academic Advising.

Horn, L., & Carroll, C. D. (2006). *Placing college graduation rates in context: How 4-year college graduation rates vary with selectivity and the size of low-income enrollment.* Washington, DC: National Center for Education Statistics.

Hughey, J., & Pettay, R. (2013). Motivational interviewing: Helping advisors initiate change in student behaviors. In J. K. Drake, P. Jordan, & M. A. Miller (Eds.), *Academic advising approaches: Strategies that teach students to make the most of college* (pp. 67–82). San Francisco, CA: Jossey-Bass.

King, N. (2004, August). *Advising underprepared students.* Presented at the NACADA Summer Institute on Advising, Milwaukee, WI.

King, N. (2007, June). *Setting the stage: Foundations of academic advising.* Presented at the NACADA Summer Institute, Burlington, VT.

Klepfer, K., & Hull, J. (2012). *High school rigor and good advice: Setting up students to succeed (at a glance).* Retrieved from http://www.centerforpubliceducation. org/Main-Menu/Staffingstudents/High-school-rigor-and-good-advice-Setting-up-students-to-succeed/High-school-rigor-and-good-advice-Setting-up-students-to-succeed-Full-Report.pdf

Koring, H., & Zahorik, D. (Eds.). (2012). *Peer advising and mentoring: A guide for advising practitioners* (2nd ed.). Manhattan, KS: National Academic Advising Association.

Layton, L. (2014, April 28). National high school graduation rates at historic high, but disparities still exist. *The Washington Post,* p. A.3. Retrieved from http://www.washingtonpost.com/local/education/high-school-grad-uation-rates-at-historic-high/2014/04/28/84eb0122-cee0-11e3-937f-d3026234b51c_story.html

Louis, M. C. (2011). Strengths interventions in higher education: The effect of identification versus development approaches on implicit self-theory. *The Journal of Positive Psychology, 6*(3), 204–215. Retrieved from https://www. researchgate.net/publication/238595779_Strengths_interventions_in_ higher_education_The_effect_of_identification_-versus_development_ approaches_on_implicit_self-theory_The_Journal_of_Positive_ Psychology_63_204-215

Malouff, J. (n.d.). *Over fifty problem solving strategies explained.* Retrieved from http://www.une.edu.au/about-une/academic-schools/bcss/news-and-events/psychology-community-activities/over-fifty-problem-solving-strategies-explained

Maslow, A. (1954). *Motivation and personality.* New York, NY: Harper.

McGillin, V. A. (2003). Academic risk and resilience: Implications for advising at small colleges and universities. In M. K. Hemwall & K. C. Trachte (Eds.), *Advising and learning: Academic advising from the perspective of small colleges and universities* (Monograph No. 8, pp. 43–52). Manhattan, KS: National Academic Advising Association.

McGrath, S. M., & Burd, G. D. (2012). A success course for freshmen on academic probation: Persistence and graduation outcomes. *NACADA Journal, 32*(1), 43–52.

Melguizo, T. (2008). Quality matters: Assessing the impact of attending more selective institutions on college completion rates of minorities. *Research in Higher Education, 49*(3), 214–36.

Miller, M. A. (2013a). *How to determine who is at-risk.* Retrieved from http://www.nacada.ksu.edu/Resources/Clearinghouse/View-Articles/How-to-determine-who-is-at-risk.aspx

Miller, M. A. (2013b). Structuring our conversations: Shifting to four dimensional advising models. In A. H. Carlstrom & M. A. Miller (Eds.), *2011 NACADA national survey of academic advising* (Monograph No. 25). Retrieved from http://www.nacada.ksu.edu/Resources/Clearinghouse/View-Articles/Structuring-Our-Conversations-Shifting-to-Four-Dimensional-Advising-Models.aspx

Miller, M. A., & Murray, C. (2005). *Advising academically underprepared students.* Retrieved from the http://www.nacada.ksu.edu/Resources/Clearinghouse/View-Articles/Academically-underprepared-students.aspx

Missouri State University. (n.d.). *17 FAQ's from faculty about SI.* Retrieved from http://pass.missouristate.edu/assets/si/faculty_faq.pdf

Moberg, F., & Simonsen, S. H. (n.d.). *What is resilience? An introduction to social-ecological research.* Stockholm, Sweden: University of Stockholm, Stockholm Resilience Centre. Retrieved from http://www.stockholmresilience.org/download/18.10119fc11455d3c557d6d21/1398172490555/SU_SRC_whatisresilience_sidaApril2014.pdf

Munsch, P., Borland, K.W., Duberstein, A., Miller, M.A., Gilgour, J., & Warren, M. (2015). *From remediation to graduation: Directions for research and policy practice in developmental education.* Washington, DC: ACPA: College Student Educators International. Retrieved from http://www.myacpa.org/sites/default/files/Developmental%20Education%20Monograph%20FINAL.pdf

National Center for Education Statistics. (2015). *IPEDS 2015-16 data collection system.* Retrieved from https://surveys.nces.ed.gov/ipeds/VisInstructions.aspx?survey=6&id=30077&show=all#chunk_305

National Survey of Student Engagement. (2015, July 23). *Engagement indicators & high-impact practices.* Retrieved from http://nsse.indiana.edu/pdf/EIs_and_HIPs_2015.pdf

Northern Illinois University. (n.d.). *A brief introduction to student development theory.* Retrieved from http://www.niu.edu/engagedlearning/themed_learning/A%20Brief%20Introduction%20to%20Student%20Development%20Theory.pdf

Obama, B. H. (2009). *Remarks of President Barack Obama–As prepared for delivery address to joint session of congress.* Retrieved from http://www.whitehouse.gov/the_press_office/Remarks-of-President-Barack-Obama-Address-to-Joint-Session-of-Congress/

O'Banion, T. (2009). An academic advising model. *NACADA Journal, 29*(1), 83–89. (Reprinted from *Junior College Journal, 42,* 1972, pp. 62, 63, 66–69)

Price, D. V., & Tovar, E. (2014, May 8). Student engagement and institutional graduation rates: identifying high-impact educational practices for community colleges. *Community College Journal of Research and Practice, 38,* 766–782. doi:10.1080/10668926.2012.719481

Q&A with Alexander Astin. (2012, July). *The Bulletin, 80*(4). Retrieved from http://www.acui.org/publications/bulletin/article.aspx?issue=36081&id=18393

Renn, K. A., & Arnold, K. D. (2003). Reconceptualizing research on college student peer culture. *Journal of Higher Education, 74*(3), 261–292.

Ross, T., Kena, G., Rathbun, A., KewalRamani, A., Zhang, J., Kristapovich, P., & Manning, E. (2012, August). *Higher education: Gaps in access and persistence study* (NCES 2012-046). Retrieved from the National Center for Education Statistics website: https://nces.ed.gov/pubs2012/2012046.pdf

Rothstein, R. (2004). The achievement gap: A broader picture. *Educational Leadership, 62*(3), 40–43.

Sanford, N. (1962). *The American college.* New York, NY: Wiley.

Schreiner, L. A. (2013). Strengths-based advising. In J. K. Drake, P. Jordan, & M. A. Miller (Eds.), *Academic advising approaches: Strategies that teach students to make the most of college* (pp. 105–120). San Francisco, CA: Jossey-Bass.

Shaffer, L. S., & Zalewski, J. M. (2011). A human capital approach to career advising. *NACADA Journal, 31*(1), 75–87.

Shotton, H. J., OoSahwe, S. L., & Cintron, R. (2007). Stories of success: Experience of American Indian students in a peer-mentoring retention program. *The Review of Higher Education, 31*(1), 81–107.

Simon, C. C. (2012, November 2). Major decisions. *New York Times.* Retrieved from http://www.nytimes.com/2012/11/04/education/edlife/choosing-one-college-major-out-of-hundreds.html

Staley, D. J., & Trinkle, D. A. (2011, February 7). The changing landscape of higher education. *EDUCAUSE Review.* Retrieved from http://er.educause.edu/articles/2011/2/the-changing-landscape-of-higher-education

Steele, G. (2013). *Decision making: Interest and effort.* Retrieved from http://www.nacada.ksu.edu/Resources/Clearinghouse/View-Articles/Decision-Making.aspx

Tinto, V. (1993). *Leaving college: Rethinking the causes and cures of student attrition* (2nd ed.). Chicago, IL: University of Chicago Press.

Toner, M. (2015, Winter). The (less-) big picture. *The Presidency: The American Council on Education Magazine for Higher Education Leaders.* Retrieved from http://www.acenet.edu/the-presidency/columns-and-features/Pages/The-Less-Big-Picture.aspx

Trinity College Dublin. (2015). Self-management. Retrieved from https://www.tcd.ie/Student_Counselling/student-learning/undergraduate/topics/self-management/

Valencia, R. (2015). *Students of color and the achievement gap: Systematic challenges, systematic transformations.* New York, NY: Routledge, Taylor & Francis.

Varney, J. (2013). Proactive advising. In J. K. Drake, P. Jordan, & M. A. Miller (Eds.), *Academic advising approaches: Strategies that teach students to make the most of college* (pp. 137–154). San Francisco, CA: Jossey-Bass.

Vianden, J., & Barlow, P. J. (2015). Strengthen the bond: Relationships between academic advising quality and undergraduate student loyalty. *NACADA Journal, 35*(2), 15–27.

Winston, R. B., Miller, T. K., Ender, S. C., & Grites, T. J. (Eds.). (1984). *Developmental academic advising.* San Francisco, CA: Jossey-Bass.

CHAPTER 6

Academic Recovery in the First Year

Nova Schauss Fergueson

For the last several decades, stakeholders in and out of the academy have directed considerable resources to initiatives designed to help students make a successful transition to college. Many of the institutional strategies—including learning communities, first-year seminars, and supplemental instruction—have been linked to improved academic performance and increased retention (Kuh, Kinzie, Schuh, & Whitt, 2005; McClenney & Waiwaiole, 2005). Despite these institutional investments, many students struggle academically in the first year, including some who enter higher education without significant risk factors. For this reason, advisors need to recognize student vulnerabilities and offer solutions for academic recovery as part of a comprehensive advising strategy for first-year students. Perhaps recognition of need for academic intervention and recovery creates the biggest challenge for advisors, but underperforming students must come to advisor attention before they can receive appropriate support. Many students enter higher education without any of the academic risk factors typically associated with underpreparation or an otherwise at-risk status (see chapter 5) but subsequently fall short on the benchmarks for college success; however, as promising students flounder, others with a significant number of risk factors demonstrate remarkable academic success.

Important personal characteristics such as motivation, self-efficacy, and self-regulated learning (Schreiner, 2012) may drive some students to achieve despite certain disadvantages. Therefore, advisors must appreciate the uniqueness of a student's story when developing and implementing first-year academic recovery interventions (Miller & Murray, 2005). The advisor who focuses too much on students encountering the greatest quantifiable difficulties may unwittingly overlook the students whose academic performances border on failure. The Education Advisory Board (2014) refers to the group of underperforming promising students as the *murky middle*, and these students may pose the greatest and most unexpected challenge to advisors. Those envisioning a comprehensive system of support for first-year students through academic recovery need nuanced understanding about the students in academic difficulty.

After identifying students in need of recovery, advisors must identify their degree of responsibility for helping the student set and meet expectations for reinstatement of good academic standing. While not answerable for student performance, advisors often play a significant and expected role in the process; however, they cannot deliver all components of an academic recovery program. Campus partners, including those in units such as financial aid, housing, student accounts, academic coaching, tutoring, and mental health services, among others, provide important collaborative inputs in a comprehensive and student-focused approach to academic recovery. When exploring the broad aspects of academic recovery programs, advisors reading this chapter must firmly resist bearing the burden of such efforts alone. However, as key contributors to recovery initiatives, they also need to know the theories undergirding recovery practices and implement specific strategies to support students experiencing academic difficulty.

Institutional Approaches to Academic Recovery

Institutional definitions of good academic standing vary, but they typically include a threshold GPA. They may also include satisfactory completion of a specified number of credits by predetermined milestones (e.g., number passed within a fixed number of academic terms). Similarly, the response to first-year students who lose their good academic standing also varies considerably. Most responses fall along a continuum from voluntary to mandatory participation in a recovery program (Gehrke & Wong, 2007). The continuum of recovery efforts, the ways students experience those strategies, and proactive steps of advisors combine to affect the success of support initiatives designed for students seeking to improve their academic standing.

Voluntary Recovery Systems

Some academic recovery programs feature no formalized system or oversight for students in negative academic standing (Duffy, 2010; Engle, Reilly, & Levine, 2003; Scrivener, Sommo, & Collado, 2009). Students are expected to seek out clarity or information regarding the academic standing policy on their own. If policy information is delivered to students, institutional staff conduct no additional outreach to ensure students accurately understand it. In fact, no structured interactions with staff members, requirements related to course load or specific course enrollment, or referrals to academic support services, such as tutoring or academic coaching, follow. When they encounter academic difficulty, students receive neither prompt to take a specific action nor any consequence (e.g., a registration hold) that might inspire help seeking. Instead, students must take the initiative in contacting staff for questions or concerns.

In practice, the simple voluntary recovery model may function as follows: A first-year student who earns a term GPA below 2.0 is placed in academic warning status. An e-mail informs the student of this academic standing along with an outline of the institutional policy, a statement articulating the GPA required for reinstatement to good academic standing, and a description of the consequence(s) of failing to improve grades in the subsequent term. The name and contact information of a university staff member responsible for oversight of academic standing concludes the message along with the invitation to address the representative with questions or concerns related to the policy. No further action is required on the part of the student, and no additional follow-up is undertaken by institutional representatives except for documentation that the student was informed of negative academic standing via an official e-mail.

Intermediate Recovery Systems

Some institutions introduce greater structure or formality into academic recovery systems, but the programs typically do not mandate specific student action (Hsieh, Sullivan, & Guerra, 2007; Isaak, Graves, & Mayers, 2006). At some colleges and universities, the nature of the intervention varies by student population or academic unit, creating inconsistency in the support offered. In some situations, holds or other restrictions may not immediately affect registration activity.

In practice, an intermediate level of intervention may function as part of a larger program. For example, at some institutions, students pursuing a major within the natural sciences may take significantly longer to recover from academic difficulty than students pursuing other academic interests; therefore, a program developed in response targets first-year students within the natural sciences who fail to earn the threshold GPA during their first term at the institution. Students in this category cannot adjust their class schedule or register for the subsequent term until they meet with an advisor to develop an academic success plan. After a plan is established at the meeting, the registration hold is lifted. First-year students in other departments exhibiting comparable academic difficulties may be encouraged to meet with an advisor to develop an academic success plan, but no registration hold is placed and students experience no adverse consequences if they choose not to follow the advice.

Mandatory Recovery Systems

Other institutions offer highly structured and coordinated academic intervention programs and consistently apply them across campus to ensure all students receive comparable levels of support (Butler, Blake, Gonzalez, Heller, & Chang, 2016; Mann, Hunt, & Alfred, 2003; Molina & Abelman, 2000). These institutions may also encourage proactive communication about academic policies to students using methods students likely appreciate. For example, an advisor may begin a conversation about an institutional policy with statements such as "I know this policy can often be confusing. Let's go through it together and see where there are questions" or "Talk me through your understanding of this policy. How do you think it impacts your current academic standing?" When they check for understanding and practice active listening, advisors increase accurate understanding of policies and limit misinterpretations or confusion.

Advisors or support staff working within a mandatory recovery system practice proactive, rather than reactive, outreach to students in poor academic standing, and interventions may include insight-oriented intrusive advising (Vander Schee, 2007). Students encounter limited access or registration holds that prevent them from enrolling until they have undertaken specific activities demonstrating compliance. Typical oversight for this population is centralized.

In practice, this model may function as follows: Academic recovery rates among all first-year students throughout the institution are assessed, which shows that specific academic departments have significantly higher rates of students on academic warning after their first term. Recognizing that first-year students often change majors, an institution-wide intervention system is developed for all first-year students on academic warning after their first term. A registration hold is applied and only lifted after a student completes an academic success plan with an advisor. In this way, all first-year students on academic warning, regardless of major, receive comparable support.

Assessing the Program

Certain institutional models or practices contribute to the meaningful support that advisors and other educators give to students. Despite the evidence that they provide proper levels of assistance, these practices warrant regular review and modification as student populations, funding, and staff support fluctuate. In this assessment process, administrators and advisors alike must ask: Does the current intervention structure support students in academic recovery? How do we know that students are using and benefiting from these efforts?

To exert the greatest influence, recovery systems cannot be established in the advising silo. Despite good reasons for differentiating particular aspects of a system to meet needs of specific student populations or promising outcomes of new interventions piloted on a small scale, advisors must understand the reach and impact of an institution-wide effort. Significant differences within an institution related to effectiveness of academic recovery interventions may require modifications to the system in part or in whole.

When discussing an institutional approach to academic recovery, advisors can point to thriving campuses as described by Schreiner (2012). At thriving institutions, everyone prioritizes student academic engagement and performance, psychological well-being, and interpersonal relationships. However, to maintain standards for the framework, they must commit to intentional efforts and high expectations for the academic recovery process. A holistic approach applies most aptly to first-year students in academic distress because they rarely confront isolated difficulties with course content (Schreiner, 2012). First-year students encounter myriad transitions, often simultaneously, including a new physical environment, redefinition of their role within the family unit, financial burdens, and exploration of identity (see chapter 3). Institutional leadership performs a disservice when conveying a message that academic performance is valued over interpersonal and intrapersonal experiences. Therefore, knowing the multifaceted concerns of first-year students, advisors can advance the conversation beyond academic success and challenge others at the institution to envision a culture that encourages holistic well-being.

Whatever the institutional strategy to academic recovery, advisors may find proactive (formerly *intrusive*) and developmental advising valuable approaches to advising first-year students in academic distress (see chapter 2). By using these longstanding practices (Crookston, 1972/2009; Earl, 1987), advisors anticipate student needs and intervene in a manner that honors the full experience of students (Miller & Murray, 2005). Because many variables contribute to academic distress, students need to identify and resolve the issues thwarting their pursuit of educational and personal goals, and the intrusive and developmental practices may prove particularly useful for students with little college experience (Miller, 2010). Advisors can investigate and learn to apply a structured intervention, such as The Move Forward Program (MFP) at The University of Texas Austin, Electrical and Computer Engineering (2014). MFP advisors actively and holistically seek undergraduates in need of added resources. Through this approach, advisors learn of students on the cusp of academic warning or probation but not yet spotted on the institutional radar. Using a proactive approach, MFP advisors identify and intervene before struggling students fall into negative academic standing.

Theories Supporting Academic Recovery

Practitioners engaged in proactive advising gain a unique awareness of a student's complete educational experience and know that a high GPA does not always indicate long-term academic success. Similarly, a mediocre GPA does not necessarily mean a student struggles with academic content. Numerical indicators as sole measures of academic success may lead to overlooking the social, emotional, and cognitive influences that affect a student's academic well-being. However, by grounding practice with theory, advisors enhance the credibility of the advising field and those working within it. Therefore, by identifying the theoretical frameworks for approaching the academic recovery process, advisors develop thoughtful and well-designed interventions. Some of the most applicable and far-reaching concepts come from the field of educational psychology and include hope and self-authorship theories.

Hope Theory

Snyder's (1995) hope theory supports efforts to increase student motivation or self-efficacy, which undergirds academic success. Hope theory overlaps with both mindset (Dweck, 2008) and strengths-based advising (Schreiner & Anderson, 2005). It suggests that a student's level of hope is connected with academic success, as demonstrated by quantitative measures such as GPA as well as persistence and graduation rates (Snyder, Lopez, Shorey, Rand, & Feldman, 2003). Through targeted student interventions, such as assignments of reflective narrative writing and exercises enhancing metacognition, advisors can incrementally improve a student's self-efficacy.

Self-authorship Theory

The transition to adulthood involves a shift away from blindly subscribing to the opinions of external authorities to developing personally defined values, beliefs, and opinions—a process that Baxter Magolda (2008) called *self-authorship*. Students in academic distress may need to reconcile the demands of external forces (e.g., parental pressure, societal expectations, university policies) and their emerging sense of self as they reflect on their academic reality. Advisors can express care and offer the appropriate level of challenge as students negotiate this process (Baxter Magolda, 2008).

First-year students, regardless of academic performance, navigate external pressures, and although each faces unique situations, advisors recognize typical scenarios of first-year students. For example, the honors student accustomed to earning straight As may fear failure upon receiving the first B– and question his or her identity as a high achiever. The student who dreams of a career in nursing may feel devastated when finding biological sciences uninteresting. While students in negative academic standing are forced to reconcile their educational goals with their current academic performance, advisors must recognize that the self-discovery process represents normal, if challenging, experiences for students regardless of their academic profile. They also must reassure students that they can engage in effective self-authorship.

Strategies Based on Nine Noncognitive Psychosocial Factors

Supporting first-year students through academic recovery requires timely intervention strategies because any delay may diminish the likelihood for academic recovery. Therefore, systematic approaches for advising students in academic distress should conform to the institutional culture and the needs of first-year students as they navigate recognizable, precarious situations. Perhaps the most immediate and important advising strategy involves reframing the context of a student's academic challenge, recovery, and success. Building an advising tool kit of ways to teach students to change their perspective requires ongoing exploration of effective strategies and related research.

Build Student Resiliency

Psychosocial factors are essential to building resiliency and include a student's attitudes, behaviors, and motivations (Habley, Bloom, & Robbins, 2012). They have alternatively been defined as "motivation, investment of effort, self-efficacy, and ability to regulate [one's] own learning" (Schreiner, McIntosh, Cuevas, & Kalinkewicz, 2013, p. 11). These factors have proven powerful when used in conversations about academic recovery because they address predictors for student success (Bowman, 2010; Robbins et al., 2004; Sedlacek, 2004). Students enter higher education with varying degrees of these noncognitive factors, and those with well-developed self-efficacy possess greater resiliency in the face of adversity, including academic difficulty (Sedlacek, 2004).

First-year students with poorly developed noncognitive factors can strengthen them through advising interventions (Robbins et al., 2004). For example, first-year students can answer advisor inquiries, such as

- Tell me about a time when you worked really hard to accomplish some-thing. What steps did you take to create a successful outcome?

- Who were the most instrumental people in getting you from high school to college? What advice do you think they'd give you about the challenge you're currently facing?

- It's very normal to enjoy certain subjects more than others. If you could create your dream college class, what would it be, and what would happen in the classroom?

Through these open-ended explorations, students identify personal strengths, re-call experiences of resilience, recognize key support systems, and translate prior knowledge to academics.

Teach Metacognition

By acquiring introductory knowledge about learning and memory, advisors gain the ability to teach metacognition—ways to think about thinking—to increase students' personal agency regarding academic behaviors (Karpicke, Butler, & Roediger, 2009; Mastascusa, Snyder, & Hoyt, 2011; Willis, 2006). To understand metacognition, one needs to know the ways information is stored and retrieved in the brain. For example, by explaining that spaced and consistent repetition of concepts creates strong and intact neuropathways that help a person retain and retrieve information (Mastascusa et al., 2011), advisors can refute any stated advantage of cramming the night before an exam. Descriptions of these processes may prove particularly salient to students who value science or evidentiary proof, such as STEM majors.

Furthermore, advisors can challenge students to consider the benefit of repetition when preparing for quizzes, exams, and class discussions. A first-year music major may appreciate the way this tactic corresponds to regular practice of a musical arrangement. Likewise, a student learning a new language will appreciate the value of repetition when exposed to vocabulary, pronunciation, and grammatical rules. Regardless of the context, by developing metacognition first-year students recognize their own power in directing their academic experiences, a significant component of academic recovery.

Change Student Mindset

Advisors should explain the value of a growth mindset (Dweck, 2008) to students because of the correlation between students' effort and their academic performance (Robbins et al., 2004). According to Dweck (2008), a growth mindset allows one to develop and expand ability and potential through time and effort. Because of the empowering nature of this perspective, a growth mindset proves a powerful ingredient when overcoming challenging experiences such as academic difficulty. Advisors will recognize that

> students who believe that hard work, focus, and effort will positively affect their own success often effectively regulate their responses to the external environment. This ... enables students to feel a sense of control and engenders confidence when faced with academic challenges. (Schreiner et al., 2013, p. 11)

When students demonstrate awareness of personal strengths and believe that hard work leads to success, moments of failure simply become feedback mechanisms they use to adjust their approach toward a better outcome. According to Dweck's (2008) research, growth mindset is best instilled through choices in language. Instead of praising students for natural intelligence or talent, advisors should praise them for the effort and persistence put into the accomplishment. Statements such as the following encourage a growth mindset:

- You worked really hard to understand such complex ideas.

- Your commitment to staying focused, attending office hours with your professor, and trying new study strategies is very impressive.

- I really admire the way you decided to take control of the situation and try a different approach.

Show Empathy

No quick fix or convenient resource will adequately address a student's every academic challenge. In those moments, simply being present and empathetically listening to the student navigating the trying time often proves more helpful than providing a litany of well-intentioned quick fixes. Empathy is the act of vicariously feeling the emotions of another person. It involves imagining the person's feelings when failing an exam or ending a significant relationship. Advisors in empathy avoid judgment while taking on the perspectives and emotions of a student. By comparison, when offering sympathy, a person maintains a separation between people. An advisor practicing sympathy expresses pity or sorrow for the student, but does not experience the feelings personally. Students engaged in academic recovery may require more than a list of academic resources and review of the academic standing policy; they may need a support system and empathy.

Those considered at risk for academic difficulty may matriculate with substandard academic preparation, limited educational support networks, reduced cultural capital, conflicting family obligations, and relatively low socioeconomic status (Swecker, Fifolt, & Searby, 2013); therefore, they may particularly appreciate an empathetic advisor who can provide multifaceted support. Advisors who walk beside students from a position of empathy, rather than sympathy, develop meaningful relationships that may culminate in one of the few that endure through graduation (Drake, 2011).

Establish Meaningful Relationships

People who build meaningful relationships increase the protective factors of care and support (Henderson & Milstein, 1996), and supportive campus environments are associated with student psychological well-being and sense of belonging (Hausmann, Ye, Schofield, & Woods, 2009) as well as persistence in college (Robbins et al., 2004). In describing the role of advisors in helping students with relationships, Habley (1994) noted that advising offers one of the few longstanding one-to-one relationships on campus; therefore, advisors may hold tremendous potential to enhance student resilience during times of academic difficulty.

Relationship building encompasses empathy. Students who feel safe may admit defeat or failure within the context of a meaningful relationship, allowing them to take the first step toward academic recovery. A genuine and caring relationship between an advisor and advisee provides a safe place for students to acknowledge failure, process the experience, and craft a solution (see chapter 5).

Specific first-year populations will encounter challenges that amplify the need for meaningful relationships within the institutional setting. For example, immigrants may experience conflicting demands between family and school, significant financial need, lack of academic preparation or language barriers, little emotional support, and impermanent legal status (Stebleton, 2011). Despite possible needs for advising, many immigrant students hesitate to seek or accept support and may consult peer groups for assistance (Brilliant, 2000). Positive and genuine early interactions rooted in an ethos of care and support with advisors lay the foundation for engagement by reticent students in the academic recovery process (Stebleton, 2011).

Encourage Reflection

Students with a positive perspective toward obstacles, and life in general, may reframe negative experiences into learning opportunities (Seligman, 2011). The act of reflection, either verbally or in writing, can help students learn to reframe events and recognize their own ability to overcome difficulties (Keyes & Haidt, 2003; Seligman, 2011). In a traditional advising context, an advisor might prompt a first-year student to discuss past experiences with academic difficulty by asking questions, such as

- What did you feel in the moment?
- How do you view the experience now?
- Did you face the challenge again? Did you handle it differently the second time?
- What actions most affected the outcome?

In a different tactic, the advisor asks the student to imagine that the same situation happened to a friend: "What advice would you give your friend to move around this obstacle?" An indirect approach, such as visualizing a friend encountering the challenge, may encourage sharing from students reluctant to discuss their personal background. Intentional and guided reflection characterizes strengths-based advising.

Practice Strengths-Based Advising

A strengths-based advising approach prompts students to identify the ways their personal strengths equip them to traverse difficult roads (see chapter 2). Through this strategy, advisors avoid identifying students' weaknesses and instead intentionally focus on highlighting strengths (Schreiner & Anderson, 2005). In one-to-one meetings advisors may first inquire about successes of the previous terms using one of the following conversation starters:

- Tell me about your greatest success last term.
- Looking back, what are you most proud of?
- What do you feel most confident about this term?
- What accomplishment would most impress your high school teacher/coach/mentor?

Students struggling academically may seem hyperfocused on their perceived academic shortcomings and benefit from a conversation that guides them into seeing their strengths during the academic recovery process. In so conversing, advisors need to point out the importance of cocurricular activities in which a student has excelled; those with a disappointing academic performance may have found a strong social circle, joined an athletic team, secured an on-campus job, or discovered a new academic interest. Each of these accomplishments may form the basis on which to proceed toward a new pathway to succeed academically. Holistic student success extends beyond grades on a transcript.

Assess Student Interests and Skills

A variety of assessments—the Myers-Briggs Type Inventory (The Myers-Briggs Foundation, 2016), the Strong Interest Inventory (CPP, 2016), ACCUPLACER (College Board, 2016), and StrengthsQuest (Gallup, 2010)—help students identify their skills and interests as well as offer suggestions on ways they translate them into an academic environment. Campus career counselors and testing service professionals can offer guidance on the most appropriate instruments for individuals or groups to use. They can also provide training in administering the instruments and interpreting the results.

The tests can be offered in one-to-one advising settings, within group advising situations, or through first-year seminars or academic recovery courses. The advisor can return to the assessment periodically as appropriate, perhaps as students disclose uncertainty with regard to a major, encounter academic difficulty in a course, or question their ability to succeed in college.

Engage in Motivational Interviewing

Through motivational interviewing, advisors use open-ended questions to prompt students in self-reflection about actions and behaviors that contributed to their current situation (Miller & Rollnick, 2002). Students may know the changes needed but fail to commit to actively making necessary corrections. Motivational interviewing helps students identify the barriers preventing them from altering their negative attitudes or behaviors, and it leads to concrete strategies to overcome the identified obstacles. Questions that encourage reflections and solutions include:

- What will be different if you commit to the academic success plan we developed?
- How will you know that you have been successful?
- What does it look like when academics are your top priority?

Through direct inquiry, advisors facilitate reflection whereby students identify differences between their stated goals and reported behaviors. By working with students from a position of empathy (Brown, 2010), advisors can lower defensiveness and empower students to develop strategies that will move them toward academic recovery.

Because of limited time with students, the advisor must readily identify the strategies that fit best with one's personal advising philosophy, delivery style, and student need. Many of the interventions discussed in this chapter require minimal time to develop, yet when repeated and used in conjunction with each other, they can create a dramatic impact on academic recovery.

AIMING FOR **EXCELLENCE**

The following discussion questions and activities give advisors concrete ideas and strategies for expanding their knowledge and applying the information shared in this chapter to their advising practice:

- Assess your institution's level of structure (voluntary, intermediate, or mandatory) in efforts to help students in negative academic standing. Do you think students receive the appropriate level of intervention at your institution? Does the current structure support students in a timely manner? Does it anticipate student needs to mitigate unintentional or ongoing academic difficulties?

- Determine the data needed to advise students in academic recovery more effectively, including those provided via external agencies (e.g., Education Advisory Board, Complete College America, John N. Gardner Institute for Excellence in Undergraduate Education). What additional data sets or reports would help stakeholders create a comprehensive picture of the academic recovery experience? What questions do the data answer? How can data be thoughtfully and consistently used to inform academic recovery interventions?

- Develop or further articulate theoretical frameworks by which you support students needing academic recovery. Specify the ways that your theoretical approach intentionally informs intervention strategies.

- Identify three interventions within or in addition to the nine outlined in this chapter to incorporate into advising practice. Determine modifications needed to support unique student populations.

- Record ideas, challenges, and successes experienced when working with students in academic recovery. Share these observations with supervisors and colleagues as a way to start conversations about existing or potentially new intervention strategies to foster success among first-year students.

Summary

At the core, effective academic recovery models and practices are intentional, institution-specific, and appropriate to the student or student group. To develop, implement, and assess academic recovery programs, stakeholders must take adequate time and create realistic, measurable expectations. Robust and dynamic comprehensive systems require a lasting commitment on the part of administrators and practitioners alike. However, even in the absence of a thoughtfully constructed institutional initiative, advisors can implement academic recovery interventions in their own advising practice. By identifying strategies from within the nine outlined in this chapter, advisors can guide students to recovery and inform new or existing institutional programs that benefit struggling students.

As one of the few consistently available institutional resources for students traveling on their educational journey, advisors can positively influence students in academic difficulty. While providing academic planning and support constitutes the role of most advisors, their reach extends far beyond curriculum and degree plans. Therefore, advisors should embrace meaningful ways to assist new students as they navigate academic difficulty and work toward recovery.

References

Baxter Magolda, M. B. (2008). Three elements of self-authorship. *Journal of College Student Development, 49*(4), 269–284.

Bowman, N. A. (2010). The development of psychological well-being among first-year college students. *Journal of College Student Development, 51*(2), 180–200.

Brilliant, J. J. (2000). Issues in counseling immigrant college students. *Community College Journal of Research and Practice, 24,* 577–586.

Brown, B. (2010). *The gifts of imperfection.* Center City, MN: Hazelden.

Butler, M., Blake, N., Gonzalez, A., Heller, E., & Chang, F. (2016). Appreciative advising: Retaining academic probation students. *Journal of Appreciative Education, 3*(1), 1–17. Retrieved from http://libjournal.uncg.edu/index.php/jae/article/view/1170/882

College Board. (2016). *ACCUPLACER.* Retrieved from https://accuplacer.collegeboard.org/students

CPP. (2016). *Strong Interest Inventory.* Retrieved from https://www.cpp.com/products/strong/index.aspx

Crookston, B. B. (2009). A developmental view of academic advising as teaching. *NACADA Journal, 29*(1), 78–82. (Reprinted from *Journal of College Student Personnel, 13,* 1972, pp. 12–17)

Drake, J. K. (2011). The role of academic advising in student retention and persistence. *About Campus, 16*, 8–12.

Duffy, K. (2010). *A mixed methods study of community college students on academic probation: The limiting effect of academic doublespeak* (Doctoral dissertation, St. John Fisher College). Retrieved from http://fisherpub.sjfc.edu/education_etd/7

Dweck, C. S. (2008). *Mindset: The new psychology of success.* New York, NY: Ballantine.

Earl, W. R. (1987, September). Intrusive advising for freshmen. *Academic Advising Today, 9*(3). Retrieved from http://www.nacada.ksu.edu/Resources/Clearinghouse/View-Articles/Intrusive-Advising-for-Freshmen.aspx

Education Advisory Board. (2014). *What's the buzz around the "murky middle"?* [web log post]. Retrieved from https://www.eab.com/technology/student-success-collaborative/student-success-insights/2014/09/ssc-making-headlines

Engle, C., Reilly, N., & Levine, H. (2003). A case study of an academic retention program. *Journal of College Student Retention Research, Theory & Practice, 5*, 365–383.

Gallup. (2010). *StrengthsQuest.* Retrieved from http://www.strengthsquest.com/home.aspx

Gehrke, S., & Wong, J. (2007). Students on academic probation. In L. Huff & P. Jordan (Eds.), *Advising special populations: Adult learners, community college students, LGBTQ students, multicultural students, students on probation, undecided students* (Monograph No. 17, pp. 135–149). Manhattan, KS: National Academic Advising Association.

Habley, W. R. (1994). Key concepts in academic advising. In the *Summer Institute on Academic Advising session guide.* NACADA: The Global Community for Academic Advising, Manhattan, KS.

Habley, W. R., Bloom, J. L., & Robbins, S. (2012). *Increasing persistence: Research-based strategies for college student success.* San Francisco, CA: Jossey-Bass.

Hausmann, L. R. M., Ye, F., Schofield, J. W., & Woods, R. L. (2009). Sense of belonging and persistence in White and African American first-year students. *Research in Higher Education, 50*, 649–669.

Henderson, N., & Milstein, M. M. (1996). *Resiliency in schools: Making it happen for students and educators.* Thousand Oaks, CA: Corwin Press.

Hsieh, P., Sullivan, J. R., & Guerra, N. S. (2007). A closer look at college students: Self-efficacy and goal orientation. *Journal of Advanced Academics, 18*, 454–476.

Isaak, M. I., Graves, K. M., & Mayers, B. O. (2006). Academic, motivational, and emotional problems identified by college students in academic jeopardy. *Journal of College Student Retention Research, Theory, & Practice, 8*, 171–183.

Karpicke, J., Butler, A., & Roediger H., III. (2009). Metacognitive strategies in student learning: Do students practice retrieval when they study on their own? *Memory, 17*(4), 471–479.

Keyes, C. L. M., & Haidt, J. (Eds.). (2003). *Flourishing: Positive psychology and the life well-lived.* Washington, DC: American Psychological Association.

Kuh, G. D., Kinzie, J., Schuh, J. H., & Whitt, E. J. (Eds.). (2005). *Student success in college: Creating conditions that matter.* San Francisco, CA: Jossey-Bass.

Mann, J., Hunt, M., & Alfred, J. (2003). Monitored probation: A program that works. *Journal of College Student Retention Research, Theory, & Practice, 5*, 245–254.

Mastascusa, E. J., Snyder, W. J., & Hoyt, B. S. (2011). *Effective instruction for STEM disciplines: From learning theory to college teaching.* San Francisco, CA: Jossey-Bass.

McClenney, K. M., & Waiwaiole, E. N. (2005). Focus on student retention: Promising practices at community colleges. *Community College Journal, 75*(6), 36–41.

Miller, L. K. (2010). *The impact of intrusive advising on academic self-efficacy beliefs in first-year students in higher education* (Doctoral dissertation, Loyola University of Chicago). Retrieved from http://ecommons.luc.edu/luc_diss/151/

Miller, M. A., & Murray, C. (2005). *Advising academically underprepared students.* Retrieved from http://www.nacada.ksu.edu/Resources/Clearinghouse/View-Articles/Academically-underprepared-students.aspx

Miller, W. R., & Rollnick, S. (2002). *Motivational interviewing: Preparing people for change.* New York, NY: Guilford.

Molina, A., & Abelman, R. (2000). Style over substance in interventions for at-risk students: The impact of intrusiveness. *NACADA Journal, 20*(2), 5–15.

The Myers-Briggs Foundation. (2016). *MBTI basics.* Retrieved from http://www.myersbriggs.org/my-mbti-personality-type/mbti-basics/

Robbins, S. B., Lauver, K., Le, H., Langley, R., Davis, D., & Carlstrom, A. (2004). Do psychosocial and study skill factors predict college outcomes? A meta-analysis. *Psychological Bulletin, 130*, 261–288.

Schreiner, L. A. (2012). From surviving to thriving during transitions. In L. A. Schreiner, M. C. Louis, & D. D. Nelson (Eds.), *Thriving in transitions: A research-based approach to college student success* (pp. 1–18). Columbia, SC: University of South Carolina, National Resource Center for The First-Year Experience and Students in Transition.

Schreiner, L. A., & Anderson, E. (2005). Strengths-based advising: A new lens for higher education. *NACADA Journal, 25*(2), 20–29.

Schreiner, L. A., McIntosh, E. J., Cuevas, A. E. P., & Kalinkewicz, L. (2013, November). *Measuring the malleable: Expanding the assessment of student success.* Paper presented at the Association for the Study of Higher Education, St. Louis, MO.

Scrivener, S., Sommo, C., & Collado, H. (2009, April). *Getting back on track: Effects of a community college program for probationary students* (Opening Doors Project Report). Retrieved from the MDRC website: http://www.mdrc.org/sites/default/files/full_379.pdf

Sedlacek, W. E. (2004). *Beyond the big test: Noncognitive assessment in higher education.* San Francisco, CA: Jossey-Bass.

Seligman, M. (2011). *Flourish: A visionary new understanding of happiness and well-being.* New York, NY: Free Press.

Snyder, C. R. (1995). Conceptualizing, measuring, and nurturing hope. *Journal of Counseling & Development, 73*(3), 355–360.

Snyder, C. R., Lopez, S. J., Shorey, H. S., Rand, K. L., & Feldman, D. B. (2003). Hope theory, measurements, and applications to school psychology. *Social Psychology Quarterly, 18*(2), 122–139.

Stebleton, M. J. (2011). Understanding immigrant college students: Applying a developmental ecology framework to the practice of academic advising. *NACADA Journal, 31*(1), 42–54.

Swecker, H. K., Fifolt, M., & Searby, L. (2013). Academic advising and first-generation college students: A quantitative study on student retention. *NACADA Journal, 33*(1), 46–53.

The University of Texas Austin, Electrical and Computer Engineering. (2014). *The Move Forward Program.* Retrieved from http://www.ece.utexas.edu/undergraduate/move-forward-program

Vander Schee, B. A. (2007). Adding insight to intrusive advising and its effectiveness with students on probation. *NACADA Journal, 27*(2), 50–59.

Willis, J. (2006). *Research-based strategies to ignite student learning.* Alexandria, VA: Association for Supervision and Curriculum Development.

SECTION III

ADVISING FOR STUDENT ENGAGEMENT

CHAPTER 7

Advising Special Populations in the First Year

Ryan Tomasiewicz

A positive transition from high school to college contributes to future academic success such that college and university stakeholders offer support and programming that address potential barriers to persistence. Regardless of the institutional efforts made to ease the difficulties, the level to which students successfully transition depends, in part, on their previous educational endeavors, lived histories, and connections made with others upon matriculation. Among these factors, high-quality interactions with a caring person on campus, such as an academic advisor, establish the initial relationship that may define the first-year experience for some (Drake, 2011). Advisors who understand the needs of first-year students and take advantage of established advising theory and practice may be best equipped to encourage a sense of belonging, which has been shown to positively affect student satisfaction and persistence (Grites, 2013). Furthermore, advisors need to recognize that first-year students represent a highly diverse population (Grewe, 2007).

The diversity of first-year students means that advisors must gain significant knowledge about the potential barriers to their successful transition as well as practice nuanced advising strategies to deal with such challenges. When they demonstrate understanding and evoke effective strategies, advisors represent the university as people who care about and assist students with navigating academic requirements, exploring intellectual curiosities, and adjusting to a new learning and (for some) living environment (Drake, 2011).

Because each student presents individual challenges, advisors must develop cultural competencies (Cunningham, 2016) and foster critical consciousness to establish advising practices that increase each student's self-efficacy and resilience (Schauss & Thomas, 2015). To help students overcome barriers to success in the first year, advisors must identify the special populations at their institutions and learn about their particular concerns. During this process, advisors must recognize ways students' backgrounds differ from their own and acknowledge the underlying assumptions that frame their own interactions with others. To achieve the necessary cultural competency and apply the best strategies for helping with the college transition, advisors turn to scholarship about students and advising (Schulenberg & Lindhorst, 2008). Practice based on knowledge of the student, institution, self, and theory results in advising that advances the success of the diverse students seeking higher education today.

Special Populations Defined

Awareness of the unique attributes of special populations, characterized as subgroups of students experiencing disadvantages in the academic environment and in need of targeted attention, has evolved significantly over time (ACT, 2010; Grites, 1982; Strommer, 1995). Historically, these U.S. populations—women, certain ethnic groups, those with low socioeconomic status, first-generation students, and people with disabilities—were recognized as marginalized in higher education settings (Grites, 1982) because they faced significant additional barriers to their transition to and successful completion of college than the White men on whom the first U.S. academies were based (LeMelle, 2002; Thelin, 2011). Recently, the list of underrepresented or at-risk college students has expanded to include student athletes, military veterans, and adult learners as well as those who participate in the workforce while attending college (Strommer, 1995) or who have limited access to technology or adequate study facilities (Bulger & Watson, 2006). Furthermore, current research is directed at commuter, English-as-a-second-language, LGBTQ, honors, and international students, among others, attending U.S. colleges and universities (ACT, 2010). In addition, early academic enrichment programs (Kulik, Kulik, & Shwalb, 1983; Roueche & Roueche, 1993; Swail, 2000) focus on specific at-risk populations to assist students perceived as less likely to graduate than their counterparts.

Although prior research provides useful guidance and programs abound for those considered at risk, advisors must develop and use their cultural competency, practical experience, and knowledge of theory to recognize and best advise students who belong to several special populations and thus straddle multiple identities (Archambault, 2016). To simplify the discussion, the working definition of *special populations* used in this chapter describes any student cohort with either visible or invisible qualities or needs that may significantly affect the transition to college and attainment of educational goals.

Multiple Identities

A solid step toward understanding special populations and meeting their needs involves exploration of the singular identities or subgroups encountered in daily interactions. When conducting research on special populations, advisors must remember that "while there is much that can be learned from generalizations about cultures, care must be taken to avoid applying stereotypes or over-simplification of these ideas" (Cunningham, 2016). For example, research suggests that first-generation students are less prepared for college-level math and English and more likely to have family or job responsibilities than peers whose parents attended college (Stebleton & Soria, 2012). Students from low-income or first-generation backgrounds are four times more likely than their peers to leave an institution after one year (Engle & Tinto, 2008); however, neither of these generalizations necessarily applies to the student engaged with the advisor at any particular moment. Despite their knowledge about a special population, advisors must take care to avoid prejudging a person's college readiness or situation (e.g., not all struggling military veterans are experiencing posttraumatic stress).

Although not universally applicable, the research into special populations may inspire appropriate inquiries that help advisors narrow possible reasons for student challenges. For example, a prompt such as "Tell me about your time in the military" may elicit responses that increase advisor understanding of the student's situation. Basic information about special populations available online in the NACADA Clearinghouse serves as a starting point, but advisors should regularly review the broader scholarship to keep informed of current trends and language regarding specific populations. Furthermore, to assist individual students, advisors must appreciate the intersection of identities or multiple identities; that is, they need to know about the "ongoing construction of identities and the influence of changing contexts on the experience of identity development" (Jones & McEwen, 2000, p. 408).

As members of multiple groups, students may experience feelings of congruence or divergence with the identities attached to them. For example, a woman student athlete in a STEM discipline may identify with any combination or none of these special populations at any particular moment. As a student athlete, the advisee tries to balance commitment to sport and academic endeavors (e.g., practice, study table, internships) (Broughton & Neyer, 2001; Howard-Hamilton & Sina, 2001; Watt & Moore, 2001). As a woman in a STEM discipline, such as physics, she may experience and cope with gender bias (Williams, Phelps, & Hall, 2014). Moreover, in addition to membership in well-established student populations, the advisee reflects her social, educational, and personal background, which may include visible or invisible manifestations of ethnicity, academic acuity, or disability.

Salient Identities

In addition, multiple identities take on various levels of importance or may change entirely during a student's time in college (Jones & McEwen, 2000). For example, a critical event, such as a drastic turn in financial stability, emerging questions about sexual identity, or diagnosis with a chronic illness may create a shift in the saliency of each identity. *Saliency* describes the way a person understands identity at a particular moment and the evolving importance of it:

> Identity salience represents one of the ways, and a theoretically most im-
> portant way, that the identities making up the self can be organized. Iden-
> tities, that is, are conceived as being organized into a salience hierarchy.
> This hierarchical organization of identities is defined by the probabilities
> of each of the various identities within it being brought into play in a giv-
> en situation. Alternatively, it is defined by the probabilities each of the
> identities have of being invoked across a variety of situations. The loca-
> tion of an identity in this hierarchy is, by definition, its salience. (Stryker
> & Serpe, 1982, p. 206)

Students navigate multiple cultures and identities throughout life and may experience the greatest changes in salience during the first year of college in the context of their cognitive development (Abes, Jones, & McEwen, 2007). The most knowledgeable and prepared advisors will successfully communicate based on the student's salient identity, which may change as students reconcile different dimensions of themselves. Therefore, the best advisors develop their self-knowledge and proficiency for working with each student who comes for advising (Archambault, 2015). They create nuanced strategies to support individuals negotiating their own circumstances, and they adjust practice to account for potential evolution of traits identified through research in a particular population.

Scholarship That Informs Advising

Advisors can build an initial foundation of critical knowledge by understanding students' histories, backgrounds, and experiences (Orozco, Alvarez, & Gutkin, 2010) through student development theories, which provide general explanations on ways most traditional-aged students evolve during college. Classic theories focus on psychosocial (Chickering, 1969; Chickering & Reisser, 1993), ethical and intellectual (Perry, 1970, 1981, 1999), and moral development (Kohlberg, 1984). Identity development theories inform the practice of advising as well. Advisors must digest these theories and evaluate their effectiveness for use with special population students (Evans, Forney, Guido, Patton, & Renn, 2009).

Because of the population data used by researchers, some of the approaches found in the literature may not prove particularly applicable to international students and students from specific cultural communities in the United States. Roufs (2015) provided a readable overview of relevant advising theories, and Archambault's (2015) chapter on cultural competencies goes into further detail on relevant identity models. Also, the online NACADA Clearinghouse offers information on student development theories and related approaches helpful to advisors.

Advisors who learn student development and identity theories recognize the dissonance many students experience during their first year of college. A sense of disequilibrium may emerge after a student receives the first distressing results of a test, actively considers (or reconsiders) majors to pursue, or tries to determine future life goals. Students disappointed with college grades that do not match those earned in high school may feel particularly and increasingly lost in the first year. For students identifying as members of special populations, feelings of isolation may be compounded by lack of fellowship with those who share their point of view or understand their circumstances. Therefore, to lessen the negative impact of dissonance, advisors must help students analyze and reflect on their experiences and encourage the positive gains that have contributed to their personal growth and successful achievement of goals (Gruber & Moffitt, 2014).

Recognizing Student Distress

Many first-year students worry about whether they will fit in with others at the institution, and each one experiences a period of adjustment; however, for students from special populations, these feelings can manifest into cause for concern. Feelings of difference and the challenges associated with their unique situations may make feelings of isolation acute. Moreover, the biases of others can inhibit student confidence and academic performance. Findings from three areas of psychological research may help advisors recognize and ameliorate typical negative perceptions and emotions that can impinge on success for first-year students: social belonging theory, imposter syndrome, and stereotype threat.

Social belonging theory. Advisors encourage feelings of belonging at the college or in the desired major to help students gain resilience during moments of setbacks and hardships. In fact, by explaining the experience as temporary and typical of most transitions, advisors promote a sense of belonging that eases college adjustment (Walton & Cohen, 2011).

The opposite condition, belonging uncertainty, may result from negative stereotypes that "cause people to wonder whether others will fully include, value, and respect them ..." (Walton, n.d., para. 9), and students may monitor their college experiences for indicators of belonging. For example, typical interactions or emotions—such as receiving critical feedback or feeling lonely—may seem like proof that the person does not belong in college, which may undermine the student's motivation and achievement.

Evidence that students assess their belonging in college has emerged in published research. For example, based on the suggestion that they would have few friends in a field of study, Black students questioned their belonging and potential success in the field and discouraged their peers from pursuing it (Walton & Cohen, 2007). On his website, Walton (n.d.) identified interventions that address this negative perception among students, suggesting "My social-belonging intervention aims to prevent such corrosive attributions by providing a nonthreatening narrative for feelings of nonbelonging in school" (para. 10).

Imposter syndrome. Sometimes known as *imposter phenomenon* or *perceived fraudulence,* imposter syndrome may affect any student—first time, special population, or doctoral. According to clinical psychologists Clance and Imes (1978), students who experience imposter syndrome may not attribute their academic success to their own efforts, or they may believe they received undeserved accolades. As a result, these students consider themselves frauds and fear that others will discover their inauthenticity and failings (Leary, Patton, Orlando, & Funk, 2000). Because students may consider themselves unlike others in their environment, possibly due to stereotypes about their difference, prudent advisors watch for signs of imposter syndrome in students from special populations.

Imposter syndrome can lead to serious states of distress including fear, doubt, shame, anxiety, and guilt (Sakulku & Alexander, 2011), which affect a student's sense of belonging and shape views of institutional fit and academic achievement. Fear ultimately leads to disengagement; advisors may see signs of stress, such as failure to turn in assignments, which may lead to complete abandonment of course work. Sakulku and Alexander (2011) provided an outstanding overview on imposter phenomenon, including the way perceived fraudulence can affect and present in special populations.

Stereotype threat. In addition to imposter syndrome and feelings of disconnect, some students face risks from stereotype threat, which pervades special populations in many academic situations. Stereotype threat refers to being at "risk of confirming, as self-characteristic, a negative stereotype about one's group" (Steele & Aronson, 1995, p. 797). The fear of possibly confirming a negative stereotype can significantly interfere with the student's academic performance.

Advisors as well as instructors can encourage students at risk of stereotype threat by de-emphasizing the stereotypes. For example, Spencer, Steele, and Quinn (1999) found in their research that women who received reassurance that both men and women had performed equally on a math test subsequently earned the same scores as men on the test; however, women who did not receive this information received lower scores than men who took the test.

Negative thought patterns and behaviors resulting from stereotype threat can undermine the potential of students by triggering a psychological state that interferes with their academic performance and integration on campus (Croizet et al., 2004, p. 729). Advisors may find articles by Schmader, Johns, and Forbes (2008), who have published on the outcomes of stereotype threat, particularly useful. Also, in *Whistling Vivaldi,* Steele (2011) suggested simple and extremely effective methods for reducing stereotype threat, and the website ReducingStereotypeThreat.org provides useful information about scholarship on stereotype threat.

Leveraging Student Strengths

Recent theories and strategies for use in ameliorating threats to identity have materialized from research in advising and educational psychology, including hope and self-authorship theories, growth mindset techniques, and motivational interviewing (see chapter 6). By becoming familiar with and using appropriate positive approaches, advisors address the well-being, character, and strength of students in special populations to clarify students' motivations and achievement (Pajares, 2001). Specifically, by addressing concerns from a position of student strength, advisors help advisees move forward, despite setbacks created by membership in a special population at a particular institution, to productive places.

Advisors may find strengths-based and appreciative advising, which both highlight positive student attributes over weaknesses, particularly useful with first-year students in special populations (see chapters 2 and 6). Strengths-based advising (Schreiner & Anderson, 2005) focuses on the recognition of success and growth that emboldens students to overcome obstacles before they seem overwhelming. Appreciative advising, based on appreciative inquiry techniques, is applied to help students optimize their educational experience through a six-stage process of reflection, goal setting, and planning (Bloom, Hutson, & He, 2008). As discussed throughout this book, strategies that emphasize students' strengths also help them develop resilience, a characteristic critical to successful goal completion for many in special populations.

Advisors armed with knowledge of student development and identity theories, as well as other frameworks for practice emerging from educational and psychological research, and with familiarity of student experiences with belonging, imposter syndrome, and stereotype threat can guide students through difficulties. Furthermore, they recognize the thinking and behavioral hallmarks of students coping with stressors and apply advising approaches to prevent or mitigate issues that may derail students from reaching their learning goals.

Developing Cultural Competencies and Fostering Critical Consciousness

An advisor's ability to interact with first-year students from various populations largely depends on the advisor's cultural awareness and competence. All first-year students benefit from advising that helps them understand and navigate the postsecondary institution, but because of their particular challenges, students from special populations may reap the most from an advisor's careful and intentional cultivation of cultural competence. Students juggling multiple identities and at risk for belonging uncertainty, imposter syndrome, or stereotype threat need an ally who recognizes the conflict of norms and assumptions that they may be trying to reconcile.

Since the 1970s, college attendance has increased dramatically, contributing to "an extraordinarily diverse array of national, racial/ethnic, and socioeconomic backgrounds. [Students] bring great vitality to an institution, but also place significant new demands on faculty knowledge and skill" (Association of American Colleges & Universities, 2002, p. vii). Campus cultures, composed of values, beliefs, systems, biases, and tendencies that frame one's interpretations and understanding of the space (Kuh & Whitt, 1988), give students experience in interactional diversity (Hu & Kuh, 2003). However, the extent of diversity varies by institution, and not all who make efforts to engage students with dissimilar perspectives successfully engender the climates, attitudes, and behaviors that support learning from multiple viewpoints (Dey, Ott, Antonaros, Barnhardt, & Holsapple, 2010).

In the United States, the college culture may include convocation, graduation, and other academic rituals and traditions. It may also manifest vestiges of selective populations, such as Greek fraternity and sorority letters, or of historical or religious beliefs, rituals, and celebrations not reflective of some peoples. Exclusive groups, timing of scheduled breaks, and organized parades may give some students comfort or convey a sense of pride, but they could also be perceived as placing the importance of one tradition over another (Bolman & Deal, 2013). Students and staff experience these displays of culture through a filter of their own lived experience and may not notice the ways these expressions marginalize some students. Advisors, as the students' guide and ally, must develop heightened sensitivity to the campus climate to reassure students who may find the culture confusing or isolating. They also need to use their consciousness to contribute to policies that promote inclusion and student success.

Cultural Competence

While recognizing the potential impact of culture, advisors use knowledge, skills, and awareness to develop the sensitivity that leads to competence (Pope, Reynolds, & Mueller, 2004). Archambault (2015) presented five questions to use for beginning and continuing exploration of oneself in the development of cultural competencies:

- How does the student's experience differ from my own?
- Am I making assumptions about this student based upon both visible and invisible areas of diversity?
- How do my assumptions about all students on this campus seem to fit or not fit this student?
- What student characteristics contribute to academic successes or challenges?
- What types of support does this student (and this campus) possess to address specific areas of diversity that he or she represents? (pp. 189-191)

When they answer these questions and absorb the abundant information about advising special populations, advisors facilitate genuine conversations with students while minimizing the harmful effects of misunderstandings and misinformation. In these interactions, a culturally aware advisor recognizes that norms of the dominant culture are not universally accepted and will not make assumptions based on them. For example, a direct gaze in conversation and punctuality for a meeting carry implications of respect in the United States, but in other cultures, these gestures may seem rude or not particularly important.

Becoming aware of one's assumptions enhances understanding of the student, ability to respond in a nuanced manner, and culturally competent advising.

To reach a state of cultural competence, in addition to the assumptions they make about students, advisors take a long look at themselves, including family and community backgrounds. This type of honest reflection helps an advisor determine knowledge gaps that may contribute to prejudiced reactions to students. By first acknowledging one's own culture and then applying acquired understanding in consideration of others, advisors care for the whole student (i.e., mental, physical, and financial health) (Jordan, 2015).

Environmental Scan

To apply their cultural competence, advisors need to conduct an environmental scan to investigate the institution's history, politics, culture, and norms. The objective of the scan, to see an institution from the perspective of another (e.g., a student using a wheelchair, a parent, or an engineering major), provides the means by which advisors hone cultural competency.

To inform academic advising, Fleming, Howard, Perkins, and Pesta (2005) suggested that scanners first look at campus characteristics; for example, they should determine the size, type, and makeup of the institution. In addition, they should review institutional data on the current special populations and the support programs and systems available to them, such as the unit handling accommodations for students with learning disabilities and summer programs for underprepared first-year students. With these data, advisors can identify and address specific needs rather than assumed obstacles, such as those described in the literature or based on bias.

According to Fleming et al. (2005), the second phase of the environmental scan involves exploration of peer interactions, classrooms, and other physical spaces. The peer environment defines the various roles of students at an institution and all of the support or challenges they encounter when interacting with their peers. The classroom defines much of the academic learning space for first-year students and situates faculty members and students in the same place for interactions related to learning. In addition to classrooms, the larger physical environment is composed of the community, including the architecture and landscape as well as nonacademic campus spaces (e.g., local shopping centers, entertainment venues, athletic and recreation facilities, and residence halls). The atmosphere created in these frequented student locales may affect the feelings of welcome and support felt by various special populations. Therefore, the best environmental scan includes an assessment that institutional data and visual identification of accessibility cannot completely provide (Fleming et al., 2005).

The institutional history and developing trends offer insight into the choices made regarding physical spaces, and thus exploration of the past helps advisors develop a context for the evolution and impact on the advising environment. By looking at the features in student and local newspapers, highlights on institutional and commercial websites, and conversations in social media forums, advisors can learn about the perception of the institution as it currently stands. Taking all the information together, an advisor can determine if remnants of any offensive historical context remain (e.g., an outdated social hierarchy, an offensive school mascot, or a demonstration of intolerance).

In addition to developing cultural awareness and competencies, advisors of first-year students benefit from understanding the theoretical frameworks that enable them to expand their approaches (Archambault, 2016). Every advisor can, little by little, broaden the skills needed to advance practice (Folsom, 2015); by merely moving out of their comfort zones and challenging themselves, advisors enhance their cultural competency (Harding & Miller, 2013). For example, advisors gain understanding when attending campus events unlike those advanced in their own ethnic or cultural circles or those that counter their preconceived ideas of others. With open-mindedness, advisors experience, to some degree, the campus as one from a culture unlike their own. Therefore, some of the best growth experiences begin with exploration of new experiences that create the understanding and enhance the skills necessary to "engage and intervene appropriately and effectively across cultures" (Harding & Miller, 2013, p. 20).

Critical Consciousness

Kumagai and Lypson (2009) referred to the integration and ongoing assimilation of cultural experience and knowledge as *critical consciousness*. First explained by Freire (1970), critical consciousness is composed of a

> moral awareness which propels individuals to dissemble from their cultural, social, and political environment, and engage in a responsible critical moral dialogue with it, making active efforts to construct their own place in social reality and to develop internal consistency in their ways of being (Mustakova-Possardt, 1998, p. 13).

Critical consciousness is based on critical thinking and awareness that increase fluency and communication with individuals from unfamiliar cultures and backgrounds. Archambault (2016) suggested that the advisor address complicated situations by recogniz[ing] the many components that comprise the whole of the student and us[ing] a multifaceted approach to address ... concerns. The ability to shift between approaches and to recognize the student's needs, rather than those of the advisor, marks a culturally competent professional. (p. 110)

By fostering critical consciousness, advisors apply theory to practice when advising students who identify with special populations.

Pratt-Johnson (2006) referred to the recognition of parts of a whole, using the example of the layers of an onion, when discussing the approach to cross-cultural communication. The first interaction, likely the first registration appointment, gives advisors the opportunity to see the outer layer of the student composed of reported demographics, such as test scores, previous educational experience, home environment, gender, and race or ethnicity. These facts about a student may lead to assumptions that give an incomplete or inaccurate view of the whole student, so advisors must create an environment in which the layers of identity can be peeled back over time. In developing the rapport needed to appreciate a student's salient and latent identities, the advisor recognizes that, unlike the onion, identities are not simply added as individual layers; rather, they are intertwined and not easy to pull apart (Torres, Howard-Hamilton, & Cooper, 2011).

The advising goal includes gaining an enhanced understanding of the educational experiences of students, especially those who identify as members of special populations. The advisor can use general knowledge of other students in initial interactions with a first-year student who identifies in multiple special populations—such as a woman student athlete and aspiring physicist—to offer guidance for making sense of and navigating college. However, by engaging critical consciousness, advisors eventually recognize the salient identities presented by advisees and then build rapport (Ohrablo, 2014). They also accumulate the experience, informed by studying applicable theories, to develop a philosophy of advising (Freitag, 2011) that provides both the framework and the flexibility to respond to students with diverse needs.

Theory to Practice

Advisors must put theories into practice to accomplish basic student outcomes, including educational fluency and agency, removal of barriers to access and achievement, and cultivation of a sense of belonging for everyone (Hoffman, Richmond, Morrow, & Salomone, 2002). Advisors need to remain aware of several important times during the first year when concerted efforts with students from special populations effect positive change.

Initial interactions. Advisors must make data-informed decisions, but data from the academic record provide only some of the useful input. Therefore, advisors should complement the statistics with information directly provided by the student. The first sessions set the tone for future interactions, and an advisor's cultural competency and critical consciousness determine the disclosure offered by a student.

Students feel comfortable discussing their future plans with trusted advisors in welcoming environments (Folsom, 2007). Advisors develop ongoing trust by preparing for their meetings with students, especially special populations, by asking appropriate exploratory questions and actively listening to gain understanding (Jordan, 2015). These open-ended questions should prompt students to share their histories, backgrounds, and experiences. For example, an advisor may ask, "How did you come to the decision to pursue medicine?" Or "What challenges do you expect to face when preparing for nursing school?" With informed and well-considered questions, advisors can unearth the student's dreams, concerns, and possible challenges, such as test anxiety or financial obligations related to family responsibilities.

These initial encounters also help create a sense of belonging in the student. Because of the empowerment felt by being a part of community (Hoffman et al., 2002), scholars have found that students who feel connected to an institution will develop loyalty to it (Vianden & Barlow, 2015). Advisors who show deep interest in their students demonstrate the ways the institution values them (Vianden, 2016), and this relationship contributes to student resiliency (Miller & Murray, 2005).

Proactive advising and academic difficulties. Particularly when working with special populations, advisors proactively invite (or require) students to an academic planning meeting early in the term. During this initial session, advisors teach students to anticipate challenges and form strategies for dealing with them. Together, the student and advisor also determine the best timing and frequency of subsequent appointments.

Some students seek an advising appointment only to ask process questions ("how do I...?"). Although the student may be looking for quick relief for an immediate problem and thus disclose little of substance, the prepared advisor seizes these brief interactions to gather information through active listening and critical thinking (Archambault, 2015; Jordan, 2015). Advisors make use of their knowledge on student development and familiarity with identity theories and special populations to seamlessly move the dialogue to matters of consequence.

The determination about the level of proper intrusiveness creates a clear advising challenge. First-year students do not arrive in the advisor's office with a list of issues to discuss. By asking exploratory questions, advisors can uncover not only the specific adjustment issues the student experiences but also the student's perceptions about these challenges. For example, through directed questions, the advisor may discover that the student athlete majoring in business wants to drop a course to maintain the GPA and rate of progress toward graduation necessary for eligibility to play a sport and keep a scholarship. With this disclosure in mind, the advisor assists the student athlete in making good choices and offers support for handling the pressures of varsity athletics and full-time academics.

Answers to probing questions may reveal that the honors student who failed a calculus exam had never experienced such disappointment in an academic setting. With this information about the student's history, the advisor explains the context for these temporary and surmountable obstacles by suggesting that preparation, not intelligence, may have contributed to the outcome. Then the advisor offers reassurance that the student can improve test performance through specific steps useful in preparing for college-level exams. Also, the culturally competent advisor listens for evidence of stereotype threat and helps the student identify and overcome it. In summary, responses to open-ended, probing questions provide advisors with critical information for directing the conversation, suggesting a change in behavior, or offering a referral.

Advisors must know the referral sources for all students. A culturally competent advisor knows that some dominant issues emerge at specific times and can identify the best advocates for students, especially those in special populations who may encounter nuanced situations. A listening advisor with critical consciousness can determine among the many specialized services to offer guidance most relevant for the issue at hand. These advisors also recognize when a student needs a nudge into the next stage of development. The advisor can leverage a trusted network to facilitate student advancement.

Career and major exploration. Career and major exploration conversations evolve over time. Although the advisor broaches the subject of major and career choices in early encounters, the details become more critical in later terms. These conversations encourage students to explore their goals with a knowledgeable advisor who can provide information about the various paths, obstacles, and opportunities of majors under consideration. To best assist exploring students, advisors need to know them and set the proper goals for each conversation. Some contemplate fields out of personal interest; others may express an interest in a field with which they have little practical knowledge; others declare majors and careers out of a sense of responsibility to their families. Regardless of their circumstance or rationale, many students feel anxious when discussing career choice (see chapter 9).

First-year students facing unique challenges associated with their status in a special population may require more support from advisors than those who feel uncertain, unknowledgeable, or uninspired. The woman student athlete may feel pressured to complete all the courses required for a physics major while meeting obligations to her sports team, which include athletic practices, conditioning, and travel. She may not know another woman working in the field of physics and wonders if she will receive support from others in the field. She may be dealing with imposter syndrome or stereotype threat.

Furthermore, advisors must use their cultural awareness to recognize that not all available resources will help every student in the exploration process. For example, students who need to seek paid employment or continue athletic training over the break cannot take advantage of career explorations such as summer career-related jobs or internships. In addition, undocumented or international students without specific work permissions and documents cannot apply for certain employment opportunities. A culturally competent advisor asks follow-up questions so that barriers can be overcome or alternative opportunities found for advancing a career option or creating a competitive résumé.

Subsequent term registration or educational plans. If only discussing course planning and registration procedures, the advisor will miss a critical opportunity to facilitate student completion of academic, career, and personal goals. Competent advisors know the information and resources students need, and they should reach out to first-year students to increase their educational fluency. Advisors know that students need reminders and instructions to negotiate the complexities of college processes, but advisors also need to act as guides and allies. Furthermore, advisors must discover and communicate to students in special populations the best methods for handling unique additional barriers and taking advantage of opportunities. Advisors use first-year encounters to fill information gaps, address immediate issues, and encourage students to explore the possibilities afforded by their college education.

When meeting a student at future appointments, advisors should reevaluate past conversations because students' self-knowledge and understanding increase over time and under developing circumstances. For example, a new medical condition can affect a student's long- and short-term academic performance, and it may prompt a shift in career and educational goals. As a first-year college student gains self-awareness, the advisor may need to offer reassurance regardless of the progress made in prior advising encounters. Advisors will also appreciate when students experience an epiphany, such as when they hear enough individuals with similar stories to realize: "I am not the only one!" or "This place accepts me for who I am!" This welcomed affirmation may come in August or February of the first year, but it accompanies a changed perspective that influences a student's educational path and future. The culturally conscious advisor prepares for the zigs and zags of a student's life and capitalizes on the salient aspects as they unfold in the student's narrative.

AIMING FOR **EXCELLENCE**

The following discussion questions and activities give advisors concrete ideas and strategies for expanding their knowledge and applying the information shared in this chapter to their advising practice:

- Find and assimilate institutional data to better understand the demographics of students and trends in enrollment; look for the outliers, not because they are different, but because they represent students who need advising as well.

- Expand critical thinking around cultural competence by completing the *Measuring Intercultural Sensitivity: The Intercultural Development Inventory* (Hammer, Bennett, & Wiseman, 2003) or *The Intercultural Conflict Style Inventory: A Conceptual Framework and Measure of Intercultural Conflict Resolution Approaches* (Hammer, 2005).

- Start your environmental scan by eating where students eat, attending campus events, reading the student newspaper, and volunteering for student activities. Adjust the scan based on the campus context (i.e., commuter, virtual, or a multilocation campus).

- Read articles from the NACADA Clearinghouse for information regarding special populations. Choose one population to learn more about and ask a colleague to select a different group so you can discuss them both.

Summary

All advisors, regardless of title or area of responsibility, must extend their experience to students in special populations and recognize and address their specific needs. For example, advisors help students with time management, eligibility, and other problems unique to student athletes, but they also help women pursuing STEM disciplines overcome feelings of isolation, ally with African American students negotiating a predominately White campus, and advocate for students with learning disabilities to access resources. All students present multiple and changing identities that may affect their transition to college and successful persistence to their second college year. All advisors bear responsibility for understanding the whole of each student in need of advising. Therefore, each advisor must prepare for any student encounter and continually develop the cultural competencies and critical consciousness necessary to offer effective assistance to students seeking to meet educational goals.

The literature on special populations grows daily, but it all points to the need of advisors to remain nimble, adjusting their knowledge in specific academic fields as well as in the changing demographics of incoming students. As they seek knowledge to understand students' and institutions' histories, backgrounds, and experiences, advisors connect students to advocates who also help them achieve their academic, personal, and professional goals.

Advisors must use multiple advising approaches as necessary to address a student's current developmental needs with sensitivity and in ways that promote a sense of belonging. Most students benefit from standard advising approaches (e.g., strengths-based, teaching, developmental, and prescriptive) when applied at the best time in the right way. However, growth does not manifest identically in every student. Advisors must recognize the culture shock of first-year students and patiently explain policies and resources as many times as necessary.

Advisors who develop education fluency encourage students to achieve their hopes and dreams, and by connecting them to the institution and removing barriers, they foster a sense of belonging that counters any imposter-like feelings. Although an advisor's relationship will differ with each student, every advisor must embrace one overriding goal: "Students can learn, they are valuable as people, their experience and ideas have legitimacy in and out of the classroom" (Terenzini et al., 1994, p. 70).

References

Abes, E. S., Jones, S. R., & McEwen, M. K. (2007). Reconceptualizing the model of multiple dimensions of identity: The role of meaning-making capacity in the construction of multiple identities. *Journal of College Student Development, 48*(1), 1–22.

ACT. (2010). *What works in student retention? Fourth national survey report for all colleges and universities.* Retrieved from http://www.act.org/content/dam/act/unsecured/documents/Retention-AllInstitutions.pdf

Archambault, K. L. (2015). Developing self-knowledge as a first step toward cultural competence. In P. Folsom, F. Yoder, & J. E. Joslin (Eds.), *The new advisor guidebook: Mastering the art of academic advising* (2nd ed., pp. 185–201). San Francisco, CA: Jossey-Bass.

Archambault, K. L. (2016). Knowing and reaching our students. In T. J. Grites, M. A. Miller, & J. Givans Voller (Eds.), *Beyond foundations: Developing as a master advisor* (pp. 107–122). San Francisco, CA: Jossey-Bass.

Association of American Colleges & Universities. (2002). *Greater expectations: A new vision for learning as a nation goes to college.* Washington, DC: Author.

Bloom, J. L., Hutson, B. L., & He, Y. (2008). *The appreciative advising revolution.* Champaign, IL: Stipes.

Bolman, L. G., & Deal, T. E. (2013). *Reframing organizations: Artistry, choice, and leadership.* San Francisco, CA: Jossey-Bass.

Broughton, E., & Neyer, M. (2001). Advising and counseling student athletes. *New Directions for Student Services, 2001*(93), 47–53.

Bulger, S., & Watson, D. (2006). Broadening the definition of at-risk students. *The Community College Enterprise, 12*(2), 23–32. Retrieved from http://www.schoolcraft.edu/pdfs/cce/12.2.23-32.pdf

Chickering, A. W. (1969). *Education and identity.* San Francisco, CA: Jossey-Bass.

Chickering, A. W., & Reisser, L. (1993). *Education and identity* (2nd ed.). San Francisco, CA: Jossey-Bass.

Clance, P. R., & Imes, S. A. (1978). The imposter phenomenon in high achieving women: Dynamics and therapeutic intervention. *Psychotherapy: Theory, Research & Practice, 15*(3), 241–247.

Croizet, J-C., Despres, G., Gauzins, M-E., Huguet, P., Leyens, J-P., & Meot, A. (2004). Stereotype threat undermines intellectual performance by triggering a disruptive mental load. *Personality and Social Psychology Bulletin, 30*(6), 721–731.

Cunningham, L. (2016). *Multicultural awareness issues for academic advisors.* Retrieved from http://www.nacada.ksu.edu/Resources/Clearinghouse/View-Articles/Multicultural-a84.aspx

Dey, E. L., Ott, M. C., Antonaros, M., Barnhardt, C. L., & Holsapple, M. A. (2010). *Engaging diverse viewpoints: What is the campus climate for perspective-taking?* Washington, DC: Association of American Colleges & Universities.

Drake, J. K. (2011). The role of academic advising in student retention and persistence. *About Campus, 16*(3), 8–12.

Engle, J., & Tinto, V. (2008). *Moving beyond access: College success for low-income, first-generation students.* Washington, DC: Pell Institute for the Study of Opportunity in Higher Education. Retrieved from http://files.eric.ed.gov/fulltext/ED504448.pdf

Evans, N. J., Forney, D. S., Guido, F. M., Patton, L. D., & Renn, K. A. (2009). *Student development in college: Theory, research, and practice.* San Francisco, CA: Jossey-Bass.

Fleming, W. J. B., Howard, K., Perkins, E., & Pesta, M. (2005, July 13). The college environment: Factors influencing student transition and their impact on academic advising. *The Mentor: An Academic Advising Journal.* Retrieved from dus.psu.edu/mentor/old/articles/050713bf.htm

Folsom, P. (2007). Creating a welcoming advising atmosphere. In P. Folsom (Ed.), *The new advisor guidebook: Mastering the art of advising through the first year and beyond* (pp. 110–111). San Francisco, CA: Jossey-Bass.

Folsom, P. (2015). The new advisor development chart. In P. Folsom, F. Yoder, & J. E. Joslin (Eds.), *The new advisor guidebook: Mastering the art of academic advising* (2nd ed., pp. 19–35). San Francisco, CA: Jossey-Bass.

Freire, P. (1970). *Pedagogy of the oppressed.* New York, NY: Continuum.

Freitag, D. (2011). *Creating a personal philosophy of academic advising.* Retrieved from http://www.nacada.ksu.edu/Resources/Clearinghouse/View-Articles/Personal-philosophy-of-academic-advising.aspx

Grewe, A. (2007). Adapting academic advising strategies to meet the needs of a diversified student body. *Academic Advising Today, 30*(2). Retrieved from https://www.nacada.ksu.edu/Resources/Academic-Advising-Today/View-Articles/Adapting-Academic-Advising-Strategies-to-Meet-the-Needs-of-a-Diversified-Student-Body.aspx

Grites, T. J. (1982). Advising for special populations. *New Directions for Student Services, 1982*(17), 67–83.

Grites, T. J. (2013). Developmental academic advising: A 40-year context. *NACADA Journal, 33*(1), 5–15.

Gruber, D., & Moffitt, J. (2014). Using reflective writing to enrich academic advising. *Academic Advising Today 37*(2). Retrieved from www.nacada.ksu.edu/Resources/Academic-Advising-Today/View-Articles/Using-Reflective-Writing-to-Enrich-Academic-Advising.aspx

Hammer, M. R. (2005). The intercultural conflict style inventory: A conceptual framework and measure of intercultural conflict resolution approaches. *International Journal of Intercultural Relations, 29*(6), 675–695.

Hammer, M. R., Bennett, M. J., & Wiseman, R. (2003). Measuring intercultural sensitivity: The intercultural development inventory. *International Journal of Intercultural Relations, 27*(4), 421–443.

Harding, B., & Miller, M. A. (2013). *Cultivating the potential in at-risk students.* (Pocket Guide No. 11). Manhattan, KS: NACADA: The Global Community for Academic Advising.

Hoffman, M., Richmond, J., Morrow, J., & Salomone, K. (2002). Investigating "sense of belonging" in first-year college students. *Journal of College Student Retention: Research, Theory and Practice, 4*(3), 227–256.

Howard-Hamilton, M. F., & Sina, J. A. (2001). How college affects student athletes. *New Directions for Student Services, 2001*(93), 35–45.

Hu, S., & Kuh, G. D. (2003). Diversity experiences and college student learning and personal development. *Journal of College Student Development, 44*(3), 320–334.

Jones, S. R., & McEwen, M. K. (2000). A conceptual model of multiple dimensions of identity. *Journal of College Student Development, 41*(4), 405–414.

Jordan, P. (2015). Effective communication skills. In P. Folsom, F. Yoder, & J. E. Joslin (Eds.), *The new advisor guidebook: Mastering the art of academic advising* (pp. 213–225). San Francisco, CA: Jossey-Bass.

Kohlberg, L. (1984). *The psychology of moral development: The nature and validity of moral stages* (Vol. 2). New York, NY: HarperCollins.

Kuh, G. D., & Whitt, E. J. (1988). *The invisible tapestry. Culture in American colleges and universities* (ASHE-ERIC Higher Education, Report No. 1). Washington, DC: Association for the Study of Higher Education.

Kulik, C. L. C., Kulik, J. A., & Shwalb, B. J. (1983). College programs for high-risk and disadvantaged students: A meta-analysis of findings. *Review of Educational Research, 53*(3), 397–414.

Kumagai, A. K., & Lypson, M. L. (2009). Beyond cultural competence: Critical consciousness, social justice, and multicultural education. *Academic Medicine, 84*(6), 782–787.

Leary, M. R., Patton, K., Orlando, A., & Funk, W. W. (2000). The impostor phenomenon: Self-perceptions, reflected appraisals, and interpersonal strategies. *Journal of Personality, 68*(4), 725–756.

LeMelle, T. J. (2002). The HBCU: Yesterday, today and tomorrow. *Education, 123*(1), 190.

Miller, M. A., & Murray, C. (2005). *Advising academically underprepared students.* Retrieved from http://www.nacada.ksu.edu/Resources/Clearinghouse/View-Articles/Academically-underprepared-students.aspx

Mustakova-Possardt, E. (1998). Critical consciousness: An alternative pathway for positive personal and social development. *Journal of Adult Development, 5*(1), 13–30.

Ohrablo, S. (2014). *Advising is more than a yes/no business: How to establish rapport and trust with your students.* Retrieved from http://www.nacada.ksu.edu/Resources/Clearinghouse/View-Articles/Advising-is-More-Than-a-YesNo-Business--How-to-Establish-Rapport-and-Trust-with-Your-Students.aspx

Orozco, G. L., Alvarez, A. N., & Gutkin, T. (2010). Effective advising of diverse students in community colleges. *Community College Journal of Research and Practice, 34*(9), 717–737.

Pajares, F. (2001). Toward a positive psychology of academic motivation. *The Journal of Educational Research, 95*(1), 27–35.

Perry, W. G. (1970). *Forms of intellectual and ethical development in the college years: A scheme.* New York, NY: Holt, Rinehart, and Winston.

Perry, W. G. (1999). *Forms of intellectual and ethical development in the college years: A scheme.* San Francisco, CA: Jossey-Bass.

Perry, W. G. (1981). Cognitive and ethical growth: The making of meaning. In A. W. Chickering (Ed.), *The modern American college* (pp. 76–116). San Francisco, CA: Jossey-Bass.

Pope, R. L., Reynolds, A. L., & Mueller, J. A. (2004). *Multicultural competence in student affairs.* San Francisco, CA: Jossey-Bass.

Pratt-Johnson, Y. (2006). Communicating cross-culturally: What teachers should know. *The Internet TESL Journal, 12*(2). Retrieved from iteslj.org/Articles/Pratt-Johnson-CrossCultural

Roueche, J. E., & Roueche, S. D. (1993). *Between a rock and a hard place: The at-risk student in the open-door college.* Washington, DC: American Association of Community Colleges.

Roufs, K. (2015). Theory matters. In P. Folsom, F. Yoder, & J. E. Joslin (Eds.), *The new advisor guidebook: Mastering the art of academic advising* (2nd ed., pp. 67–81). San Francisco, CA: Jossey-Bass.

Sakulku, J., & Alexander, J. (2011). The impostor phenomenon. *International Journal of Behavioral Science, 6*(1), 73–92.

Schauss, N., & Thomas, K. (2015, June). The 'f' word: Why teaching resiliency is critical. *Academic Advising Today, 38*(2). Retrieved from https://www. nacada.ksu.edu/Resources/Academic-Advising-Today/View-Articles/ The-%E2%80%98F%E2%80%99-Word-Why-Teaching-Resiliency-is-Critical.aspx

Schmader, T., Johns, M., & Forbes, C. (2008). An integrated process model of stereotype threat effects on performance. *Psychological Review, 115*(2), 336–356.

Schreiner, L. A., & Anderson, E. (2005). Strengths-based advising: A new lens for higher education. *NACADA Journal, 25*(2), 20–29.

Schulenberg, J. K., & Lindhorst, M. J. (2008). Advising is advising: Toward defining the practice and scholarship of academic advising. *NACADA Journal, 28*(1), 43–53.

Spencer, S. J., Steele, C. M., & Quinn, D. M. (1999). Stereotype threat and women's math performance. *Journal of Experimental Social Psychology, 35*, 4–28.

Stebleton, M. J., & Soria, K. (2012). Breaking down barriers: Academic obstacles of first-generation students at research universities. *The Learning Assistance Review, 17*(2), 7–10.

Steele, C. M. (2011). *Whistling Vivaldi: How stereotypes affect us and what we can do (issues of our time).* New York, NY: W. W. Norton.

Steele, C. M., & Aronson, J. (1995). Stereotype threat and the intellectual test performance of African-Americans. *Journal of Personality and Social Psychology, 69*, 797–811.

Strommer, D. W. (1995). Advising special populations of students. *New Directions for Teaching and Learning, 1995*(62), 25–34.

Stryker, S., & Serpe, R. T. (1982). Commitment, identity salience and role behavior: Theory and research example. In W. Ickes & E. S. Knowles (Eds.), *Personality, roles, and social behavior* (pp. 199–218). New York, NY: Springer-Verlag.

Swail, W. S. (2000). Preparing America's disadvantaged for college: Programs that increase college opportunity. *New Directions for Institutional Research, 2000*(107), 85–101.

Terenzini, P. T., Rendon, L. I., Upcraft, M. L., Millar, S. B., Allison, K. W., Gregg, P. L., & Jalomo, R. (1994). The transition to college: Diverse students, diverse stories. *Research in Higher Education, 35*(1), 57–73.

Thelin, J. R. (2011). *A history of American higher education.* Baltimore, MD: The Johns Hopkins University Press.

Torres, V., Howard-Hamilton, M. F., & Cooper, D. L. (2011). *Identity development of diverse populations: Implications for teaching and administration in higher education* (ASHE-ERIC Higher Education Report Vol. 29, No. 6). San Francisco, CA: Jossey-Bass.

Vianden, J. (2016). Ties that bind: Academic advisors as agents of student relationship management. *NACADA Journal, 36*(1), 19–29.

Vianden, J., & Barlow, P. J. (2015). Strengthen the bond: Relationships between academic advising quality and undergraduate student loyalty. *NACADA Journal, 35*(2), 15–27.

Walton, G. M. (n.d.). *Research.* Retrieved from http://gregorywalton-stanford.weebly.com/research.html

Walton, G. M., & Cohen, G. L. (2007). A question of belonging: Race, social fit, and achievement. *Journal of Personality and Social Psychology, 92*(1), 82–96.

Walton, G. M., & Cohen, G. L. (2011). A brief social-belonging intervention improves academic and health outcomes of minority students. *Science, 311,* 1447–1451.

Watt, S. K., & Moore, J. L. (2001). Who are student athletes? *New Directions for Student Services, 2001*(93), 7–18.

Williams, J. C., Phelps, K. W., & Hall, E. V. (2014). *Double jeopardy? Gender bias against women in science.* Retrieved from http://www.toolsforchangeinstem.org/tools/double-jeopardy-report

CHAPTER 8

Engaging First-Year Students in Academic Planning

Melissa L. Johnson

Academic planning, broadly interpreted, involves building a community of students and educators who focus on the needs of both the learner and society as well as the academic mission of the institution (Rowley & Sherman, 2004). Shifting and competing interests among stakeholder needs and academic mission, particularly as trending market forces affect student desires for specific majors and career opportunities, challenge administrators to create a community for learning (Dey & Hurtado, 2005). Academic advisors can play a critical role in promoting student understanding about the values inherent in the educational mission and the skills gained through learning experiences with others (Gordon, 1998). This chapter provides an overview of ways academic advisors encourage first-year students to take ownership of their education through academic planning and to engage as full partners in the advising process.

Advising as a Learning Process

Learning is a "flowing process" (Fried, 2006, p. 5) in which identity is created through a series of interdependent connections between core internal beliefs and external interactions with the environment. Previous views on student learning were rooted in a positivist epistemology that explained knowledge construction and meaning making outside the realm of academic learning (Fried, 2006). More recently, constructivist educators have explained learning as an active process in which the individual gains new knowledge through the linkages of personal experiences and prior knowledge. According to prevailing thought, in a constructivist learning environment, students can articulate learning as well as reflect on the activities and observations undertaken during the learning process (Jonassen, Howland, Marra, & Crismond, 2008). Whereas positivism projects an objective view of learning, constructivism accounts for the subjective nature of learning in which "every story has two sides" (Fried, 2006, p. 2).

Academic advisors advance meaningful learning by creating intentional environments in which students actively process and reflect on the knowledge they are gaining both in and out of the classroom. Danis (1987) provided a useful guide to academic planning with undergraduates that remains relevant today: "choose a major that satisfies you ... exhaust every informational resource at your disposal ... [and] get practical experience" (pp. 87-88). These recommendations provide a launch point for constructivist learning activities discussed as part of the academic planning process.

Theoretical Foundations for Academic Planning

Development and other adult learning theories explain the importance of academic planning with first-year students. From Chickering and Reisser's (1993) vectors of psychosocial development to Baxter Magolda's (2004) description of self-authorship, the theoretical bases of academic planning undergird the practices that encourage first-year students to persevere. Several theoretical models and their connection to academic planning with first-year students warrant review.

Developing Competence and Purpose

Chickering and Reisser (1993) viewed development as a series of stages or tasks, most commonly referred to as *vectors*. Two of those vectors, developing competence and developing purpose, directly correlate to academic planning. By developing intellectual competence, students learn to master content, generate new reference points, and increase skill-building capacity. As students enhance their intellectual competence, they demonstrate their higher order thinking skills by using complex ways of learning and knowing through analysis, evaluation, and creation (Anderson & Krathwohl, 2001).

Students operating with intellectual competence look at multiple sides of an issue, synthesize information from a variety of sources to make decisions, and reflect on their learning (Chickering & Reisser, 1993). Feedback contributes to intellectual competence, but students do not always receive specific input about their capabilities. Academic advisors can provide explicit feedback about students' strengths and weaknesses as well as the other skills and abilities observed through their interactions with students. That is, they can review academic records (e.g., GPA), discuss student perceptions of their own of abilities and deficiencies ("I've never been any good at math"), and respond to requests for help in a specific area ("I'm having trouble staying focused"). Advisors also motivate students to build intellectual competence by discussing multiple approaches to creating academic plans, encouraging them to find their own voice through course work and extracurricular activities, helping them identify and apply their strengths in academic and career development opportunities, and frequently reflecting on the plans with them.

A more advanced vector, developing purpose, focuses on assessment of interests, clarification of goals, establishment of plans, and persistence despite barriers (Chickering & Reisser, 1993). Intentionality characterizes successful movement along this vector, with students making an effort to choose their priorities, act with purpose, and move toward their goals. At this point in development, students balance their career aspirations with personal interests and other commitments.

College students, like others, may struggle to plan for a future or a goal beyond their experience (Chickering & Reisser, 1993). This difficulty may acutely affect students new to higher education. In these cases, academic advisors can encourage experimentation with and flexibility in creating academic plans so that students can pursue multiple interests. First-year students expressing confusion or indecisiveness about future goals may particularly benefit from advisors who advocate for exploration, but such an approach may also prove necessary for students who have foreclosed on a decision with little or inappropriate consideration of viable alternatives (Shaffer & Zalewski, 2011) (see chapter 9). All first-year students should work closely with advisors to clarify their personal and vocational interests so they can consider the desired outcomes of their college education. As early as the student's first session, the advisee–advisor team can construct a plan for seizing academic and extracurricular opportunities that encourage exploration and meaning making.

Transition Theory

Schlossberg's transition theory (Anderson, Goodman, & Schlossberg, 2012) explains three types of events and the impact of each on a person. Anticipated events are predicted to occur (e.g., a student's graduation from college) and stand opposite of unanticipated or unscheduled events (e.g., an unexpected internship offer that changes the course of a student's trajectory). A nonevent was expected to occur but did not (e.g., a student not gaining admission into graduate school or achieving the GPA needed to continue in a major). Regardless of type, an event triggers a transition for the individual.

Four factors influence a person's ability to cope with a transition: situation, self, support, and strategies (Anderson et al., 2012). Key ingredients of the situation include the cause of the transition, the timing and duration of it, previous experience with similar circumstances, control over and reaction to it, and compounding factors associated with it (e.g., other stressors). In examining the self, personal and demographic characteristics—such as gender, age, socioeconomic status, health, race/ethnicity, and culture—can affect the transition, as can psychological resources such as self-efficacy and resilience as well as values and coping aids (see chapter 3).

Meaningful support includes the types, functions, and measurements of social assistance available. It incorporates intimate relationships, families, friends, institutions, and communities. Two functions—honest feedback and affirmation—characterize support, which is measured by the degree it remains stable or transitory. Furthermore, to cope with situations, individuals try to modify and control circumstances as well as manage the stress created by the situation (Anderson et al., 2012).

Academic advisors shepherd students navigating through various transitions. From the initial contact during orientation to checkpoints through the first year, an advisor can serve as a sounding board, proactive guide, and co-constructive planner with students. The impact of a transition initially rests on the students' appraisal of whether it is positive, negative, or irrelevant (Anderson et al., 2012). Students may feel the elated rush of a positive transition, but a negative transition could cripple a person with little resiliency to bounce back. An event initially perceived as irrelevant may reemerge with a profound positive or negative impact, especially for students not intentionally reflecting upon the initial transition experience. For example, dropping a course may create significant problems for a student who later struggles with the alternative sequence of classes. Advisors teach students to reframe negative or irrelevant transitions by providing resources and referrals as well as by reestablishing focus on the ultimate outcomes of a student's goals and purpose.

First-year students experience certain types of events without precedent. Knowledge of the resources available to help manage transitions can improve a new student's ability to cope (Anderson et al., 2012). At many institutions, an academic advisor accompanies a student from enrollment through graduation, discussing options and brainstorming ideas, and students looking for a stabilizing influence may appreciate this consistent partnership; however, before advisors can exert the most positive influence in transition experiences, students must recognize them as valuable resources. To ensure that every transitioning student receives the benefit of such a partnership, practicing advisors reach out to first-year students through orientation advising, first-year seminar visits, advising assignments, social media and e-mail announcements, and residence hall programming. They establish partnerships with both faculty members and student affairs administrators who make contact and develop rapport with students (see chapter 10). Furthermore, by adopting an advising syllabus (Trabant, 2006), advisors clarify the details of and responsibilities for the advising relationship so that students understand the purpose for, opportunities offered through, and expectations of both parties (see chapter 2). A syllabus or similar document explains the unique benefits available through academic advising, especially during one of the many college student transitions.

Self-authorship

Self-authorship is defined as the "capacity to internally define [one's] own beliefs, identity, and relationships" (Baxter Magolda, 2004, p. xvi). The capacity for self-authorship emerges in phases: First, the person follows external channels and when arriving at a crossroads begins listening to internal voices. Then, the person starts authoring her or his own life and developing an internal foundation. Because they rely heavily on the beliefs and values of external voices while in college, many young adults do not move beyond the first phase until after they leave college (Baxter Magolda, 2004).

Three dimensions characterize growth in self-authorship: epistemological, intrapersonal, and interpersonal. The epistemological dimension shapes the determination or construction of knowledge. The intrapersonal dimension focuses on self-awareness and beliefs, and the interpersonal dimension reflects ways of building relationships with others (Baxter Magolda, 2004). First-year students may come to college dependent on others—parents, faculty members, or academic advisors—to tell them the knowledge to gain. Authority figures need to challenge student assumptions so that new students can begin to develop their own views and construct their own knowledge (Hodge, Baxter Magolda, & Haynes, 2009).

First-year students may seek out academic advisors during the academic planning process to gain approval for their ideas. The plans they articulate may represent a conglomeration of predetermined career paths, parental expectations, and knowledge of subjects they feel they have mastered or with which they feel confident. Rather than dictating the academic plan for students, academic advisors nudge students toward self-authorship by co-constructing these plans with them. Effective advisors engage students in critical questioning and reflection about their future to encourage them to consider their own internal voices while making decisions. This process can start as early as orientation, continue through course selection discussions, and reemerge during discussions about resources as students gather information about a variety of opportunities that may complement their academic journeys (see chapter 3).

Other findings related to self-authorship show that authentic learning tasks provide opportunities for students to apply their knowledge to real-life scenarios (Baxter Magolda, 2004). Through these experiences, students expand previous knowledge on topics by constructing new models of understanding (Jonassen et al., 2008). To encourage self-authorship, academic advisors should discuss participation in authentic learning experiences, such as internships, service-learning and global engagement initiatives, and undergraduate research, early in the student's academic career, and they should assist in fitting these opportunities into academic plans. In later years, after the students engage in these experiences, advisors should advocate for reflection so that students can process the meaning of these undertakings and continue to build upon the foundation of learning laid through these explorations.

Learning-Centered Advising

Theoretical foundations of student and adult development, as discussed in the context of academic planning with first-year students, create the basis for further productive interactions with students. Upon creating rapport and a strategy for helping students meet their goals, academic advisors drill down into the heart of academic planning by adopting the philosophy of advising as teaching (Crookston, 1972/2009). This approach is used by those who consider academic advising as more than a series of authoritative decision-making sessions; rather, those advocating the advising-as-teaching approach encourage a developmental conversation between advisors and students through which learning emerges as the by-product. Through this developmental context, students take an active role in decision making, collaborate on problem solving with their advisors, and share in the learning outputs (Crookston, 1972/2009) (see chapter 2).

Lowenstein (2005) advanced the concept of advising as teaching by describing *learner-centered advising;* this paradigm suggests that the academic advisor can affect a student's understanding of the entire curriculum, including courses taken for a major, general education requirements, and in other areas of study. Lowenstein explained, "The excellent advisor helps the student to understand, and indeed in a certain sense, to create the logic of the student's curriculum" (p. 65). Rather than focusing on educating students through an individual course, as a teacher does, the advisor focuses on educating students through the overall curriculum. As they develop competence and gain experience in their courses and out-of-class activities, students begin to generate knowledge about their education as a whole. Academic advisors help students construct meaning from the knowledge they have developed.

According to Lowenstein (2005), through excellent advisors, students understand the ways parts of their curriculum support each other because advisors and students engage in critical conversations about the meaning of various requirements. For example, an advisor may discuss the purpose of general education requirements and the ways the perspectives gained in those courses might complement knowledge in the student's chosen discipline, or the advisor may relate that the spark of interest from a general education class can initiate a new direction of inquiry.

Excellent advisors also support students in sequencing their learning experiences (Lowenstein, 2005); that is, they teach students the reasons for a particular order of completing courses and participating in activities. Although prerequisites in a course description make clear the order of certain courses in sequence, the student may not understand the reasons for the progression. Furthermore, advisors can help students see the rationale behind less-obvious or otherwise unexamined options for a well-considered academic plan. For example, an undergraduate interested in conducting social science research would benefit from course work in statistics, and a student seeking a study abroad experience may find value in taking the appropriate foreign language in advance of program participation.

Through conversations with their advisors, students can learn to identify the transferable skills they are developing (Lowenstein, 2005). To assist students making intentional decisions about their curriculum, advisors ask them to reflect on the skills they might gain in courses that seem irrelevant to the academic plan. Also, advisors advance the conversation by discussing not only student learning but also by asking "What are you doing in class?" Quick consultations led by questions for reflection and exploration engender thinking that students use to identify the skills gained in courses and the ways to apply them in the future.

In addition, advisors who work with students to synthesize their overall curriculum (Lowenstein, 2005) reveal the full picture when various components of an education fit together. As a guide or as a coach (Lowenstein, p. 71), the advisor uses teachable moments to encourage reflection on student plans. The student, meanwhile, constructs his or her version of the curriculum based on the information shared by the advisor, knowledge gained through each component, and the understanding developed as a result of these combined factors. Much like the journey to self-authorship, in which an adult learns to consider but not completely rely upon external voices (Baxter Magolda, 2004), students can make the transition from relying upon their advisors to explain the curriculum-building process to making those connections themselves with an advisor's guidance. As they better understand the place of each component within their curriculum, students will likely learn more from each individual component (Lowenstein, 2005).

Using Technology to Support Academic Planning

Students continue to come to college with a wide range of technological experiences and expectations. According to a 2014 survey (Dahlstrom & Bichsel, 2014) with a representative sample of 10,000 U.S. undergraduates, 67% of respondents believed they had acquired adequate technological skills before entering college. Students also reported getting more involved in courses (49%) and more connected to instructors (54%) when technology is used than when it is not (Dahlstrom & Bichsel, 2014). Based on the learning-centered advising model, one can surmise that technology use in academic planning can exert a similar positive influence on students in an advising session as it does for them in the classroom. Technology enhances knowledge construction, provides an authentic context to support learning by doing, and serves as a reflective tool and social medium (Jonassen et al., 2008).

Learning Management Systems

A learning management system (LMS) supports face-to-face courses and delivers online instruction. Features within an LMS may include customizable modules, or folders, containing course resources organized by week or topic, discussion forums, calendars, announcements, messaging systems, web authoring and grading tools, and assessments. Available at 99% of U.S. higher education institutions (Lang & Pirani, 2014), the LMS gives all students access to an e-learning platform. Although primarily used in course-based environments, advisors can harness the features and analytics for academic planning (see chapter 10).

Students using LMSs for face-to-face and online courses see the potential applications for academic planning. According to the survey conducted by Dahlstrom and Bichsel (2014), 69% were very or extremely interested in having personalized support and degree progress information available through their LMS. Another 68% of surveyed students responded positively to suggestions that administrators and faculty members use LMS analytics to create personalized messages about students' academic progress. In fact, 89% of respondents indicated at least moderate interest in use of analytics to provide course recommendations.

Using the findings from the Dahlstrom and Bichsel (2014) survey, advisors could create a virtual advising environment through the LMS and enroll new students in the same manner as the registrar adds them in classes. Advisors could use the announcement and calendar features to post prescriptive information, such as important policies and academic deadlines, and thereby free meeting times for conversations about the academic curriculum. Because of the convenient messaging aspects of the LMS, students may connect with their advisors frequently, deepening and enhancing the relationship between them. Activity modules, web-authoring tools, and assessments encourage student reflection upon the knowledge they have gained and provide a basis for conversation starters during the advising session.

Electronic Portfolios

Through the purposeful collection of digital artifacts that showcase a student's efforts, progress, and achievements, the electronic- or e-portfolio represents a student's best work over time, demonstrates achievement of certain standards, or serves as an external performance evaluation shared with stakeholders (Jonassen et al., 2008). Reflection characterizes both the process of assembling the e-portfolio and is articulated as a specific component within the collection. An instructor or advisor assigns the specifications of the e-portfolio by considering the overall purpose, the learning outcomes to be demonstrated, the artifacts that might represent each outcome, and the intended audience (Jonassen et al., 2008).

An instructor-assigned e-portfolio might represent a body of work throughout one course or throughout a student's entire education. Such a collection of artifacts prompts students to synthesize the various components of the curriculum as well as consider the greater purpose behind their own education. Alongside their students, advisors can review the e-portfolio in progressive stages that culminate in a capstone appointment at graduation.

In sessions held during the student's first college year, advisors may use the e-portfolio to develop student learning outcomes and subsequently to discuss opportunities for meeting those outcomes through courses and activities. This planning tool may aid first-year students in understanding the sequenced learning experiences necessary to meet long-term objectives (Lowenstein, 2005). Advisors can also use e-portfolios to flip the advising learning experience by allowing students to review their academic decision making and planning prior to the advising session (Ambrose, Martin, & Page, 2014). By preparing before the meeting, the student and advisor can capitalize on their time together to discuss the outcomes associated with the e-portfolio. Through their reflection of academic decisions and plans as part of the flipped learning experience, students also maximize their own investment in their education (Ambrose et al., 2014).

Although stand-alone e-portfolio platforms are available at a range of price points, some LMSs include an e-portfolio component at no additional cost. Likewise, students can use free blogging applications to create e-portfolios at many institutions. The LMS and blog options for an e-portfolio provide free, shareable spaces for students to curate their artifacts and reflections.

Concept Mapping

Concept maps help students "to generate ideas, to design a complex structure, to communicate complex ideas, to aid learning by explicitly integrating new and old knowledge, and to assess understanding or diagnose misunderstanding" (Dykeman & Mackenzie, 2009, p. 197). The learner begins the mapping process by addressing a focus question, identifying concepts related to that question, and then drawing the connections on a visual map (Novak & Canas, 2007). This graphical representation of relationships among ideas can produce a powerful, purposeful learning opportunity.

In the classroom, instructors use concept mapping to teach a deeper understanding of topics covered in the course. In advising, concept mapping may help students visualize the relationships among curricular components and make plans for meeting the previously identified learning outcomes. Johnson, Podjed, and Taasan (2013) presented online concept mapping in a first-year seminar to help students brainstorm opportunities for involvement throughout their undergraduate careers. The authors found that the assignment helped students "visualize, organize, and prioritize their goals" (p. 81) as well as conduct in-depth research for determining the opportunities to include on their maps.

Similar to instructors in a first-year seminar, academic advisors can encourage students to develop concept maps of their long- and short-term educational goals. They can collaborate with first-year students to construct maps on paper during an advising session, or students can use online tools to create a concept map that they share electronically with the advisor (see chapter 11). The online map presents advantages in term of saving, editing, and sharing it with others, including those on social media.

Although not the only technological tools available for advisors and advisees, LMSs, e-portfolios, and concept maps are easily accessible, customizable, and affordable. In addition, they confer opportunities to construct intentional plans and spaces for reflection with first-year students in support of their entire educational curriculum for the remainder of their degree program.

AIMING FOR **EXCELLENCE**

The following discussion questions and activities give advisors concrete ideas and strategies for expanding their knowledge and applying the information shared in this chapter to their advising practice:

- Attend a curriculum committee meeting for an academic unit and participate in discussions about the placement of certain courses within the major curriculum so you can articulate them clearly to students.

- Attend a general education committee meeting to participate in discussions about the purpose of various requirements so you can explain them clearly to students.

- Create an academic planning space within the institutional LMS and conduct usability testing with student volunteers.

- Download the 2005 Lowenstein article, "If Advising Is Teaching, What Do Advisors Teach?" from the *NACADA Journal* and host a common reading with other advisors. Discuss how current advising models support the academic curriculum.

- Download the 2011 Freitag article, "Creating a Personal Philosophy of Academic Advising" from the NACADA Clearinghouse of Academic Advising Resources. If you have a personal philosophy of advising, how does the stated epistemology of learning affect your approach to academic planning with students? If you do not have a personal philosophy of advising, develop one.

- Familiarize yourself with opportunities on and off campus that may complement a student's academic plan, such as undergraduate research, study abroad, and an internship, which may have a profound impact on a student's ability to make meaning of their curriculum.

Summary

In a constructivist learning environment, educators emphasize meaning making and knowledge construction. By helping students understand and reflect upon all the forces converging as part of their curriculum, the best academic advisors take a consistent, central role in this learning process (Drake, 2011; Lowenstein, 2005). First-year students, in particular, may not take charge over their decisions (Baxter Magolda, 2004) and may need encouragement to engage critically with academic planning.

Advisors serve as a guide through the first year by understanding the plethora of transitions students undergo (Anderson et al., 2012), especially those that affect their search for meaning and sense of purpose (Chickering & Reisser, 1993). Although they can leverage a variety of tools to help students process and reflect upon their educational journey, academic advisors play the most important part in active co-construction of the meaning that underscores academic plans and makes first-year students feel confident in making decisions about their future.

References

Ambrose, G. A., Martin, H. E., & Page, H. R. (2014). Linking advising and e-portfolios for engagement: Design, evolution, assessment, and university-wide implementation. *AAC&U Peer Review, 16*(1). Retrieved from https://www.aacu.org/peerreview/2014/winter

Anderson, L., & Krathwohl, D. R. (2001). *A taxonomy for learning, teaching, and assessing: A revision of Bloom's taxonomy of educational objectives.* New York, NY: Longman.

Anderson, M. L., Goodman, J., & Schlossberg, N. K. (2012). *Counseling adults in transition: Linking Schlossberg's theory with practice in a diverse world* (4th ed.). New York, NY: Springer.

Baxter Magolda, M. B. (2004). *Making their own way: Narratives for transforming higher education to promote self-development.* Sterling, VA: Stylus.

Chickering, A., & Reisser, L. (1993). *Education and identity* (2nd ed.). San Francisco, CA: Jossey-Bass.

Crookston, B. B. (2009). A developmental view of academic advising as teaching. *NACADA Journal, 29*(1), 78–82. (Reprinted from *Journal of College Student Personnel, 13*, 1972, pp. 12–17)

Dahlstrom, E., & Bichsel, J. (2014). *ECAR study of undergraduate students and information technology, 2014.* Retrieved from the EDUCAUSE website: https://net.educause.edu/ir/library/pdf/ss14/ers1406.pdf

Danis, E. J. (1987). Academic planning as a career strategy. *NACADA Journal,* 7(1), 87–89.

Dey, E. L., & Hurtado, S. (2005). College students in changing contexts. In P. Altbach, R. O. Berdahl, & P. J. Gumport (Eds.), *Higher education in the twenty-first century: Social, political, and economic challenges* (2nd ed., pp. 315–339). Baltimore, MD: The Johns Hopkins University Press.

Drake, J. K. (2011). The role of academic advising in student retention and persistence. *About Campus, 16*(3), 8–12.

Dykeman, M., & Mackenzie, J. (2009). Concept mapping. In A. Mills, G. Durepos, & E. Wiebe (Eds.), *Encyclopedia of case study research* (pp. 197–201). Thousand Oaks, CA: Sage.

Freitag, D. (2011). *Creating a personal philosophy of academic advising.* Retrieved from http://www.nacada.ksu.edu/Resources/Clearinghouse/View-Articles/Personal-philosophy-of-academic-advising.aspx

Fried, J. (2006). Rethinking learning. In R. Keeling (Ed.), *Learning reconsidered 2: Implementing a campus-wide focus on the student experience.* Washington, DC: ACPA, ACUHO-I, ACUI, NACA, NACADA, NASPA, and NIRSA.

Gordon, V. (1998). New horizons: Learning from the past and preparing for the future. *NACADA Journal, 18*(2), 5–12.

Hodge, D., Baxter Magolda, M. B., & Haynes, C. (2009). Engaged learning: Enabling self-authorship and effective practice. *Liberal Education, 95*(4). Retrieved from https://www.aacu.org/publications-research/periodicals/engaged-learning-enabling-self-authorship-and-effective-practice

Johnson, M. L., Podjed, S., & Taasan, S. (2013). Engaging honors students in purposeful planning through a concept mapping assignment. *Honors in Practice, 9,* 73–84. Retrieved from http://digitalcommons.unl.edu/nchchip/226/

Jonassen, D., Howland, J., Marra, R. M., & Crismond, D. (2008). *Meaningful learning with technology* (3rd ed.). Upper Saddle River, NJ: Pearson Prentice Hall.

Lang, L., & Pirani, J. (2014, May 20). *The learning management system evolution: CDS spotlight report.* Retrieved from http://www.educause.edu/ecar

Lowenstein, M. (2005). If advising is teaching, what do advisors teach? *NACADA Journal, 25*(2), 65–73.

Novak, J., & Canas, A. (2007). Theoretical origins of concept maps, how to construct them, and uses in education. *Reflecting Education, 3*(1), 29–42.

Rowley, D. J., & Sherman, H. (2004). *Academic planning: The heart and soul of the academic strategic plan.* Lanham, MD: University Press of America.

Shaffer, L. S., & Zalewski, J. M. (2011). "It's what I have always wanted to do." Advising the foreclosure student. *NACADA Journal, 31*(2), 62–77.

Trabant, T. D. (2006). *Advising Syllabus 101.* Retrieved from http://www.nacada.ksu.edu/Resources/Clearinghouse/View-Articles/Creating-an-Advising-Syllabus.aspx

CHAPTER 9

Dangers of Foreclosure

Leigh S. Shaffer and Jacqueline Zalewski

Academic advisors have gained increasing awareness of a developmental and academic problem called *identity foreclosure,* common among college students, especially those in their first year (Albright, Martel, & Webster, 2012; Menke, 2015; Ross, 2013; Schwartz, 2006; Shaffer & Zalewski, 2011). Foreclosure refers to premature commitments to plans and goals despite minimal or no effort to explore options or to understand oneself. We published an extensive review of empirical research into the nature and causes for foreclosure, describing ways academic advisors can recognize foreclosure and facilitate further personal development that leads to well-considered academic and career preparation decisions (Shaffer & Zalewski, 2011). Drawing selectively on that review, we describe common causes of foreclosure, practical means to identify it, and techniques for working with students by aiding them in academic recovery when needed and engaging them in renewed career exploration.

Cases Demonstrating Foreclosure

A series of brief case studies illustrate typical ways that foreclosure students present to academic advisors. Fictitious names are attributed to students in these narratives, which are based on scenarios presented in previous publications as noted.

> Anne, a first-year student, wants to be a nurse and was admitted to the university in her second major of choice. She applied unsuccessfully to nursing programs at several other colleges, but her scores on nursing entrance exams and her high school science grades failed to meet admissions standards. Now that she has matriculated, Anne wants to apply for an internal transfer into the nursing program, and she intends to enroll exclusively in humanities and social science courses to build an

impressive GPA. She explains to her advisor that she has no interest in a major other than nursing, and she "doesn't want to give up her dream." (Albright et al., 2012)

Bob, the first in his family to attend college, receives encouragement from his parents, who make significant sacrifices to pay as many of his expenses as possible. Bob is admitted as an accounting major, but when he meets with an advisor from the Accounting Department, he demonstrates very little enthusiasm for his declared program of study. In fact, he states that he dislikes mathematics and finds the business topics "painfully" boring. When his advisor begins discussing exploration of alternative careers and majors, Bob explains, "My parents said—in no uncertain terms— that they 'are not going to waste their money on tuition and expenses for a worthless degree.'" Bob's parents want him to learn marketable skills and chose accounting for him because "there are always jobs for accountants." (Pizzolato, 2006; Shaffer & Zalewski, 2011)

The youngest of four children born to a fifth-generation farmer, Charles embraced his status as the heir apparent for the farm when one of his older siblings died and the others made career choices outside agriculture. Charles always wanted to farm, and with the takeover of the family business, he hopes to ensure it remains solvent so his children can one day inherit it. Charles matriculates to the state university to study agriculture and sees no need to undertake career exploration. (Keating, 1996)

Dawn was a two-time all-state basketball player in high school and was heavily recruited by several nationally prominent women's basketball programs. After accepting an athletic scholarship and matriculating into her dream school, she met with her assigned athletic advisor to begin the scheduling process. When asked about her plans after college, Dawn replied, "I'm a baller; that's me; that's what I do. I'm gonna go pro and play as long as I can." She did not want to discuss fields of study because she expected to earn "a boatload of money" in the WNBA. She summed up her attitude toward choosing an academic major with, "I just want to make sure to pick one that won't be an obstacle to maintaining my NCAA eligibility." (Beamon, 2012; Menke, 2015)

During the summer orientation program, Ed and two of his high school friends declared as sociology majors. They attended the first advising meeting together. The advisor asked, "How did you come to share this interest in sociology?" After a sheepish glance to his friends, Ed explained, "We thought that sociology would be a pretty easy subject for us, and the course work would be even easier if we work on assignments and study together." When she asked them about the careers they hoped to enter with a sociology degree, they admitted to giving very little thought to their lives after graduation. Ed volunteered, "I'm not bothered much about what happens after graduation because all that really matters is having a college degree." (Shaffer, 1997/2009; Shaffer & Zalewski, 2011)

These students demonstrate identity foreclosure because each has committed to an academic major and a career direction with little consideration of possible alternatives. However, each case depicts a different set of circumstances and social pressures that have encouraged premature decisions about their educational and vocational futures.

Causes and Consequences of Foreclosure

Erikson (1958) introduced the term *foreclosure* to refer to one undesirable—and often unsuccessful—approach taken by adolescents to address their problems in forming a personal identity. According to Erikson's theory, adolescents and young adults struggle to develop a sense of personal identity that guides them in their life course; that is, they experience an *identity crisis*. The development of the self requires an individual to enter adulthood through education or vocational training (Baumeister, 1987). This emerging identity can be characterized as a set of commitments to relatively permanent orientations toward family, friends, the larger society and its institutions as well as beliefs, attitudes and values, and means of making a living, among others. In the end, the young person resolves the crisis by adopting a set of commitments that create a sufficient platform for living a meaningful and productive life. Modern societies recognize that adolescents need time for this exploration; allow for a certain level of experimentation with lifestyles and social relationships; and tolerate the inevitable awkwardness, inconsistency, and reversal of direction that coincide with these tentative efforts at self-direction. If this process goes well, then the adolescent will emerge from the period of crisis with a stable, internally consistent sense of self; he or she will have achieved an identity.

This process of exploration, however, brings a level of apprehension that can become burdensome. Students may attempt to minimize their anxiety by making and announcing an identity choice that they believe will garner approval by important persons in their lives, including parents. The most important facet of this new identity will be their intention to pursue a legitimate occupation or career.

When they matriculate to postsecondary institutions, students who have foreclosed often engage in self-defeating behaviors, such as selecting majors for which they are poorly prepared and careers for which they are ill suited either intellectually or motivationally (Shaffer & Zalewski, 2011). Anne demonstrates this self-defeating behavior. In high school, she performed poorly in science classes. Furthermore, during the college application process, she received clear indications that, based on her low scores and grades on required admissions exams, program experts found her skills incompatible with the nursing curriculum. Despite this feedback, she rigidly pursues admission to a nursing program and refuses to initiate career exploration on her own.

Fear of Disappointing Others

In addition to defending themselves from the anxieties of identity searches, many students make foreclosed decisions about their careers and their academic majors because of family influence. Parents often express preferences—and even mandates—for their children's educational and career choices. Parental control of students' choices is reported for international student populations (Pizzolato, 2006; Shaffer & Zalewski, 2011). For example, Uzman (2004) found that foreclosure students in a Turkish university had accepted their parents' values for fear of being rejected. Sometimes familial influences are expressed in the choice of institution, such as when a student attends the alma mater of a parent and thereby becomes a *legacy admit* (Martin & Spenner, 2009).

Parents paying some or all of a student's educational costs who threaten to withdraw emotional and financial support if their student deviates from the parent-prescribed major and career plans encourage foreclosure (Simmons, 2008). For example, Bob accedes to his parent's conditional offer of support for college expenses by pursuing the practical major, accounting, that they selected for him. Pizzolato (2006) reported one student's account of parental influence that reinforced a foreclosed identity choice:

> I've been going to be a microbiologist for my whole life. That's what my parents really wanted. Who really knows why?! The idea of getting a degree and working in a lab for the rest of my life didn't seem like a good life. I wanted to work in inner city schools, but my parents said they'd stop paying my bills if I wasn't going to be a bio major. (p. 37)

Some families want to perpetuate career traditions; for example, some may expect children to maintain the family line of physicians or attorneys (Petitpas, 1978; Waterman & Waterman, 1976). Charles faces perhaps the most complicated situation for a prospective college student: the legacy of inheriting a business (Keating, 1996), in this case, the farming operation. Family farms typically represent indivisible accumulations of capital that have created the basis for both family wealth and identity. Each generation of a farm family negotiates the selection of the potential heir, who is expected to work the farm and keep it in the family (Keating, 1996).

In addition to pressures from family members, some students feel compelled to foreclose on career exploration because of membership in a larger community. Many gifted students are encouraged to enter high-prestige occupations such as physician, lawyer, engineer, and business leader (Greene, 2006; Shaffer, 2015). Those with sponsors also feel compelled to complete a degree chosen for them; for example, many international students receive funds from their family or home government to meet a specific need for experts at home, such as nurses, scientists, or agricultural specialists. In cases of sponsorship, students may have known their final educational and career destinations for as long as they can remember, and some view these appointed careers as obligations or burdens (Pizzolato, 2006; Shaffer & Zalewski, 2011).

As a result of these complicated expectations, advisors who suggest exploration or reconsideration of a declared major or career path may elicit a variety of student reactions. Some students may feel deeply threatened when they consider the possible consequences of questioning the directives of their government or family. This fear may manifest in resistance, either stated or not, to the advisor's suggestions (Archambault, 2016).

Lack of Vision

In addition to the complicated situations presented by international students, academic advisors encounter specific forms of identity foreclosure based on the characteristics of special populations of domestic students, such as student athletes (Menke, 2015; Shaffer & Zalewski, 2011). With elite-level skills and high-profile accomplishments, Dawn foreclosed on identity and career exploration because she intends to play in the WNBA. Although some athletes, like Dawn, perceive that their talents will propel them to the professional ranks, those who cling to little hope for a professional career may also make hasty decisions because the demands of participating in intercollegiate athletics leave them little time or energy to reflect on aspects of life unassociated with sports (Menke, 2015; Shaffer & Zalewski, 2011).

Through the profile of student athletes and the people who work with them, academic advisors will realize that foreclosure, commonly observed of many in the student body, presents in distinct ways according to the socialization process of students who identify in specific categories. For example, student athletes feel a unique sense of loss at the prospect of retirement or confront fears of a future without competitive sports (Shurts & Shoffner, 2004) that may complicate their expectations.

Adherence to Credentialism

In stark contrast to the reasons based on serious issues, students seeking to make early life choices and persist with little reflection, like Ed and his friends, think that decisions about majors carry little importance. Peers, parents, and community members sometimes share a belief in *credentialism*, the notion that obtaining a college degree is sufficient to guarantee success in getting a job (Collins, 1977). Those who subscribe to credentialism regard choice of major as a mere requirement for graduation and believe that completion of any degree will lead to a desirable lifestyle (Shaffer, 1997/2009). For this reason, those advocating credentialism push students to make quick and permanent decisions, especially during the college application process. Although choices made under these pressured circumstances may be both premature and superficial, students justify taking the path of least resistance by adopting the decisions of their peers, selecting a major in which they feel certain to attain success (graduate), or choosing a career path that will please significant others (Rysiew, Shore, & Leeb, 1999). Although they might benefit from reexamination of their expressed commitment to a major and a career path, students who chose speciously may not appreciate the reasoning for reconsidering their choices and resist the suggestion to explore alternatives. As with those who felt burdened to make a logical or imposed decision, students who choose haphazardly may engage in active reconsideration only when faced with disenchantment or academic failure (Albright et al., 2012; Schwartz, 2006).

Identifying Foreclosure in First-Year Students

When building a relationship with new students, advisors need to recognize signs of identity foreclosure. Mature major selection and career decision making follows a period of exploration and reflection, which the advisee should readily recall when prompted. Because commitment without exploration characterizes foreclosure, advisors can probe the depth of each student's rationale by asking key questions about their selection process; for example, "How did you decide that you wanted to be a nurse?" Answers such as "I have always wanted to be a nurse" demonstrate an early commitment indicative of one who has never questioned the evident choice (Albright et al., 2012). Advisors should inquire more of those who provide a definitive but nonspecific answer. Specifically, follow-up questions should elicit evidence of an identity search and career exploration, such as "What other careers have you considered?" "What did you do to discover what being a nurse is like?" or "How do you know that you will enjoy being a nurse?" Advisors who face resistance to these questions can reassure advisees that choices made without extensive exploration do not necessarily lead to poor outcomes and then explain that research shows that choice of majors and careers made over time and with reflection is linked to better academic performance (Shaffer & Zalewski, 2011).

Academic advisors can exert a positive influence on foreclosure students by encouraging them to perform actions intended to confirm the appropriateness of early career selections, such as endeavors that improve self-awareness (including psychometric tests and inventories, job shadowing, and field experiences) and activities that improve awareness of the demands of prospective careers (often available through career development centers). By using in-depth queries, advisors may uncover signs of a foreclosed identity status. Advisors may recognize foreclosure in students who complain about activities or requirements that should bring intrinsic satisfaction for students well placed in a major. For example, advisors may seek clarification from music majors who hate practicing their instruments or accounting majors who find performing mathematical computations tedious. High-ability students who have foreclosed on high-status careers, such as law or medicine, may believe no one enjoys their jobs and that everyone of ability chooses professions because of extrinsic motivators, such as income or prestige (Shaffer, 2015). When they detect students expressing dislike for some (or all) of the characteristic activities of their chosen field, advisors should consider that the students may need to reexamine some of their decisions.

Some students who have foreclosed, particularly those who did not meet admission criteria for the preferred major, may enter as undeclared, or they may present as undecided major-changers who have matriculated into a second-choice field. They may fit the profile called *up-tighters* (Buyarski, 2009) because they are either unable or unwilling to explore alternatives, fail to matriculate in their first choice, or unrealistically expect to enroll in courses most applicable to the denied major. In each of these cases, advisors broaching career exploration can expect to encounter intransigence. When they manifest anxiety during discussion of options, advisees may be experiencing the stress they sought to escape by foreclosing their identity search in the first place. In addition to providing a supportive environment for these students within the developmental advising context, academic advisors help their advisees seek additional support from counseling professionals on their campuses.

Ironically, some foreclosure students who adhere to credentialism may express little anxiety over renewing their career and major selection process because they have made little investment in their decisions. Instead of arguing for maintaining their original plans, they may easily acquiesce to aborting their plans. While they may welcome the absence of student anxiety and resistance, advisors may soon discover that students adhering to credentialism may change their major but not their rationale for choosing. Because some undergraduates believe that any academic degree guarantees future vocational success, students espousing credentialism see no reason to revisit the process of major selection and career orientation unless their academic or progress-to-degree standing seems at risk.

Advising to Encourage Student Development

We advocate the *praxis* advising model (Hemwall & Trachte, 1999; Smith, 2002) as a useful approach for many students, including those who have foreclosed. The praxis model combines features of both the developmental and prescriptive approaches to academic advising. Hemwall and Trachte (1999) emphasized that, through a praxis approach, advisors engage students in critical self-reflection, especially concerning their educational goals and their career choices, and lead each to question an initial choice of major despite the apparent appropriateness of it. They pointed to the unique aspect of the praxis approach in the following hypothetical exchange between an advisor and student:

> An advisor might be tempted to say to her or his pre-med student, "Oh, so you want to be a physician. Okay, let's see what course choices you might have." However, an advisor who is guided by the concept of praxis might ask probing questions instead. "Tell me why you want to be a physician ..." might open an important conversation that might be missed by the advisor who assumes that the career decision was already determined. Such questions prompt the advisee to engage in critical self-reflection. (Hemwall & Trachte, 1999, p. 9)

When asked the reason for pursuit of a nursing career, students like Anne often provide socially accepted justifications for service-related careers, such as, "I want to help people" and "I want to give back to society." Others offer personally relevant indicators; for example, "I can't be a doctor" may reflect a belief that the student cannot afford medical school; "I would like to work in a professional setting like a hospital or a clinic" may signify that the foreclosed does not know the range of career opportunities in the health care field. Conversations that follow from such inquiry can create a path toward a reopened career search.

Career Interventions

For invigorating career exploration, advisors can provide foreclosure students with *career interventions*, individually designed activities aimed at enhancing the development of skills and special knowledge or at making better career-related decisions (Hartung, Savickas, & Walsh, 2015). By engaging career interventions, advisors embody Shockley-Zalabak's (2012) vision of intentional *interaction designers* (p. 13). One such interaction designer, an advisor in a pre-med program, assigned a foreclosure student to write a narrative about the way life as a physician might unfold (Shaffer, 2015). Others have taken advantage of career counseling sessions, academic career-oriented classes, computer applications (e.g., *Career HOPES* as described by Herman, 2010), self-administered career inventories, and job shadowing as career interventions. Niles and Hutchison (2009) provided a valuable discussion of designing career interventions in the context of prominent career development theories in *The Handbook of Career Advising* (Hughey, Burton Nelson, Damminger, & McCalla-Wriggins, 2009).

Ross (2013) developed an especially successful career intervention strategy, based on Gottfredson's (1981) career development theories, to use with foreclosure students. According to Gottfredson, children develop conceptions of occupations and career paths, including the criteria of people suited for it. Upon accepting an occupation as inappropriate for oneself, the child eliminates it as a possibility; for example, the young person may say, "I don't like to do math, so I probably can't be an accountant." The cognitive activity of discarding possible occupational choices characterizes the first stage of career selection that Gottfredson calls *circumspection*. However, most students undergo a limited circumspection process because of narrow and flawed preliminary understanding of the occupations considered. Also, most children demonstrate little awareness of themselves and their abilities. As a result, they may eliminate choices for trivial reasons that they could profitably reconsider in high school.

Students who narrow choices to a single career without the benefit of a mature process of exploration often foreclose on their options. Foreclosure students who encounter any kind of barrier to their chosen career path may feel apprehension and express recalcitrance because they do not see any viable options. Ross (2013) suggested that advisors encourage students to reconsider a wide range of academic programs and majors available by recapitulating the circumspection process. Ross led students through a list of potential majors offered at an institution and asked them to specify the reasons they had eliminated some majors and considered others. This activity helps foreclosure students recognize that any inaccurate or immature perceptions of majors and motivates them to reconsider them.

Ross (2013) reported that participating students typically identified a small number of alternatives to explore without provoking the levels of anxiety and resistance experienced by foreclosure students forced to reopen the identity exploration process. Ross also explained that advisors who directed students to career interventions, such as internships, informational interviews, or experiential learning activities (e.g., service-learning) found success in getting students to look purposefully into options.

Career Advising

Finally, the 3-I career advising process described by Gordon (2006) offers another successful approach for advising students who have foreclosed. Through Gordon's model, students prepare to make mature career decisions by *inquiring* into their own skills, interests, and intriguing careers, *informing* themselves about the educational requirements to qualify for those careers, and *integrating* the information into a workable plan for pursuing choices.

Student athletes, such as Dawn, often foreclose their identity and career searches on the assumption that they will earn a living playing professional sport. Student athletes may not only overestimate their own skills and abilities but may also hold unrealistic expectations about the number of athletes who reach the professional ranks. Among those who realize the improbability of playing as a professional athlete, some may not hold realistic ideas about the opportunities for pursuing a nonperformance career in sports, such as coaching, scouting, or teaching, and as result, fail to prepare for such occupations.

Menke (2015) described a variation of the 3-I process by suggesting that students first address integration. In this process, advisors allow student athletes to discover their own foreclosure by helping them see that they cannot integrate their vision of a sports career because they did not know the requirements for specific occupations. For example, in Dawn's case, learning that no more than 1% of all collegiate women basketball players are annually drafted into the WNBA inspired her to learn about the educational credentials needed to coach high school basketball.

AIMING FOR **EXCELLENCE**

The following discussion questions and activities give advisors concrete ideas and strategies for expanding their knowledge and applying the information shared in this chapter to their advising practice:

- Download the 2011 Shaffer and Zalewski article, "'It's What I Have Always Wanted to Do': Advising the Foreclosure Student" and host a brown-bag lunch or coffee hour to discuss the article with other advisors. Discuss potential problems foreclosure students may face in college and brainstorm different approaches to encouraging them to engage in further exploration of their plans and goals.

- Create a set of follow-up questions to help identify foreclosure students.

- Develop effective working relationships with professionals in other units who may assist with designing and implementing career interventions for foreclosure students. Identify options that give students first-hand exposure to potential careers, such as job shadowing programs, volunteer work experiences, service-learning courses, and career internships.

- Host a brown bag luncheon to discuss Gordon's (2006) 3-I career advising process and discuss ways to use this approach to advise foreclosure students. Discuss the opportunities and challenges for career exploration associated with each academic major.

- Attend advisor training programs and participate in developmental activities that help academic advisors integrate career advising into their interactions with students. If facilitators do not address the foreclosure process or characteristics of the foreclosure student, partner with others to introduce foreclosure to career advisors and those who help transition first-year students.

Summary

Exploratory students in a state of foreclosure often engage in self-defeating behaviors, including selecting majors and careers for which they show little motivation or relevant academic preparation. They present special challenges for academic advisors because many appear mature but resist changing their plans despite unpleasant evidence for likely failure or long-term unhappiness with their choices.

Academic advisors who develop the habit of asking first-year advisees to describe the process used to choose a major must also listen for evidence of a conscious search and reflection prior to making their selection. Advisors prepare to encounter anxiety and resistance from some of their students and understand that these reactions often serve as warning signals that the student has foreclosed on major and career choices. These students may need help in coping with academic and developmental challenges during their first year of college.

References

Albright, J. S., Martel, K. M., & Webster, B. D. (2012). No more missed opportunities: Using the foreclosure model to advise pre-nursing and nursing students. *Academic Advising Today, 35*(4). Retrieved from https://www.nacada.ksu.edu/Resources/Academic-Advising-Today/View-Articles/No-More-Missed-Opportunities-Using-the-Foreclosure-Model-to-Advise-Pre-Nursing-and-Nursing-Students.aspx

Archambault, K. L. (2016). Knowing and reaching students. In T. J. Grites, M. A. Miller, & J. Givans Voller (Eds.), *Beyond foundations: Developing as a master academic advisor* (pp. 107–122). San Francisco, CA: Jossey-Bass.

Baumeister, R. F. (1987). How the self became a problem: A psychological review of historical research. *Journal of Personality and Social Psychology, 52*(1), 163–176.

Beamon, K. (2012). "I'm a Baller": Athletic identity foreclosure among African-American former student-athletes. *Journal of African American Studies, 16*(2), 195–208. doi:10.1007/s12111-012-9211-8

Buyarski, C. A. (2009). Career advising with undecided students. In K. F. Hughey, D. Burton Nelson, J. K. Damminger, & B. McCalla-Wriggins (Eds.), *The handbook of career advising* (pp. 217–289). San Francisco, CA: Jossey-Bass.

Collins, R. (1977). Some comparative principles of educational stratification. *Harvard Educational Review, 47*(1), 1–27.

Erikson, E. H. (1958). *Young man Luther.* New York, NY: Norton.

Gordon, V. N. (2006). *Career advising: An academic advisor's guide.* San Francisco, CA: Jossey-Bass.

Gottfredson, L. S. (1981). Circumscription and compromise: A developmental theory of occupational aspirations. *Journal of Counseling Psychology, 28*(5), 545–579.

Greene, M. J. (2006). Helping build lives: Career and life development of gifted and talented students. *Professional School Counseling, 10*(1), 34–42.

Hartung, P. J., Savickas, M. L., & Walsh, W. B. (Eds.). (2015). *APA handbook of career intervention* (Vols. 1-2). Washington, DC: American Psychological Association.

Hemwall, M. K., & Trachte, K. C. (1999). Learning at the core: Toward a new understanding of academic advising. *NACADA Journal, 19*(1), 5–11.

Herman, S. (2010). Career HOPES: An internet-delivered career development intervention. *Computers in Human Behavior, 26*, 339–344. doi:10.1016/j.chb.2009.11.00

Hughey, K. F., Burton Nelson, D., Damminger, J. K., & McCalla-Wriggins, B. (Eds.). (2009). *The handbook of career advising*. San Francisco, CA: Jossey-Bass.

Keating, N. C. (1996). Legacy, aging, and succession in farm families. *Generations, 20*(3), 61–64.

Martin, N. D., & Spenner, K. I. (2009). Capital conversion and accumulation: A social portrait of legacies at an elite university. *Research in Higher Education, 50*(7), 623–648. doi: 10.1007/s11162-009-9136-9

Menke, D. J. (2015). 3-I career advising process: Implications for college athletes with foreclosed identity. *NACADA Journal, 35*(1), 22–28.

Niles, S. G., & Hutchison, B. (2009). Theories of career development to inform advising. In K. F. Hughey, D. Burton Nelson, J. K. Damminger, & B. McCalla-Wriggins (Eds.), *The handbook of career advising* (pp. 68–96). San Francisco, CA: Jossey-Bass.

Petitpas, A. (1978). Identity foreclosure: A unique challenge. *Personnel & Guidance Journal, 56*(9), 558–561.

Pizzolato, J. E. (2006). Complex partnerships: Self-authorship and provocative academic-advising practices. *NACADA Journal, 24*(1), 33–45.

Ross, K. (2013). Applying career and identity development theories in advising. *Academic Advising Today, 29*(3). Retrieved from http://www.nacada.ksu.edu/Resources/Academic-Advising-Today/View/Articles/Applying-Career-and-Identity-Development-Theories-in-Advising.aspx

Rysiew, K. J., Shore, B. M., & Leeb, R.T. (1999). Multipotentiality, giftedness, and career choice: A review. *Journal of Counseling Development, 77*, 423–430.

Schwartz, M. (2006). Preparing to advise high-achieving students. *Academic Advising Today, 29*(3). Retrieved from http://www.nacada.ksu.edu/Resources/Academic-Advising-Today/View/Articles/Preparing-to-Advise-High-Achieving-Stdents-.aspx

Shaffer, L. S. (2009). A human capital approach to academic advising. *NACADA Journal, 29*(1), 98–105. (Reprinted from *NACADA Journal, 17*[1], 1997, 5–12)

Shaffer, L. S. (2015). Academic advising. In P. J. Hartung, M. L. Savickas, & W. B. Walsh (Eds.), *APA handbook of career intervention: Vol 2. Applications* (pp. 85–98). Washington, DC: American Psychological Association.

Shaffer, L. S., & Zalewski, J. M. (2011). "It's what I have always wanted to do." Advising the foreclosure student. *NACADA Journal, 31*(2), 62–77.

Shockley-Zalabak, P. (2012). Advisors as interaction designers. *NACADA Journal, 32*(1), 12–17.

Shurts, W. M., & Shoffner, M. F. (2004). Providing career counseling for collegiate student-athletes: A learning theory. *Journal of Career Development, 31*(2), 95–109.

Simmons, A. N. (2008). A reliable sounding board: Parent involvement in students' academic and career decision making. *NACADA Journal, 28*(2), 33–43.

Smith, J. S. (2002). First-year student perceptions of academic advisement: A qualitative study and reality check. *NACADA Journal, 22*(2), 39–49.

Uzman, E. (2004). Identity status of university students with different levels of social support. *Eurasian Journal of Educational Research, 15*, 110–124.

Waterman, A. S., & Waterman, C. K. (1976). Factors related to vocational identity after extensive work experience. *Journal of Applied Psychology, 61*(3), 336–340.

SECTION IV

STRENGTHENING FIRST-YEAR
ADVISING PRACTICES

CHAPTER 10

Advisors' Tools, Resources, and Partnerships

Susan Poch

Working with first-year students is simultaneously demanding and rewarding. Unlike their predecessors, first-year students today are more likely to claim first-generation status, cite financial gain as the primary reason to attend college, present with mental health issues and learning disabilities, and experience challenges in achieving academic success (McElwee, 2013). Now, more than ever, faculty and primary-role advisors for distance or on-campus students bear responsibility for facilitating academic success. Therefore, advisors must locate and develop tools that create a rich array of resources to support the changing abilities and interests of first-year students. This chapter presents the tools, resources, partnerships, and communities critical to advisors' professional success.

Tools for Success

A number of tools influence advisors' ability to fulfill their responsibilities to students and other stakeholders (NACADA: The Global Community for Academic Advising [NACADA], 2005). In addition to those techniques, theories, and resources for assisting first-year students through the transition from high school to college, including suggestions for questionnaires that encourage student self-reflection and self-assessment (see chapter 3), some important technological tools offer means to support student goals. Especially for one-to-one advising, technology that links to broader institutional information provides answers to student questions and helps both parties prepare for meetings. In addition, advisors can use technology to engage students in the important conversations that build rapport. Therefore, technology is a critical component for advising first-year students today, and for those studying at a distance, it forms the very foundation for advisor–advisee interactions.

Predictive Analytics

Predictive analytics programs and early-warning systems expand advisor knowledge of first-year students in ways not possible before the Information Age (see chapter 5). Bryant (2016) explained,

> Advising departments invest in technologies that will help keep track of students, establish early warning systems, communicate with students, connect students to resources, and engage students at a personal level. The results can be powerful when these technologies make predictive analytics easy to leverage. (p. 1)

In addition to online resources such as Campus Technology, the NACADA Clearinghouse of Academic Advising Resources offers articles on and links to advising-relevant technologies, including early-warning systems and early-alert systems. Because technology changes rapidly and leaders in higher education put it to practice with increased sophistication, advisors and administrators need to vet these and similar resources continuously when deciding the technologies to apply in various situations (Steele, 2014).

Predictive analytic programs, based on prior student experiences and success patterns in specific courses, deliver curricular data to advisors (McCarty, 2014). Although they do not directly relate to a sole student, the analytics data give advisors some general information to guide first-year students through enrollment in challenging courses and in meeting expectations in milestone courses (Aguilar, Lonn, & Teasley, 2014). For example, course data on the performance of students with certain college-readiness test scores may be shared through analytic programs. Course planners and advisors can use these data to answer specific questions such as "Do most students with threshold SAT math scores pass a chemistry course required for the pre-med curriculum?" If data show that a significant percentage of students with suboptimal SAT math scores do not earn passing grades, advisors can discuss tutoring options with class participants before, rather than after, the first course examination. Despite the value of predictive analytics, advisors must caution against making assumptions about first-year students' abilities based on these generalized data. For specific students, advisors should attend to the alerts provided by early-warning systems.

Early-Warning Systems

Early-warning or early-alert systems collect and disperse information about specific students. Unlike predictive analytics, the computer-based early-alert systems provide data on grades and absences as well as notes from instructors that give advisors timely indications that a student is exhibiting academic distress. Many alert systems are based on multiple means for collecting grades or input from professors to create a foundation for important academic conversations. For example, an early alert about a student's difficulties gives an advisor an opportunity to proactively reach the student, who may not realize that some behaviors, such as missing an assignment or skipping class (tracked by the system), may lead to an academic crisis. Furthermore, early-warning systems provide an avenue for instructional faculty and advisors to collaborate and communicate as they support first-year students.

Another communication tool, the institutional student information system, such as Banner or PeopleSoft, monitors academic progress and course grades. It can also supply critical data to advisors about a student's academic accomplishments and path to degree completion. This information is required to advise students who may need to take developmental courses (see chapters 4 and 5), bring advanced placement or college credit, or have earned test scores that deem them qualified for advanced courses.

Advisors may also use e-portfolio technology to help first-year students conceptualize and demonstrate their accomplishments in curricular, cocurricular, and extracurricular activities. E-portfolios offer means for students to reflect on their experiences and encourage their continued engagement in chosen academic and extracurricular activities (Ambrose, Martin, & Page, 2014) (see chapter 8). This integration of technology and activity not only provides data for appropriate decision making in advising, but it sends a strong message to students that people at the institution care about student success.

Communication and Instructional Technology

Although communication with first-year students is acknowledged as a key function of advising, rapport is not always easily established. Some advisors find that electronic forms of communication (e.g., e-mail, texts, podcasts, websites) enhance relationship building and dialogue with students adept in these media (Lipschultz & Musser, 2007); advisors appreciate their value for addressing routine information so more time can be devoted to capitalizing on learning opportunities (Multari, 2004). Communication-oriented technology, used effectively, delivers important information prior to an advising session, thus streamlining the communications so advisors can enhance their interactions with first-year students.

Some advisors have adapted standard classroom technology for advising applications. Learning management systems (e.g., Blackboard or Angel) serve as repositories for student-accessible information, such as assignments, due dates, activities, and discussions related to a specific course. It can be used by advisors, especially faculty members already using such tools in class, to relay information about important dates or to assign tasks (e.g., finding and reading a degree audit). Furthermore, faculty members and primary-role advisors may provide valuable input for systems designed to meet common goals that provide consistent sources of information for students, especially in circumstances where advisors share responsibility or an advisor leaves the position. By using a learning management system for academic advising concerns, first-year students practice navigating through the same technology used in their credit-based courses.

Although much of the technology popular in higher education is designed for student use, advisors who spend time fully understanding these tools also benefit. By learning the latest features and tips, advisors remain up-to-date with the new technology (Haydon, 2004) that many first-year students use in their studies, and as a result, advisors can help students with practical guidance. Many institutions have targeted training sessions to improve the competence and confidence of primary-role and faculty advisors using technology.

As a follow-up to an advising interaction, advisors may refer first-year students to academic resources such as tutoring and academic coaching as well as study skills and time management workshops, which are sometimes delivered via technology. Advisors use these resources for encouraging first-year students to engage with other caring faculty and staff members.

Resources and Partnerships

Just as a network of technology and academic resources provides advisors a means to refer students, strong partnerships and specific resources contribute to advisor success. By building these partnerships, advisors develop the skills and confidence that inspire the understanding, compassion, knowledge, and, when appropriate, empathy necessary for reaching first-year students. Advisors relying on these partnerships to find solutions to complex advising issues partake in the comradery that encourages others and builds an advising community. Conversely, advisors of first-year students disconnected from resources or partnerships may feel isolated, and this detachment could lead to burnout (Huebner, 2011). Advisors who fully engage in social and workplace support receive intangible advantages for practice, such as increased competence and self-awareness.

As suggested in chapter 1, advisors need awareness of first-year students' characteristics, needs, and challenges. Because they experience new and recurring pressures, advisors who identify and create a suite of relevant resources learn to handle difficulties in ways that advance their professional development. Although a wide variety of advising supports are featured in the institutional structure, such as the tools named in this chapter, others need to be generated.

Orientation Programs for Students

Advisors seeking to develop a network of resources and partnerships can start by identifying institutional information and activities directed to first-year students. Students' initial introduction to campus life often resembles other aspects of first-year programming, such as seminars, residence hall events, transition workshops, and other student and academic affairs initiatives designed for newcomers. Well-structured first-year programs help students transition to the institution and to higher education. The featured programs or convocations serve as traditional rites of passage where first-year students are welcomed, celebrated, supported, and integrated into the campus community (Gavazzi, 2012). While important for first-year students, these orientation activities also provide excellent inroads for advisor access into the experiences of first-year students and a means to survey many important resources available to them.

Advisors who attend orientation programs and other welcome events can hear the information given to first-year students and their parents (see chapter 4). These presentations typically feature information vital for appropriate referrals, immediate answers to advisee questions, and key messages that provide consistent explanations. Faculty advisors, because of their expertise in an academic specialty and in advising, may present material related to success in the classroom. Distance or online advisors might participate in on-campus student programming or develop informational modules for first-year students. Although the needs of online students differ in some respects from those attending the institution on site, their participation in on-campus activities may encourage engagement in the campus culture.

Primary-role and faculty advisors who participate in first-year activities often gain a sense of their students that the demographic data cannot convey, including their challenges and transition issues and the ways adversities are addressed by others. The opposite also holds true: Advisors who do not engage with first-year programs may remain unaware of their students' needs or of newly implemented campus policies and procedures related to first-year students. Without these critical pieces of information, the unaware may advise poorly or refer inappropriately. Advisor participation in first-year programs and activities—from assisting students moving into a residence hall, to advising at orientation, to answering questions about schedules and options on the first day of class—creates connections with students and student services staff that evolve into a resource network.

Professional Networks and Resources

The creation of a professional network is "essential for promoting staff [professional] development, nurturing and retaining talented advisors, [and] providing excellent student services..." (Bryant, Chagani, Endres, & Galvin, 2006, p. 1). Because many advisors, particularly faculty and those off campus, work in isolation, professional networks offer inclusion and support. According to King (1993), "Advising cannot be done in isolation, and advising systems that are most successful have good working relationships with other offices on campus" (p. 7). By networking, advisors gain greater visibility and establish stronger positions from which to suggest policy changes than those not engaged in campus partnerships. In addition, the scholarship and best practices associated with advising may enrich practices in other areas of the institution. Finally, professional networks also increase the opportunity for personalized referrals that prove valuable for first-year students (Bryant et al., 2006).

At the institution. Networks and partnerships make up part of the institutional fabric developed individually by advisors, but how does one select an appropriate partnership, find a network, or start networking with others? The answers depend on an advisor's time, personal goals, and interests. The extent of networks may be dictated by an advisor's campus location. Bryant et al. (2006) pointed out, "Bringing advisors together from across campus allows them to reconnect in ways that are much more meaningful in person as compared to e-mail or phone" (p. 2); however, in some cases, advisors make connections through institutional commitment to professional networks (Bryant et al., 2006). A community of advisors, a campuswide advising group, or an identified structure for professional development may comprise the core group from which networking grows and proves most rewarding.

Network participants include colleagues in colleges, academic departments, student service offices, and advising units who work with first-year students. Faculty advisors who feel alone in advising may reach out to primary-role advisors to broaden their partnerships. Indeed, primary-role and faculty advisors in a community of like-minded coworkers find emotional comfort and social support as well as increased creativity in their advising practices (Huebner, 2011).

In addition to practical help with advising issues, advising colleagues with solid professional relationships may benefit from reciprocal attention, including recognition of challenges or burnout in each other (Huebner, 2011). The ultimate support structure is composed of caring individuals who share compliments, acknowledge each other's impact, and share the experiences of advising first-year students. This type of network benefits all and is worth the time and effort to develop.

Some professional networks evolve organically as faculty, distance, departmental, and unit advisors make connections through programs, offices, and committees across the campus. As Frost (1991) pointed out, students benefit from a system that stems from a collaborative effort between academic and student affairs (p. 2). Advisors from different campuses in a single educational system, in the same geographical location, or from connected community colleges and four-year institutions can develop cross-campus networks and further increase the scope of their resources. For example, advisors at community colleges and four-year institutions can share valuable information about first-year transfer, commuter, or other student populations who move back and forth between facilities.

Likewise, a network of colleagues can create professional development structures that accommodate unique and diverse needs of faculty, distance, and on-campus advisors. An existing program could be improved or reshaped, or advisors can initiate a new association, group, or program. The revised or new structure facilitates exchange of information about relevant areas, offices, programs, and organizations for advisors of first-year students. Individuals and groups of advisors can benefit from a coordinated professional development plan, such as the Advancing Practice program at the University of California, Berkeley. Although created for nonmandatory professional development, the program was widely viewed as a critical investment in advisors and an acknowledgement of the contributions they make to student success (E. Wilcox, personal communication, April 14, 2016). Additional ideas for advisors who wish to generate a specific self-practice and self-development plan, including those without access to formal training programs, are featured by Yoder and Joslin (2015) and Folsom (2008, 2015).

Some campuses host NACADA-affiliated or similar associations that provide professional development, updated information about campus resources, monthly opportunities for training, and a built-in network of colleagues. These associations typically invite all who advise, whether faculty, campus, or distance advisors, to participate. An individual or group interested in affiliating with NACADA should contact the NACADA Executive Office or leaders of the local advising organization.

Outside the institution. In addition to local organizations, advisors may consider attending NACADA regional and annual conferences to take advantage of more networking opportunities. Presentations directly related to first-year students and commissions or interest groups created for advising first-year students draw together practitioners and scholars from two- and four-year institutions. Likewise, opportunities to collaborate on presentations and writing projects with other advisors create a support structure for those looking to further the scholarship on advising. Sharing time and information with like-minded advisors often creates long-term relationships that transcend the conference. Advisors who can ask questions and share ideas with each other enlarge their collegial circle and supplement their resources.

Of course, not all advisors can attend conferences. Even in the case of scarce travel resources, advisors can subscribe to online journals, webinars, and electronic mailing lists hosted by NACADA and the National Resource Center for The First-Year Experience and Students in Transition. Scheduled lunch-and-learn or roundtable discussions further advance the ideas shared through these inexpensive resources.

To locate other resources and networks, advisors can investigate off-campus programs and offices that offer resources to first-year students. They can obtain a broad overview of first-year programming and support structures through NACADA and the National Resource Center websites and published research. By learning about the advising practices at other campuses and looking off campus for ideas about nearby or otherwise accessible programs, advisors generate a host of professional development opportunities.

Partnerships

Academic services. Offices and committees within and outside one's advising unit are valuable resources that provide key information related to first-year students. For example, due to increasing pressure on students to complete degrees in a timely manner, effective advisors develop relationships with others in the registrar's or bursar's office (Reynolds, 2009). In addition to an accurate degree audit program, the people in these offices keep official student records, provide information about the Family Educational Rights and Privacy Act (FERPA), and maintain the institutional academic time line. An advisor contacts the registrar's or bursar's office for questions related to evaluating Advanced Placement credit, scheduling a meeting room, requesting a registration time for a student, or inquiring about academic regulations. Therefore, advisors familiar with the organizational structures of these key offices likely know the person to contact for important information and student referrals (Reynolds, 2009).

Advisors need connections to the curriculum and academic affairs committees. Found at the college and department levels, curriculum committees develop, revise, and maintain the academic requirements for each major, minor, and certificate program within academic colleges. Faculty advisors, in particular, and primary-role advisors often find participation in this committee valuable for staying abreast of changes that affect advising.

The institutional corollary to curriculum committees, academic affairs committees also decide requirements for degrees and thereby influence advising. With the intention of providing accurate, up-to-date information to advisees and colleagues, advisors who participate in curriculum discussions learn about changes in degree, general education or core requirements, and other institutional academic mandates for first-year students.

A council or committee dedicated to all aspects of the first year includes members from residence life, orientation staff, faculty members who teach first-year courses, academic advisors, and advising administrators (see, e.g., University of Georgia, Office of the Vice President for Instruction, n.d.). Participation on an institutional first-year council expedites collaboration with colleagues in offices not directly involved with advising. To ensure that updates and ideas are consistently shared, advising representatives can serve as liaisons to their own departments or programs.

The people who work with underprepared students may confer critical understanding on the issues presented by first-year students in any college or university. Often referred to as an *academic standing office*, the people in this unit identify and notify students of academic deficiency and state the conditions for continued enrollment (see chapter 6). Because of the substantial number of underprepared first-year students (Renzulli, 2015), advisors must understand the procedures and policies for probation or reinstatement to help students in academic recovery. Advisors who serve on review boards develop policy or participate in targeted conversations with others associated with student reinstatement. By interacting with those involved in helping students on probation or otherwise at risk, advisors gain understanding about the office responsible for academic recovery and the students who benefit from those efforts.

Student life. If first-year students live on campus, residence life programs offer professional development and training opportunities that benefit advisors. Resident advisors (RAs) interact with first-year students in unique ways from their college home (think advising in pajamas!). Therefore, RAs develop perspectives that advance understanding of first-year student transitions (Acheson-Beck & Rybski, 2009), which make them valuable resources for academic advisors seeking to understand the student experience during the first weeks or month of classes. Midterm difficulties such as homesickness, broken relationships, and illness, which affect academic performance, may come to the attention of an RA before an academic advisor knows of the situation; therefore, strong relationships with RAs benefit academic advisors and students.

On some campuses, residence life staff, as part of their required programming, provide academic advising to first-year students living in a residence hall (Acheson-Beck & Rybski, 2009). These RAs receive the same training as academic advisors and may serve as students' primary advisor throughout the first term or year. Institutions that require first-year students to live on campus may assign a team of individuals consisting of an RA, academic advisor, and faculty member to support first-year students and connect them to the university community (Acheson-Beck & Rybski, 2009). Faculty-in-residence and academic advisors with offices in residence halls also serve as resources for hall staff and the campus community at large (Johnson & Cavins, 1996). While advising on the curricular and cocurricular aspects of students' first year, these advisors form important collaborative relationships and partnerships in which they learn from one another and create a resource network in support of first-year student success.

International student programs and multicultural centers. Large international student populations receive support from offices and programs specifically designed to address their needs. First-year international students experience a complex set of transition issues, including language barriers, cultural differences, and unfamiliar food choices. Students' lack of knowledge about the nature of U.S. higher education compounds any difficulties in adjustment. International students need the same guidance as domestic students and many need more assistance in navigating their first year. Many faculty and primary-role advisors are particularly skilled at working with first-year students from other countries, but those with little training or who feel unprepared for advising diverse students can partner with more experienced advisors and the staff of an international student office (Stürzl-Forrest, 2012).

An international student services or programs office may provide helpful seminars, handbooks that address transition issues, and information on student visas and first-year adjustment issues specific to their students. Advisors can find off-campus support through professional associations such as the Association for International Educators and the American Association of Community Colleges (see chapter 4).

Multicultural centers and offices that serve diverse domestic students also play a role in first-year students' persistence and success (Harding, 2009). As with international students, many first-year transition experiences create challenges for underrepresented students not necessarily experienced by the dominant population of the institution. The campus culture and environment as well as the size and location of the campus (e.g., urban vs. rural) contribute to the substance of advisor–advisee conversations and the level of a student's academic progress. Similar to residence life, some multicultural offices provide academic advising to students. Advising in a diverse student office affords a unique opportunity to understand student experiences and transition issues, and advisors outside these units can establish partnerships to enrich the advising community.

Health and other specialized services. As explained in chapter 1, more first-year students with mental health issues and learning disabilities enroll in college than in the past. Counseling and community mental health centers, disability offices, and other campus health programs prove vital to advisors' support structures. Advisors familiar with these services, resources, and programs may identify struggling students and can refer them for appropriate assistance. Primary-role and faculty advisors may be the first to observe students' actions and behaviors and can offer helpful information or walk students to the proper office (Jordan, 2007).

To broaden a resource network, advisors partner with informal support structures, such as professors and instructors of first-year courses, as well as professionals working in learning, counseling, and testing centers; admissions, financial aid, and the Dean of Students offices; and the LGBTQ program, athletics department, and career services unit. Staff in each of these areas handle different aspects of the first-year student experience, and academic advisors who understand those specific functions can take advantage of that expertise and experience. Advisors who reciprocate and share their work with first-year students also increase the awareness and understanding of advising and the ways it benefits students. Advisors who build a network of contact people and partnerships in each office can feel comfortable calling for assistance and information.

Information and Communication

An obvious but often overlooked benefit for first-year student advisors, accurate information communicated effectively to and from various units, brings together those concerned with first-year students' academic and personal welfare. Outside the college or department, accurate information, whether from a committee, an office, or a colleague, fills in knowledge gaps critical to helping students reach their goals. Inside the unit, regular advising meetings that include faculty and distance advisors offer fundamental space for discussion on policy and practice. Participation in college or institution roundtables keeps advisors apprised of requirement changes or deadlines that can affect first-year students. Internal newsletters, announcements, committee reports from college or department representatives provide other means of critical communication. Much like the technology that encourages timely discussions between advisors and their students, distribution lists, electronic mailing services for an advising community, or a group e-mail sent to everyone in a department ensure that information is shared broadly and accurately.

In addition to open lines of correct and clear communication, scheduled, structured time (e.g., staff meetings or annual gatherings) devoted to sharing advising knowledge turns out to be perhaps most critical for professional development and practice. Of course, information passed through the grapevine may keep advisors in the communication loop, but the information may not be received efficiently or accurately.

Professional Development Programs

Although most new students partake in first-year programming initiatives, many new advisors do not (Givans Voller, 2011). However, administrators can develop an advisor training program by emulating the first-year student program, complete with seminars, activities, and community-building activities that encourage advisors to develop networks and partnerships necessary for their own success. Perhaps most important, professional development should not consist of an isolated, one-time training event only for new advisors. A continuing education model for professional development ensures that new information, policies and procedures, curriculum changes, and other continuously evolving advising-related material remain updated for and communicated to all advisors on a routine basis (Givans Voller, 2011). Indeed, some institutions require annual professional development participation for both new and continuing primary-role and faculty advisors. For faculty and distance advisors, professional development opportunities are critical for informing, connecting, and supporting their practice with students.

Despite variations and shortfalls in professional development opportunities for advisors, quality training programs include components related to first-year students, such as key details on first-year orientation programs, descriptions of learning centers and learning communities, agendas for first-year seminars, information on summer bridge programs, and techniques for working with students deciding on a major. Advisor development maximizes the benefit of information sharing among experts such that capitalizing on an invitation to make a presentation to those in other offices and units promotes an essential aspect of ongoing development.

Welcoming their questions and requests for information about advising completes the communication circle and establishes solid communication pathways. Input from professionals in nonadvising offices and development programs enhances the diversity of training and deepens advisors' knowledge of and appreciation for collaboration. Experts from each institutional area that handles first-year student transition issues can offer perspectives that create a community of knowledge. Such proactive and strategic ways to increase awareness and collaborate with units outside advising need not tax resources or require presenter or attendee overcommitments.

Program managers or advising administrators can identify the training opportunities best suited to the particular unit and additionally and inexpensively support advisors with subscriptions to online journals, webinars, and electronic mail lists. Because advisors grow in their advising expertise through experience, targeted and continual professional development ensures that advisors receive every opportunity to deliver the best advising experience for first-year students (Folsom, 2008). Targeted professional development might include topics for initiating career advising for first-year students, understanding international students, or promoting education abroad opportunities. Professional development can be facilitated through a central advising unit, an advising professional organization, or a series of informal presentations offered in a staff meeting. The end goal is growth and development of advising expertise for all responsible for first-year students.

Inventory of Campus Resources

On most campuses, advisors can access the tools, partnerships, and resources described in this chapter, but they must take the initiative to locate and identify these connections. Of course, the first step involves gaining familiarity with the campus culture and resources (Miller, 2002). A network of advising colleagues can identify or communicate a list of first-year student issues and then brainstorm or acknowledge the offices or programs linked to experts in those issues. Recording the location and contact information of specific areas creates an inventory of institutional websites, relevant campus offices, print resources, and technology support to share with colleagues and advising associations or

AIMING FOR **EXCELLENCE**

The following discussion questions and activities give advisors concrete ideas and strategies for expanding their knowledge and applying the information shared in this chapter to their advising practice:

- What are the most-used technology programs on your campus? Do you know how to access and use them? Is training available to advisors new to the most-used technology?

- Participate in term start-up student activities. Attend parent and student sessions, volunteer to help with student move-in, and attend new student convocation.

- Look across campus to see whether the institution supports first-year students by providing avenues for their success: free tutoring, academic success seminars, first-year social activities, residence hall live-in requirement, first-year common reading, and convocation. Get involved in an existing program or advance plans to initiate one.

- Infuse advisor training with information that specifically addresses first-year student issues. Invite colleagues from other relevant offices to participate and discuss first-year students' transitions, academic preparedness and success, and social and interpersonal development.

- Take notice of advisor attrition on campus. Advisors who burn out or change positions may have failed to develop a strong professional network of colleagues. Upon discovering shortcomings, seek other members in the advising community and reach out to advisors at risk of burnout; look out for one another.

- Read more about advising tools, resources, and partnerships in

  » *Academic Advising Today*: http://www.nacada.ksu.edu/Resources/Academic-Advising-Today.aspx

  » *International Journal of the First Year in Higher Education* (FYHE International Journal): https://fyhejournal.com/

  » *Journal of The First-Year Experience & Students in Transition*: http://sc.edu/fye/journal/

  » NACADA Clearinghouse of Academic Advising Resources: http://www.nacada.ksu.edu/Resources/Clearinghouse/View-Articles/Campus-Collaboration-Index.aspx

  » *NACADA Journal*: http://www.nacadajournal.org/

organizations. Periodically, advisors may wish to attend a technology training together or organize a field trip to (re)acquaint themselves with the location, staff, hours of operation, available information, and services offered to students and support available for advisors (Miller, 2002).

Summary

Despite abundant support for first-year students, some of the useful tools, partnerships, resources, and networks mentioned in this chapter remain underutilized by advisors of first-year students. With a small amount of effort, advisors can seek out the less obvious but excellent, relevant, and effective resources on most campuses and in surrounding communities. A solid knowledge base of available tools and partnerships deepens advisors' awareness of their roles in first-year student success, and when it is coupled with development of strong professional networks, advisors of first-year students can build powerful support structures (Bigger, 2005). Haydon (2004) suggested that "advisors should always be learners as well as teachers" (p. 1). Thus, with investigation and identification, connection and collaboration, advisors can be continuous learners of the resources and tools that support first-year student success.

References

Acheson-Beck, S., & Rybski, J. (2009). *It takes a village: Academic advising at Miami University.* Retrieved from http://www.nacada.ksu.edu/Resources/Clearinghouse/View-Articles/Academic-advising-and-residence-life-collaboration.aspx

Aguilar, S., Lonn, S., & Teasley, S. D. (2014). Perceptions and use of an early warning system during a higher education transition program. In *Proceedings of the Fourth International Conference on Learning Analytics and Knowledge* (pp. 113–117). New York, NY: Association for Computer Machinery. doi: 10.1145/2567574.2567625

Ambrose, G. A., Martin, H. E., & Page, H. R. (2014). Linking advising and e-portfolios for engagement: Design, evolution, assessment, and university-wide implementation. *Peer Review, 16*(1). Retrieved from https://www.aacu.org/peerreview/2014/winter/linking-advising-and-eportfolios-for-engagement

Bigger, J. J. (2005). *Improving the odds for freshman success.* Retrieved from http://www.ksu.edu/Resources/Clearinghouse/View-Articles/Advising-first-year -students.aspx

Bryant, G. (2016, January 28). Unlocking predictive analytics to improve student engagement and retention. *Campus Technology.* Retrieved from https:// campustechnology.com/Articles/2016/01/28/Unlocking-Predictive-Analytics-to-Improve-Student-Engagement-and-Retention.aspx?p=1

Bryant, R., Chagani, A., Endres, J., & Galvin, J. (2006). *Professional growth for advisors: Strategies for building professional advising networks.* Retrieved from http://www.nacada.ksu.edu/Resources/Clearinghouse/View-Articles/ Building-professional-advising-networks.aspx

Folsom, P. (2008). Tools and resources for advisors. In V. N. Gordon, W. R. Habley, & T. J. Grites (Eds.), *Academic advising: A comprehensive handbook* (2nd ed., pp. 323–341). San Francisco, CA: Jossey-Bass.

Folsom, P. (2015). Mastering the art of advising: Getting started. In P. Folsom, F. Yoder, & J. E. Joslin (Eds.), *The new advising guidebook: Mastering the art of academic advising* (2nd ed., pp. 3–35). San Francisco, CA: Jossey-Bass.

Frost, S. H. (1991). *Academic advising for student success: A system of shared responsibility* (ASHE-ERIC Higher Education Report No. 3). Washington, DC: George Washington University School of Education and Human Development.

Gavazzi, S. M. (2012). *The true meaning of convocation* [web log post]. Retrieved from http://www.huffingtonpost.com/dr-stephen-m-gavazzi/the-true-meaning-of-convocation_b_1821893.html

Givans Voller, J. (2011). *Implications of professional development and reward for professional academic advisors.* Retrieved from http://www.nacada.ksu.edu/ Resources/Clearinghouse/View-Articles/Implications-for-professional-development-2011-National-Survey.aspx

Harding, B. (2009). *From bridges to coalitions: Collaborations between academic advising units and offices that support students of color.* Retrieved from http://www.nacada.jsu.edu/Resources/Clearinghouse/View-Articles/ Collaborations-between-academic-advising-units-and-multicultural-offices.aspx

Haydon, L. (2004). *If I were to write a book about academic advising for new advisors.* Retrieved from http://www.nacada.ksu.edu/Resources/Clearinghouse/ View-Articles/Advice-for-new-advisors.aspx

Huebner, C. (2011). *Caring for the caregivers: Strategies to overcome the effects of job burnout.* Retrieved from http://www.nacada.ksu.edu/Resources/ Clearinghouse/View-Articles/Advisor-Burnout.aspx

Johnson, W. G., & Cavins, K. M. (1996). Strategies for enhancing student learning in residence halls. *New Directions for Student Services, 1996*(75), 69–82. Retrieved from http://onlinelibrary.wiley.com/doi/10.1002/ss.v1996:75/ issuetoc

Jordan, P. (2007). Building relational skills: Building effective communication through listening, interviewing, and referring. In P. Folsom (Ed.), *The new advisor guidebook: Mastering the first year of advising and beyond* (Monograph No. 16, pp. 83–91). Manhattan, KS: The National Academic Advising Association. Retrieved from https://www.nacada.ksu.edu/portals/0/Clearinghouse/AdvisingIssues/documents/Jordan-communication-chapter-M6.pdf

King, M. C. (1993). Academic advising: The challenge of the 90s. *NACADA Journal, 13*(1), 6–8. Retrieved from http://www.nacadajournal.org/doi/pdf/10.12930/0271-9517-13.1.6

Lipschultz, W., & Musser, T. (2007). *Instant messaging: Powerful flexibility and presence.* Retrieved from http://www.nacada.ksu.edu/Resources/Clearinghouse/View-Articles/Instant-Messaging.aspx

McCarty, S. (2014, April 10). *Predictive analytics and the higher ed overhaul.* Retrieved from http://evolllution.com/opinions/predictive-analytics-higher-ed-overhaul/

McElwee, R. O. (2013). Teaching and advising first-year students. *Observer, 26*(4). Retrieved from http://www.psychologicalscience.org/index.php/publications/observer/2013/april-13/teaching-and-advising-first-year-students.html

Miller, M. A. (2002). How to thrive, not just survive, as a new advisor. *Academic Advising News, 25*(4). Retrieved from http://www.nacada.ksu.edu/Resources/Clearinghouse/View-Articles/How-to-Thrive--Not-Just-Survive--As-a-New-Advisor.aspx

Multari, R. J. (2004, May 26). *Integrating technology into advisement services. The Mentor.* Retrieved from https://dus.psu.edu/mentor/archives/volume-six/

NACADA: The Global Community for Academic Advising. (2005). *NACADA statement of core values of academic advising.* Retrieved from http://www.nacada.ksu.edu/Resources/Clearinghouse/View-Articles/Core-values-of-academic-advising.aspx

Renzulli, S. J. (2015). Using learning strategies to improve the academic performance of university students on academic probation. *NACADA Journal, 35*(1), 29–41. Retrieved from http://www.nacadajournal.org/doi/pdf/10.12930/NACADA-13-043

Reynolds, M. (2009). *Developing a good working relationship with the registrar's office.* Retrieved from http://www.nacada.ksu.edu/Resources/Clearinghouse/View-Articles/Developing-a-working-relationship-with-the-Registrars-Office.aspx

Steele, G. E. (2014). *Intentional use of technology for academic advising.* Retrieved from http://www.nacada.ksu.edu/Resources/Clearinghouse/View-Articles/Intentional-use-of-technology-for-academic-advising.aspx

Stürzl-Forrest, S. (2012). *Helping first semester international undergraduates taxi to academic success.* Retrieved from http://www.nacada.ksu.edu/Resources/Clearinghouse/View-Articles/Advising-first-year-international-students.aspx#sthash.4p7mUwyL.dpuf

University of Georgia, Office of the Vice President for Instruction. (n.d.). *Academic advising coordinating council.* Retrieved from https://ovpi.uga.edu/faculty-staff-resources/academic-advising-coordinating-council

Yoder, F., & Joslin, J. E. (2015). Advisor growth and development: Building a foundation for mastery. In P. Folsom, F. Yoder, & J. E. Joslin (Eds.), *The new advisor guidebook: Mastering the art of academic advising* (2nd ed., pp. 301–315). San Francisco, CA: Jossey-Bass.

CHAPTER 11

The Assessment Process: Connecting Advising and Learning

Sharon A. Aiken-Wisniewski

Hi Karleton,

Welcome to the U! I am Sharon, your academic advisor for your first year. (My contact information is attached.) As your advisor, I am here to listen to your experiences and questions, provide information on campus resources, and assist you in clarifying your academic goals. As we build our advising relationship, you will learn how to navigate the policies and processes of the campus. Throughout your first year, you will learn how to

- *identify your major through exploration,*

- *declare your major,*

- *monitor your major with a degree audit,*

- *develop a graduation plan to complete your curricular and extracurricular experiences in four years, and*

- *engage with resources that support your academic plan.*

I am excited to be part of your campus experiences. Occasionally, I will check with you to ensure the best advising experience possible for you. In fact, here's a link to a short survey of five questions that I'd like you to complete so I can start understanding your needs: www.welcomefromadvisor.edu/advisingquestionnaire. It is quick, anonymous, and helps the university offer the most beneficial advising possible.

Also, I will be at the President's Welcome on August 22nd at the Academic Advising table and wearing a name badge. Let's meet there if possible. If I don't see you and haven't heard from you beforehand, I will call you to set up an appointment as soon as the semester begins. I want to meet early and often so that we can create a clear path to meeting your college goals.

Enjoy the summer and don't hesitate to contact me as you prepare to enroll at the U.

Best,

Sharon

Transitions are exciting for everyone involved in the experience, whether a first-year student such as Karleton or an academic advisor such as Sharon. As expressed in the e-mail to Karleton, transitions require support, engagement, understanding, and some level of direction to prevent or overcome fear and anxiety. Therefore, when initially developing a relationship with a first-year student, the advisor clarifies the roles of each in the partnership and the way their respective responsibilities contribute to learning. Also, advisors should make clear that the advisee provides feedback on the interaction as a contribution to the assessment plan, which helps planners, practitioners, and administrators understand the impact of advising on student learning, belonging, retention, and completion. The items for feedback inform stakeholders on the areas of satisfaction, need, and learning as well as advising delivery. In addition to identifying learning outcomes and measures of advising contributions to learning, assessment gives administrators a way to evaluate the most effective advising techniques for establishing direction for transitioning students and their advisors and for securing resources for their support.

This chapter offers a focus on ways academic advising affects first-year learning and student success. Advisors of first-year students need to understand the process of learning from the student perspective to ensure effective delivery strategies. In addition to an introductory description of assessment, topics include development of learning outcomes and the academic advising assessment plan, advising strategies that complement learning outcomes, selection of evaluation and measurement tools, and analysis and use of data to facilitate needed change. Based on advisee feedback, the assessment plan provides practitioners with direction for advising students in the most-important first college year. Advisors who understand the assessment process can effect change for their first-year advisees as well as lead others to appreciate the value of assessment for the institution.

Assessment Plan and Process

The assessment plan offers four important measures that contribute to the successful achievement of student goals:

- The findings from an assessment can explain the impact of advising on the first-year student experience. Therefore, the plan should include a focus on ways students learn about tools, policies, and practices that influence academic goal achievement. Some measurement tools ask students to evaluate the quality of the experience or describe the advising interaction.

- The assessment plan communicates metrics on advisee retention and completion. By documenting all interactions with first-year students, advisors provide information for a comparative review of specific advising encounters with completion data to identify actions that advance (or impede) goal attainment and institutional mission.

- The plan provides practitioners information about the student experience. Measurement tools that collect student descriptions of advising communicate specific advising practices that facilitate student success.

- The metrics from a comprehensive assessment plan provide evidence for continuing or infusing new resources into the advising process. (Aiken-Wisniewski et al., 2010)

Comprehensive assessment plans allow advisors and other stakeholders to identify learning outcomes, measure the contributions made to learning, and evaluate advising techniques for effectiveness in helping first-year students transition to college. They enumerate the metrics for determining the best way to support advisor–advisee interactions and the areas in which students benefit (or not) from advising practices. The information for an assessment offers a foundation for dialogue on creating or improving programs and practices.

Advisor and Student Roles

Students share their undergraduate experiences with advisors every day. Their stories detail their perceptions of teaching styles, engagement experiences, activities in the residence hall, and noncampus events. For example, many advising conversations revolve around course exams or grades—assessment measures that students experience continuously. Students and advisors recognize that assessment in the educational process determines the learning of students and may form the basis of important dialogue, such as when exploring the importance of a test in math or political science.

Advisors explain the significance of curricular assessment to students within the context of an academic major or skill set, and they apply these same communication skills when describing the value of advising assessments to stakeholders inside and outside their own units. To establish or refine assessment plans, they immerse themselves in identification of the learning that transpires through advising.

The Advising Cycle

Advisors who understand the principles of assessment appreciate the professional growth that they experience from student feedback garnered from measurement tools. At its most basic level, assessment is created by a cyclical and systematic process of inquiry that emerges through a purposeful plan. In the case of advising, assessment is used to evaluate student knowledge and the ways they learn (Maki, 2002, 2004). Figure 11.1 shows the stages in the assessment process and the ways they connect to explain learning.

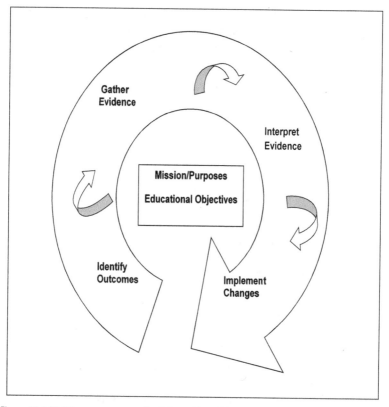

Figure 11.1. Maki's assessment cycle. Adapted from "Developing an Assessment Plan to Learn About Student Learning" by P. L. Maki, 2002, *Academic Librarianship, 28*(1–2), p. 12. Copyright P. L. Maki. Used with permission.

From the beginning, an assessment process needs a champion, someone who understands academic advising and facilitates the process. This facilitator assumes many titles, includes other human resources, such as an assessment committee, and often emerges from the ranks of advising practitioners or administrators. Each institution organizes leadership of assessment based on resources, personnel interest, and organizational culture. In this chapter, this person is referred to as the *assessment coordinator,* but he or she may hold another title on a specific campus. The coordinator facilitates the process and draws upon the advising community to participate throughout all parts of it. Advisors who actively engage as or with the assessment coordinator recognize that the benefits offset the time and planning needed to implement the assessment (Aiken-Wisniewski et al., 2010).

The assessment plan is initiated based on the development of a vision and mission as well as related objectives for unit, program, or campuswide initiatives (Campbell, 2008). When creating assessment-related documents, or the core statements on which they are based, the assessment coordinator seeks involvement from the advising community. After creating the assessment plan, advisors communicate and reinforce foundational messages to students through their advising relationships.

Next, the objectives are translated into specific student learning outcomes (SLOs) that clarify the goals for students to know, do, or value based on the academic advising process (NACADA: The Global Community for Academic Advising [NACADA], 2006). As shown in Figure 11.1, measurement tools are created to collect evidence of met and unmet SLOs.

During the interpretation stage, data collected from various measurement tools are analyzed to verify the learning gained and the points in the advising process where it was demonstrated. Advisors who understand the source of data can better determine the ways they apply to advisees.

In the last step in this cyclical process, the administrators propose changes in programming and delivery based on analysis of data, and the advising coordinator communicates the change, as part of the advising culture, that emanates from the cycle (Aiken-Wisniewski et al., 2010; Campbell, 2008; Maki, 2002, 2004; Robbins & Zarges, 2011). This strategy for continual, dynamic improvement provides metrics for data-informed decision making (see chapter 10), and the advisors who know the many resources that contribute to assessment can exert influence as well as establish and advance SLOs, advising delivery strategies, and measurement tools for first-year students.

Student Learning Outcomes for Advising

A learning outcome defines "the skills and/or knowledge we would like our students to obtain" (Gahagan, Dingfelder, & Pei, 2010, p. 11). It is specific, measurable, and addresses the information, endeavors, and beliefs that students know, do, or value after participating in academic advising (Aiken-Wisniewski et al., 2010; Martin, 2007). The development of SLOs involves three key elements:

the learner, the knowledge the learner is expected to gain, and the ways that knowledge is framed by the advisor to promote comprehension and learning (Aiken-Wisniewski et al., 2010).

First, advising administrators must learn the characteristics of the advisee population. The demographics for first-year students reflect more diversity than those of populations that matriculated in earlier generations (see chapters 1 and 7). By understanding student demographics, these administrators devise advising strategies that focus on information delivery to advance SLOs and engage the student. This focus on the learner allows for selecting and delivering advising with strategies shown useful for the identified learners in similar institutional types (see chapter 2).

Second, led by the assessment coordinator, planners collaborate to craft SLOs that articulate expectations about the knowledge, behaviors, and attitudes that students demonstrate due to advising. The assessment coordinator reviews the strategic plan, mission statement, and other documents to clarify the direction and focus for undergraduates (Campbell, 2008), and advisors identify the way these guiding statements apply to academic advising, especially for first-year students (see chapter 2). As Martin (2007) indicated,

> Learning objectives [outcomes] need to be tailored to fit the needs of the university, college, or departmental environment in which students function. They also must be shaped to fit the academic advising model in use and, of course, they must be tailored to the needs of the students being advised. (para. 10)

Furthermore, the advising coordinator and other stakeholders must know the national initiatives that inform the campus culture and advising (Aiken-Wisniewski et al., 2010; Holzweiss, 2012). The national conversation on undergraduate degree completion driven by the Lumina Foundation, Complete College America, and the U.S. Department of Education are affecting the message that advisors need to communicate (see chapter 1). Also, these groups offer resources and strategies that educators, including advisors, must merge with institutional values, tools, and techniques to enhance a student's chances of degree completion. For example, at the University of Utah (2015), the Plan to Finish initiative is composed of strategies and messages that academic advisors use to help first-year students select a major, organize courses to complete, and create a time line for graduation while considering the appropriate curricular and cocurricular activities to include in the plan (see chapter 8).

Third, the advisors must frame learning experiences specific to academic advising. One theoretical perspective, advising as teaching, explains delivery of academic advising by incorporating pedagogical concepts, such as learning outcomes, to establish the relationship between students and advisors (Hemwall & Trachte, 2003, 2005). Specifically, as an instructor explains the concepts that the students will learn in the upcoming term, advisors articulate expectations for advising as identified through SLOs (see chapters 2, 3, and 8).

Advisors who advocate for the advising-as-teaching model may find the revised version of Bloom's taxonomy useful for constructing SLOs of advising (see, e.g., Iowa State University, Center for Excellence in Teaching and Learning, 2015). They may also appreciate advice from Suskie (2009), who explained the importance of using a strong verb in building an SLO because the statement communicates the acquisition of specific behaviors, skills, processes, or content. In addition to clarifying SLOs, the assessment plan must identify resources for advising delivery, particularly those organized for first-year students.

Measurements of and Reasons for Assessment

The assessment plan for advising first-year students must communicate the type of information necessary so advisors and students can work together on clear, shared goals. The assessment coordinator and planners need to consider ways to measure key campus goals and document the contribution from advising. Some plans are based on feedback that advances student satisfaction and learning or meets specific, articulated need; others are informed by SLOs or the foundations of advising practice. The assessment plan that balances evaluation of student learning and satisfaction as well as guiding theoretical constructs, delivery strategies, and campus goals offers a holistic approach to understanding the entire student experience; it does not focus on one aspect, such as courses or majors. Through this holistic approach, the advising community and other institutional stakeholders discover student learning through advising, the strengths of current practice, and the opportunities for growth. (Aiken-Wisniewski et al., 2010)

As the mission of an educational institution, student learning drives both the curricular decisions and support initiatives disseminated to stakeholders, including students and their families. For example, descriptions of teaching and learning comprise mission statements as well as marketing materials sent to students (see chapter 4). Also, a syllabus states the SLOs and modes of delivery and evaluation (Thurmond & Nutt, 2009) (see chapter 3). The regional accreditation process in the United States provides reviews and informs the choices of SLOs for specific disciplines and support services. Using these markers for student learning, practitioners and administrators need to articulate the contributions of advising to the learning experienced by first-year students. (Aiken-Wisniewski et al., 2010)

The first-year student enters an environment with new policies, processes, and practices to learn and understand. Therefore, advisors must frame and communicate SLOs with material relevant to them. To identify or develop SLOs, advisors must understand the information, behaviors, or experiences students must know, do, or value to achieve their goals. In response, students view advisors as agents of student success. Because it informs an advising-as-teaching approach, Bloom's revised taxonomy serves as a popular tool for developing statements that address factual, conceptual, procedural, and metacognitive knowledge (Aiken-Wisniewski et al., 2010; Gahagan et al., 2010; Iowa State University, Center for Excellence in Teaching and Learning, 2015; NACADA, 2007).

Some examples of SLOs for first-year students follow. The student will

- address the advisor by name,
- schedule an appointment with an academic advisor,
- recognize the resources for tutoring in mathematics,
- identify courses that meet degree requirements for second-term registration,
- estimate a grade in a major course,
- calculate the first-year GPA as a means to ascertain academic status, and
- articulate the value of engaging with an academic advisor.

To demonstrate the intentional process, the statements include an action verb and a clause that explains the objective. Just as new students can be overwhelmed with curricular and cocurricular opportunities during the first year, advisors undertaking first-year learning assessment may also feel overwhelmed. Despite many applicable SLOs, experts recommend that those starting the assessment process select an initial few (i.e., three or four) outcomes and then increase the number each year (Aiken-Wisniewski et al., 2010; Martin, 2007).

Each assessment coordinator, advisor, or administrator writes the final SLOs based on mission and campus expectations. Martin (2007) admonished that advisors not confuse SLOs with advisor or advisee responsibilities. She offered three questions to guide advisors as they create SLOs (Martin, 2007):

- What information should the student learn through academic advising?
- What skills should the student exhibit as a result of academic advising?

- What cognitive or developmental changes should the student demonstrate due to academic advising? (p. 9)

Through the use of these questions, advisors communicate to students the results of active engagement in the advising process.

Advising Delivery

As they collaborate on SLOs and delivery strategies, advisors identify theoretical frameworks to guide the effort. These plans provide structure and direction for advising practice as well as distinguish the purpose of the advisor–student relationship. One theoretical construct—sense of belonging—is associated with persistence and academic success. Strayhorn (2012) defined sense of belonging as "students' perceived social support on campus, a feeling or sensation of connectedness, the experience of mattering or feeling cared about, accepted, respected, valued by, and important to the group" (p. 3). Advising strategies not only facilitate learning but also offer opportunities for students to connect with other members of the campus community to engender a sense of belonging that positively affects student satisfaction, persistence, and goal attainment (Strayhorn, 2012) (see chapters 2, 4, and 7).

In addition to strategies to assess learning and information on the theoretical foundations that guide advising practice, outcomes referenced in the assessment plan include student retention, completion, and time to graduation. Emerging evidence suggests that academic advising exerts a positive influence on these outcomes (Habley, Bloom, & Robbins, 2012; Klepfer & Hull, 2012; Pascarella & Terenzini, 2005). Thus, assessment coordinators and planners must track these metrics for first-year students and pursue advising strategies associated with improvements to confirm the impact of advising on these and other student experiences.

Upon confirmation of the desired outcomes, the assessment coordinator identifies campus partners who offer resources for instituting the advising assessment plan (see chapter 10). For example, the institutional analysis office may offer expertise in understanding the data. At the University of Utah (2008), such a partnership resulted in evidence that students who participated in academic advising during their first term of enrollment were more likely to be retained to the second year, earn a higher GPA, and graduate in less time than those who did not. As a result, the University of Utah implemented a mandatory advising program for all first-year students that includes an individual advising session devoted to specific SLOs. By identifying and ensuring contributions to institutional goals through the assessment process, stakeholders view academic advisors as valuable players on the institutional team (Aiken-Wisniewski et al., 2010).

Finally, some assessment plans incorporate measures of student satisfaction and needs. Metrics on these areas do not constitute the key point of an assessment plan, but collecting information on student perceptions and attitudes may confer advantages to those developing advising activities; that is, they can strive to create experiences that students appreciate or enjoy while learning through advising. Therefore, assessment planners should consider context when creating measures for student self-reports of satisfaction and need. By collecting select student-reported data, advisors learn the ways students view advising, which may also prove significant in certain campus reports. Also, student satisfaction with advising strategies may reinforce or redirect practice for development programming.

In most cases, the advisor serves the dual role of advocating for students and enforcing institutional policy. Because the advisor acts as both supporter and bearer of bad news, the constructs of satisfaction and need reflect complicated constructs that may yield unclear results on a self-report instrument. For example, students who learned from an advisor about the enforcement of a probation policy or the reason admission to a competitive major was denied may express dissatisfaction on the survey because they feel general disappointment or associate anxiousness with the information learned in advising. Because learning outcomes, not student self-reports of satisfaction, remain the focus of the assessment plan, administrators and advisors must direct much of the plan toward assessing advising strategies for advancing student learning.

Advising Strategies That Engage Learners in Content

The assessment coordinator initiates creation of the assessment plan by collecting resources that foster learning in advising practice. Toward this end, The Council for the Advancement of Standards in Higher Education (CAS) "promotes the use of its professional standards for the development, assessment, and improvement of quality student learning, programs, and services" (2015, p. 1) for all functional areas, including academic advising. In addition, CAS articulates student learning and development domains and dimensions useful for developing SLOs (CAS, 2015). Likewise valuable, the NACADA Concept of Academic Advising addresses pedagogy and SLOs (NACADA, 2006). Both CAS standards and the NACADA Concept of Advising identify the SLOs regarding knowledge, skills, and values through ongoing engagement with an academic advisor and through various advising delivery strategies.

To conclude the assessment, the plan outlines an internal review of resources that facilitate student learning. The internal review is based on answers to the following questions:

- What is the advising model? How many advisors are available to meet with students and when are they available? Are peer advisors, graduate assistants, or interns part of the advising resource pool?

- To meet the desired outcome, should individual appointments or group advising be used to foster learning? In these circumstances, how do these delivery strategies complement each other?

- What technology tools are available to facilitate learning through advising? What opportunities can be used to augment in-person advising with technology?

By understanding the availability of human resources and technology, those developing advising strategies can address the needs of first-year students, facilitate learning, and meet institutional objectives (Aiken-Wisniewski et al., 2010).

Technology for Advising and Assessment

The e-mail from Sharon to Karleton demonstrates the value of technology in advising delivery: It briefly introduced Karleton to his advisor, explained learning outcomes for the first year to be addressed through the advising relationship, and identified ways for them to meet in the near future. Karleton knows the learning outcomes before arriving on campus. Even more important, he knows the name of his advisor and how to reach her. Furthermore, through the survey, Sharon learns the best ways to connect with Karleton.

Once those committed to an assessment plan identify SLOs and the advising resources needed to meet them, they consider possible delivery strategies for learning. Individual advising sessions allow advisors to customize the information for the interaction with the student. In a face-to-face meeting, the advisor may introduce a new concept, review a policy, or check for competency on an SLO based entirely on needs of the specific student. For example, Sharon can explore Karleton's knowledge base on the SLOs outlined in the e-mail: major exploration, a degree audit, and resources for success. Sharon will use the information garnered to create a strategy to complete each SLO. The set of SLOs establishes a foundation for the development of the advising relationship and the earliest possible communication of information that students need for success in achieving goals.

The student information system as well as advisor notes and early-alert tools provide key pieces of information that encourage development of a holistic relationship while advisors thread specific concepts through their conversations with advisees (Aiken-Wisniewski et al., 2010). Through these technology tools, advisors like Sharon can review and check for advisee competency in SLOs (see chapter 10). For example, after explaining ways to generate and read a degree audit to Karleton, in future sessions or e-mails, Sharon can inquire to assess if he has achieved competency in generating a degree audit and interpreting the information gleaned from it.

Especially in situations of high student–advisor ratios, group advising offers an efficient way to deliver content relevant to SLOs (Bentley-Gadow & Silverson, 2005). The advisor introduces general information that all students need to know to achieve academic goals such as degree completion. For delivering general advising content applicable to all, unlawful disclosure of private information, such as outlined by the Family Educational Rights and Privacy Act (FERPA), need not concern the facilitator; however, each student in the group must seek individual advising to address issues specific to their educational experience. For example, after attending a group advising session on general education requirements, which apply to and constitute a learning outcome for all students, Karleton sees Sharon in her office for help determining the classes that best fit both the requirements and his educational goals. Because he learns about the requirements in a group advising session, Karleton can explore other areas with Sharon to augment his success, such as resources for personal involvement or potential majors. Participation in group advising allows the advisor to focus on a student's specific questions and concerns best addressed through individual appointments, but in some cases, the advisor will need to invoke proactive advising to encourage attendance in any advising meeting or individual session (Earl, 1987) (see chapters 2, 5, and 6).

Technology offers another means for delivering advising content (Steele, 2014). Communication advances resulting from the Information Age offer students, family members, and student support systems easy access to calendars, policies, class schedules, and academic catalogs. Students check the campus website for FAQs, schedule appointments with an advisor, or review the structured degree plan. Many institutional personnel also employ social media (e.g., Facebook, Twitter, and Instagram) to announce or update an event as well as document it in real time. Because Sharon actively uses Twitter to talk to her advisees, Karleton follows her and like other advisees receives reminders about key deadlines and events, such as the withdrawal deadline and links to procedural instructions and forms. These tools complement the general information heard in group or individual advising sessions, and access to this content through specific tools is intentionally built into SLOs. Furthermore, the technology tools provide data for analytics, offering important information for creating and revising the assessment plan (see chapter 10).

Advisors may find the following three tools the most advantageous to practice: virtual engagement applications, learning management systems (LMSs), and enhanced software for degree audits and early alerts. Traditionally, relationships were forged between an advisor and a student through face-to-face interactions. Today, when an in-person meeting cannot be conducted, persons can still develop relationships online. To increase educational options for those off site, virtual tools include online degrees, and interaction tools connect the advisor and student for synchronous exchanges through cameras, microphones, and screen sharing. While maintaining FERPA compliance, advisors can deliver the same SLOs online as in sessions held in an office.

For example, standardized SLOs are successfully delivered through an LMS, such as CANVAS, D2L, and Blackboard; these tools emerged for recordkeeping of curricular endeavors but now prove useful for tracking cocurricular activities as well. The LMS can also deliver group advising virtually. For example, a workshop on a career inventory, the requirements for a major, or instructions for using the degree audit report can be placed in the LMS for students to access repeatedly and at any time. In addition, the LMS provides data on the students who engaged in the programming, when they accessed it, and the time they used to engage in it. The information from an LMS can be used to create and administer surveys to students so they can rate their advising experience (see chapters 8 and 10).

Enhanced software products include those associated with degree planning and early academic alert. Before the advent of computers, advisors wrote degree audits by hand as a means to update a student on progress or verify graduation. Today, U.S. institutions purchase software to accomplish that task, which allows advisors more time to discuss curricular and extracurricular activities with students. For example, at Arizona State University (2014), the eAdvisor system alerts a student and advisor when a critical course is not on the student's schedule, resulting in an *off-track* status. Using a system like eAdvisor, Sharon would immediately know if Karleton dropped a general education course in math or English during this first term. For Karleton, and other exploratory students (undeclared major), the software tracks requirements in English and math as critical. In addition to acting as a degree audit and planning tool, eAdvisor alerts an advisor to a deviation from a student's graduation plan (Parry, 2012) (see chapter 5).

In addition to facilitating the advising relationship and learning, technology tools provide metrics on student actions, which inform assessment plans. First-year students face a steep learning curve through which they gain familiarity with policies, practices, people, and processes unlike those encountered in high school or employment experiences. The assessment plan clarifies the information the student receives from the advisor based on SLOs, and it helps determine the timing and manner in which information is introduced and reviewed.

Mapping for Advising and Assessment

As part of the assessment plan, mapping communicates a visual representation of the learning process for new students and their advisors. Through mapping, the SLO is paired with the advising strategies that teach concepts, ideas, and skills. The map communicates the timing for student receipt of the information from an academic advisor and the point at which the student should demonstrate competency. The mapping process also identifies delivery strategies, expected patterns for learning, and the appropriate measurement tools. Just as it serves to determine the delivery of advising, the map also indicates when advisors should employ assessment tools, such as a survey, focus group, advising observation, or interview to gather evidence of learning.

Figure 11.2 provides an example of the mapping process. It includes an institutional objective, an SLO, and information on the level of learning and complementary advising strategies for each level of learning. In this case, the map outlines SLOs and learning experiences designed to help students graduate within two or four years, and it also provides examples of strategies proven effective in assessing early learning (e.g., surveys, observations, audits). Sharon uses this map to provide structure for the information that she shares with Karleton during their initial advising interactions, and the map gives further direction on the learning accomplished from the advising relationship during the first year.

Through mapping, the coordinator, planning committee, and advisor contribute to the assessment plan such that the appropriate measurement tools emerge. In general, the map offers guidance for the timing of SLO assessment. At that point, the best measurement tools will determine competency level for the SLO and provide information for creating or revising the assessment plan.

First-year learning outcome	Level of learning	Delivery	Advising strategy	Assessment measure
Student organizes courses from institutional curriculum that complete major and degree.	Introduction	Orientation (in-person & web tools)	Advisor (in-person) explains the concept of curriculum for degree, including degree components using an informational graphic on website. Advisor shows students online campus catalog; introduces key concepts for degree completion by using information on this page; and discusses with student course requirements, course descriptions, faculty bio, and recommended extracurricular activities.	Pre–post survey during orientation term
	Review	First-term advising session (in-person or online)	Advisor (in-person or online) introduces electronic degree planning tool that lists all courses for degree, critical courses to complete degree, and course scheduling patterns by academic term. Advisor engages student in conversation on courses, resources, and extracurricular experiences to date.	Pre–post survey during first term
	Review	First term (e-mail and workshop)	Advisor sends an e-mail to student that explains degree-planning tool and extends invitation to online workshop on creating a degree plan.	Document number invited and those who attend
	Competency	Second-term advising session (in-person or online)	Student presents to advisor a degree plan by term via electronic degree plan tool. Students maps out degree and added electives. Advisor approves plan.	Evaluate a sample of students registering during second term to assess degree completion goals.

Figure 11.2. Example map of student learning outcome: Student accomplishes timely graduation.

Variety of Assessment Tools

Despite all the techniques for gathering feedback from students about academic advising, the most useful involve those that correlate to the learning being evaluated. Furthermore, before the unit engages in creating tools, they need to look at existing data-collection mechanisms. Resources being finite in higher education, the assessment coordinator should inventory information available from campus entities, especially those that include data on first-year students.

Nonadvising units use measurement tools, such as the National Survey of Student Engagement or Community College Survey of Student Engagement, for broad institutional analysis. In addition to measurement tools that provide direct data, some institutional partners can assist by allowing piggyback assessments. For example, if a first-year seminar is concluded with administration of a student survey, the assessment coordinator can ask to add items that measure the extent academic advising SLOs were met in the class. After taking a measurement inventory and establishing partnerships, the assessment coordinator identifies the information needed to develop or enhance the academic advising assessment plan; then the coordinator can turn to a variety of means to address any gaps (Aiken-Wisniewski et al., 2010) (see chapter 10).

The 21st-century consumer is continuously asked to provide feedback on experiences from air travel to car repair to dining. As a result, some people, including students, feel survey fatigue. Therefore, assessment coordinators should look beyond the survey to garner information on the impact of advising on first-year students. When surveys provide the best means to collect the needed information, the assessor should approach campus partners skilled in survey development and administration to ensure that a well-considered and effective instrument is created.

Focus groups and individual interviews provide rich descriptive data on a particular learning experience or advising strategy from a small group of students. Although these data do not quantify the experience, the small-group discussions offer an opportunity for students to describe their experience, such as the ways they learn, so advisors can adapt their delivery of advising (Robbins, 2016). Through this process, students may affirm the value of current advising strategies and communicate opportunities to enhance learning during advising (Kvale, 1996; Morgan, 1993; Rubin & Rubin, 2005).

By data mining from websites, portals, and student information systems, the assessment coordinator can determine whether a student has developed the skills that may lead to accomplishment of a certain goal. For example, many degree audit tools identify the names of those who have generated an audit and list the times the audit has been accessed. If an SLO involves generation of a degree plan by the end of the first year, advisors can access tools within the audit to determine the extent students demonstrate competence in developing their plan.

Observations of advising interactions provide data on student learning and delivery. In this situation, the observer uses a rubric to list the criteria and levels of performance for evaluations. Descriptors of each criterion for a level of performance guide the evaluation. Upon completion, a numeric scale can be positioned on the rubric to quantify, rank, or scale the scores (Brookhart, 2013; Stevens & Levi, 2005). After developing the rubric to assess learning, the coordinator can encourage advisors to participate in peer observations and thereby evaluate content delivery and learn from one another.

Finally, student portfolio projects, now used on some campuses, provide a unique means to assess SLOs. For a portfolio, either specific to or that includes academic advising SLOs, advisees collect artifacts that document their advising relationship(s) at the college (see chapters 8 and 10). For advising, documents may include degree audits, course schedule plans, personal statements, and exceptions-to-policy petition statements. Although each item does not provide evidence of learning, in a collection, they offer insight into the advisee's experience. Therefore, the portfolio creates a tangible documentation for view by academic colleagues and highlights the learning accomplished within academic advising. It provides evidence that advising contributes to intellectual development (Suckarieh, 2010; Wilson & Gerson, 2011).

Interested advisors and administrators find many opportunities to gather data and information that shape the assessment plan. Through multiple measures—evidence coming from two or more assessment tools for each SLO—coordinators build an assessment plan that yields valid and reliable results (Aiken-Wisniewski et al., 2010; Robbins, 2016; Robbins & Zarges, 2011). Once the planners identify three or four SLOs, they collect data. First, the assessment coordinator will determine the source for the data. If existing data are available from a campus partner, the coordinator collaborates to secure it. If the data must be generated in other ways, the coordinator brainstorms with others to identify tools that engage students as active participants in the assessment. Through the process, the coordinator maintains an inventory of measurement tools, their purpose, and administration frequency. Second, once data are gathered, the coordinator makes arrangements for analysis.

AIMING FOR **EXCELLENCE**

The following discussion questions and activities give advisors concrete ideas and strategies for expanding their knowledge and applying the information shared in this chapter to their advising practice:

- Create an advising assessment working group for first-year SLOs and assessment strategies. Assessment takes time, and engaging in a group process will distribute the work among colleagues.

- Organize a focus group of first-year students and ask them, "What should you know, do or value after engaging with academic advisors during their first year?" Bring their responses to their advisors for discussion.

- Participants in the advising unit or campuswide advising program should develop a list of first-year SLOs. Next they should consider a variety of ways to introduce this information to students. Finally, they should collaborate on a map for each SLO to identify delivery strategies for introducing students to each goal as well as determine the time in which students are expected to achieve competency.

- Identify one SLO that could be delivered through the campus LMS. Establish a model in the LMS that details all information relevant to the SLO that students can access at any time. If the LMS has a quiz option, learn to use this function so that students can demonstrate their learning on the SLO. Through these interactive features, generate an assessment to determine the number of students who used the LMS tool to achieve competency for the LMS-delivered SLO.

- Develop ways to communicate to first-year students the advising information, behaviors, and outcomes they should know, do, or value as they engage with their advisor. Be creative and use media relevant to the student population.

- Share with the campus community the fruits of your assessment labor to find new partners focused on student learning and success.

Analysis of the Data

A large collection of data is accumulated during the first year of a student's college experience. For example, Karleton completed an advising survey before enrolling in the institution, and Sharon documented all their interactions with notes in the advising system. Also, Karleton declared a major and established a four-year plan that lists all the courses needed to complete the degree. Finally, accomplishments of SLOs were documented through the campus LMS, which included a competency quiz. Besides listening to Karleton's overall comments on success, Sharon and the advising community documented the learning accomplished during his first year. Because the purposeful assessment plan produces a substantial data record for the first-year student, the assessment coordinator needs to detail the analysis in the plan:

- How will data from each measurement tool be analyzed?

- How much time will this analysis take?

- What campus resources are leveraged for this analysis?

- Who receives the report of the analysis?

- How many data points are needed to create generalizations, meeting criteria for significance, from certain measurement tools?

- How will qualitative data, rich in description, be collected and used to improve the advising practice?

The assessment plan that provides answers to these questions will drive the assessment cycle and provide information that advances the understanding of student learning and the advising experience (Aiken-Wisniewski et al., 2010). A thorough assessment plan, completed with answers to the questions, guarantees effective data analysis and ensures that data can be used to explore, affect, and identify areas for growth and change as well as demonstrate the value that advisors place on students' lived experiences and learning. To benefit fully from the assessment cycle, the advisor must know the information that each evaluation tool communicates about first-year student learning.

A strategy for analysis produces a deeper understanding of the strengths of the advising program and guides future improvements. As a result, the first-year advising program is informed by data collected from students, but to understand the impact of advising on first-year students, advisors must share the analysis results within the institutional community. An e-mail, announcement, presentation to Council of Deans, or social media posting highlights student learning from participation in the assessment process. Furthermore, the impacts of assessment on academic advising inform students that participation in advising yields concrete benefits and that advisors and others at the institution value their lived experience (Aiken-Wisniewski et al., 2010).

Summary

Assessment of academic advising demonstrates student engagement with learning and identifies contributions to the institutional mission of retention, completion, and time to completion. NACADA and the National Resource Center for The First-Year Experience and Students in Transition provide tools that delve into the depths and survey the breadth of student learning based on engagement with an academic advisor.

Sharon welcomed Karleton to campus and introduced college academic advising processes, including SLOs and student feedback tools, to document his first-year advising experiences. Students need this guidance as they join a higher education community. Using assessment data from previous assessment cycles, Sharon and her advising colleagues used a plan that outlined learning important for first-year students. Sharon offered information so Karleton could arrange follow-up in-person sessions where she offered advising tools for learning foundational concepts such as the general education curriculum and the degree audit system. Each encounter allowed for increases in the intensity and scope of learning.

In addition, Sharon received direct feedback from Karleton as well as indirect information taken from other assessment tools, such as those associated with the LMS and survey results. The advising connections made through the LMS and focus groups helped Karleton and Sharon understand the ways to document learning, which also demonstrated that Karleton's experiences were valued and added to the larger database for first-year advising.

As they develop strategies that complement SLOs, advisors need to consider the best way to introduce information to students and engage them in the feedback process. Through a thoughtful introduction to advising, students gain awareness of their role in the relationship and prepare to engage during the first year and later. These initial efforts result in a purposeful assessment cycle for advising first-year students, communicate the relevance of academic advising within the educational process, and positively affect the undergraduate student experience.

References

Aiken-Wisniewski, S., Campbell, S., Nutt, C. Robbins, R., Kirk-Kuwaye, M., & Higa, L. (2010). *Guide to assessment in academic advising* (Monograph No. 23). Manhattan, KS: The National Academic Advising Association.

Arizona State University. (2014). *How does eAdvisor benefit me?* Retrieved from https://eadvisor.asu.edu/

Bentley-Gadow, J. E., & Silverson, K. (2005). *The sequential advising model for group advising: Modifying delivery venues for freshmen and transfer students.* Retrieved from the http://www.nacada.ksu.edu/Resources/Clearinghouse/View-Articles/Group-advising-model.aspx

Brookhart, S. M. (2013). *How to create and use rubrics for formative assessment and grading.* Alexandria, VA: ASCD.

Campbell, S. M. (2008). Vision, mission, goals, and program objectives for academic advising programs. In V. N. Gordon, W. R. Habley, & T. J. Grites (Eds.), *Academic advising: A comprehensive handbook* (2nd ed., pp. 229–241). San Francisco, CA: Jossey-Bass.

Council for the Advancement of Standards in Higher Education. (2015). *Academic advising programs.* Retrieved from http://standards.cas.edu/getpdf.cfm?PDF=E864D2C4-D655-8F74-2E647CDECD29B7D0

Earl, W. R. (1987). Intrusive advising for freshmen. *Academic Advising News, 9*(3). Retrieved from http://www.nacada.ksu.edu/Resources/Clearinghouse/View-Articles/Intrusive-Advising-for-Freshmen.aspx

Gahagan, J., Dingfelder, J., & Pei, K. (2010). *A faculty and staff guide to creating learning outcomes.* Columbia, SC: University of South Carolina, National Resource Center for The First-Year Experience and Students in Transition.

Habley, W. R., Bloom, J. L., & Robbins, S. (2012). *Increasing persistence: Research-based strategies for college student success.* San Francisco, CA: Jossey-Bass.

Hemwall, M. K., & Trachte, K. (2003). Learning at the core: Theory and practice of academic advising in small college and universities. In M. K. Hemwall & K. Trachte (Eds.), *Advising learning: Academic advising from the perspective of small colleges and universities* (Monography No. 8, pp. 5–11). Manhattan, KS: National Academic Advising Association.

Hemwall, M. K., & Trachte, K. (2005). Academic advising as learning: 10 organizing principles. *NACADA Journal, 25*(2), 74–83.

Holzweiss, P. C. (2012). Determining skills and outcomes: What should student leaders know or be able to do? In K. M. Collins & D. M. Roberts (Eds.), *Learning is not a sprint: Assessing and documenting student leader learning in cocurricular involvement* (pp. 43–72). Washington, DC: National Association of Student Affairs Administrators.

Iowa State University, Center for Excellence in Teaching and Learning. (2015). *Revised Bloom's taxonomy.* Retrieved from http://www.celt.iastate.edu/teaching/effective-teaching-practices/revised-blooms-taxonomy

Klepfer, K., & Hull, J. (2012, October). *High school rigor and good advice: Setting up students to succeed.* Alexandria, VA: Center for Public Education, National School Boards Association. Retrieved from ww.centerforpubliceducation.org/Main-Menu/Staffingstudents/High-school-rigor-and-good-advice-Setting-up-students-to-succeed/High-school-rigor-and-good-advice-Setting-up-students-to-succeed-Full-Report.pdf

Kvale, S. (1996). *InterViews: An introduction to qualitative research interviewing.* Thousand Oaks, CA: Sage.

Maki, P. L. (2002). Developing an assessment plan to learn about student learning. *Journal of Academic Librarianship, 28*(1–2), 8–13.

Maki, P. L. (2004). *Assessing for learning: Building a sustainable commitment across the institution.* Sterling, VA: Stylus.

Martin, H. (2007). *Constructing learning objectives for academic advising.* Retrieved from http://www.nacada.ksu.edu/Resources/Clearinghouse/View-Articles/Constructing-student-learning-outcomes.aspx

Morgan, D. L. (1993). *Successful focus groups: Advancing the state of the art.* Newbury Park, CA: Sage.

NACADA: The Global Community for Academic Advising. (2006). *NACADA concept of academic advising.* Retrieved from http://www.nacada.ksu.edu/Resources/Clearinghouse/View-Articles/Concept-of-Academic-Advising-a598.aspx

NACADA: The Global Community for Academic Advising. (2007). *Student learning outcomes: Evidence of the teaching and learning components of academic advising* (Pocket Guide Series PG06). Manhattan, KS: Author.

Parry, M. (2012, July 18). Big data on campus. *New York Times.* Retrieved from http://www.nytimes.com/2012/07/22/education/edlife/colleges-awakening-to-the-opportunities-of-data-mining.html?pagewanted=all&_r=0

Pascarella, E. T., & Terenzini, P. T. (2005). *How college affects students. Volume 2: A third decade of research.* San Francisco, CA: Jossey-Bass.

Robbins, R. (2016). Assessment of academic advising: Overview and student learning outcomes. In T. J. Grites, M. A. Miller, & J. Givans Voller (Eds.), *Beyond foundations: Developing as a master advisor* (pp. 275–288). San Francisco, CA: Jossey-Bass.

Robbins, R., & Zarges, K. M. (2011). *Assessment of academic advising: A summary of the process.* Retrieved from http://www.nacada.ksu.edu/Resources/Clearinghouse/View-Articles/Assessment-of-academic-advising.aspx

Rubin, H. J., & Rubin, I. S. (2005). *Qualitative interviewing: The art of hearing data* (2nd ed.). Thousand Oaks, CA: Sage.

Steele, G. E. (2014). *Intentional use of technology for academic advising.* http://www.nacada.ksu.edu/Resources/Clearinghouse/View-Articles/Intentional-use-of-technology-for-academic-advising.aspx

Stevens, D. D., & Levi, A. J. (2005). *Introduction to rubrics.* Sterling, VA: Stylus.

Strayhorn, T. L. (2012). *College students' sense of belonging: A key to educational success for all students.* New York, NY: Taylor & Francis.

Suckarieh, G. (2010). *Implementing electronic portfolios for learning and assessment.* Retrieved from http://ascpro0.ascweb.org/archives/cd/2010/paper/CEUE199002010.pdf

Suskie, L. (2009). *Assessing student learning: A common sense guide* (2nd ed.). San Francisco, CA: Jossey-Bass.

Thurmond, K., & Nutt, C. (2009). *Academic advising syllabus: Advising as teaching in action* (2nd ed.) (Pocket Guide Series PG09). Manhattan, KS: National Academic Advising Association.

University of Utah. (2008). *University college annual report.* Retrieved from http://ugs.utah.edu/_documents/annual-reports/2007-08/University%20College.pdf

University of Utah. (2015). *Plan to finish.* Retrieved from http://plan2finish.utah.edu/

Wilson, C. A., & Gerson, T. (2011). *Advisee e-folio: Measurable effects on persistence, retention, and graduation rates.* Retrieved from http://www.nacada.ksu.edu/Resources/Clearinghouse/View-Articles/e-folio.aspx.

INDEX

NOTE: Page numbers with italicized *f* indicate figures.

A

Academic Advising Programs CAS Standards and Guidelines (Council for the Advancement of Standards in Higher Education), 20

Academic Advising Today, 194

academic affairs committee, advisors and, 189

academic coaches, first-year persistence and, 75

academic difficulties, proactive advising and, 139–140

academic planning
concept mapping and, 160
developing competence and, 152–153
developing purpose and, 152, 153
electronic portfolios and, 159–160
learning management systems and, 158–159, 161
learning process and, 151–152
learning-centered advising and, 156–158
overview of, 151
self-authorship and, 155–156
summary, 162
technology for support of, 158–160
theories on, 152–156
transition theory and, 153–155

academic recovery
assessing programs for, 110–112
assessing student interests and skills, 118
building student resilience, 113–114
empathy and, 115–116
growth mindset and, 114–115
institutional approaches to, 108–112
intermediate, 109
mandatory, 110
meaningful relationships and, 116
motivational interviewing and, 118
overview of, 107–108
reflection and, 116–117
strategies, noncognitive psychosocial factors and, 113–118
strengths-based advising and, 117
summary, 120
teaching metacognition, 114
theories supporting, 112–113
voluntary, 108–109

academic standing office, advisors and, 189

academic success plan, mandatory academic recovery and, 110

academically underprepared students
advisor relationships with academic standing office and, 189
avoiding prejudging, 129
demographics and issues for, 85–88
environmental scan of support systems for, 136

223

D

D2L, standardized SLOs delivered through, 211

Dahlstrom, E., 159

Danis, E. J., 152

data, for advising unit, 11

data, institutional, special populations and, 142

data mining, assessment and, 214–215

DataPoints, AACC's, 64, 66

deadlines, enrollment process and, 71

Dean of Students office, advisor partnerships with, 191

decision-making, first-year students and, 8

Deferred Action for Childhood Arrivals (DACA) program, 67–68

degree audits
  advising delivery and, 210
  enhanced software for, 211
  student portfolios and, 215

Delaney, J. G., 35

deliver phase, appreciative advising and, 34

demographics, 5–6, 12, 47–48, 204. *See also* diversity

design phase, appreciative advising and, 34

Development, Relief, and Education for Alien Minors (DREAM) Act, 67–68

developmental advising, 31–32, 92, 111

developmental courses. *See* remediation

D/F/withdrawal rates, 95, 97

disabilities, people with
  as first-year students, 6
  increased enrollment by, 9
  military veterans as, 7
  as special population, 128
  visual identification of accessibility and, 136

disability support services, advisors and, 11, 191

disarm phase, appreciative advising and, 34

discomfort, transition to college and, 31

discover phase, appreciative advising and, 34

diversity
  as advisor challenge, 127–128
  institutional variations in, 134
  as opportunity for first-year students, 23
  student learning outcomes for advising and, 204

don't settle phase, appreciative advising and, 34

doubt, imposter syndrome and, 132

Drake, J. K., 35

dream phase, appreciative advising and, 34

dual enrollment students, 7

Duckworth, A. L., 57

Dunlosky, J., 49

Dweck, C.S., 57, 113–114

E

eAdvisor system, Arizona State University, 211

early registration periods, expectations and, 73

early term advising
  connecting students with professors, 51
  contributing to skill development, 48–49
  identifying resources, 49–50
  offering practical encouragement, 50–51

early-warning (early-alert) systems
  advising delivery and, 210
  as advising tool, 11, 182–183
  enhanced software for, 211
  as institutional support, 96–97
  proactive advising and, 94
  using *iPASS*, 71

P

S

ABOUT THE CONTRIBUTORS

The Editors

Jennifer R. Fox is assistant dean for programming and personnel in the University of Notre Dame's First Year of Studies (FYS). She has previously served as the assistant to the dean for Strategic Planning, Outreach and Collegiate Advancement and the director of peer advising. Most of her students are engineering intents, and she has a particular interest in STEM retention as well as women in STEM. In her role as assistant dean, Fox oversees Welcome Weekend programming and supports the dean of FYS on special projects related to office operations and strategic planning. These responsibilities include preparing reports about the performance of the first-year class, the contributions of FYS advisors to national conversations on advising, and the status of various FYS initiatives undertaken in recent years.

Fox is currently the chair of the Advising First-Year Students Interest Group for NACADA: The Global Community for Academic Advising. She is also the co-chair of the University of Notre Dame's FYS National Conference on Advising Highly Talented Undergraduates, which the university hosts every other year on campus. Fox earned her BA in history from Marquette University in 2003 and her MA in higher education from Boston College in 2005.

Holly E. Martin is associate dean for advising and academic programs in the University of Notre Dame's First Year of Studies (FYS). A winner of the University's Dockweiler Award for Excellence in Undergraduate Advising, she specializes in advising theory and practice, engaged learning strategies, and intensive academic advising practices. Martin is active in NACADA: The Global Community for Academic Advising, principally as a publications advisory board member and an editorial advisory review member. She is the past chair of the

NACADA Advising First-Year Students Interest Group. She has also published in NACADA a number of times, including in the Clearinghouse on creating learning outcomes, in *Academic Advising Today* on working with student athletes, and in *Academic Advising Approaches: Strategies That Teach Students to Make the Most of College* (Drake, Jordan, & Miller, 2013) on increasing engagement through midyear student reflections. In addition to advising first-year, first-generation college students, honors students, and student athletes at the university, she is the co-chair of the FYS National Conference on Advising Highly Talented Undergraduates, which the university hosts every other year on campus.

Martin earned her BA in history and literature from St. Olaf College and her MA and PhD in literature from Notre Dame. Her areas of special interest and expertise are American, British, and Irish drama as well as interdisciplinary arts, and she has recently taught classes entitled Global Arts and Identity, Shakespeare: Plays Within Plays, and Shakespeare on Stage and Screen.

The Authors

Sharon A. Aiken-Wisniewski, PhD, is an associate professor–clinical and director of the MEd Student Affairs Program in the Educational Leadership & Policy Department at the University of Utah. Her prior position as assistant vice president for academic affairs at the University of Utah included programming responsibilities for first-year students to promote student persistence, and as associate dean for University College, she facilitated the development of an academic advising curriculum for transitioning students that emerged through an assessment process. She has facilitated presentations at conferences sponsored by NACADA, NASPA, AERA, ASHE, and the National Resource Center for The First-Year Experience and Students in Transition and served as a faculty member for the NACADA Assessment Institute for six years. Her research and publications center on emerging questions from the lived experiences of scholar-practitioners who are actively engaged with students and campus peers.

Karen L. Archambault, EdD, a long-time advocate for student success, currently serves as executive director of enrollment management at Rowan College at Burlington County (New Jersey) where she oversees recruitment, financial aid, and the registrar's office as well as several retention programs for high-risk students. In prior positions, she worked in recruitment, advising programs, and retention as well as new student programs and faculty support. While her experience spans a wide range of functional areas, Archambault's research interests are in transfer student preparation, cultural competency, and in cross-campus efforts that support student success. Archambault received her bachelor's degree from Salisbury University and her master's degrees from Old Dominion University and Trinity Washington University. She completed her doctorate in Educational Leadership at Rowan University.

Joanne Damminger is the assistant vice president for student affairs at the four campuses of Delaware Technical Community College, providing leadership for the student affairs division including academic advising; career, veteran, and disabilities services; student activities; athletics; and recruitment and admissions. She also oversees international education. Damminger's work focuses on creating shared vision and empowering student affairs professionals dedicated to increasing student success. Damminger also teaches in the Masters in Higher Education Program at Rowan University. She is a past president of NACADA and presents nationally and internationally on the topics of effective advising programs and approaches, career advising, ethics in advising, the first-year experience, and assisting students to be intentional learners. Damminger earned her doctorate in Education in Educational Leadership, a master of arts degree in Student Personnel Services, and a bachelor of arts degree in Elementary Education from Rowan University.

Nova Schauss Fergueson has a master of science degree in Counseling and Guidance from California Lutheran University in Thousand Oaks, California. She has more than a decade of experience working with first-year students in academic difficulty and was most recently the student success coordinator in the College of Engineering at Oregon State University. Her interests include resiliency development within an academic advising framework and enhancement of first-year engineering curricula to increase retention of academically underprepared students.

Carita Harrell is currently an advisor and instructor at Arizona State University. Harrell has more than 15 years of experience in higher education. She has served in the areas of advising, student retention, service-learning, counseling psychology, and community involvement through various work and volunteer positions. She has taught undergraduate- and graduate-level education, counseling, leadership, and research courses. Harrell's research efforts focus on student retention, counseling, spirituality, and higher education. Originally from Toledo, Ohio, she completed her bachelor's degree in Psychology from Bowling Green State University and her master's degree in Pastoral Counseling from Ashland Theological Seminary. She graduated with her doctorate in education in Higher and Postsecondary Education at Arizona State University, with her research focusing on student success. A passion for student success has been a core value for supporting her current research in education.

Melissa L. Johnson is the associate director of the University of Florida Honors Program. She holds a PhD in Educational Technology from the same institution, and her dissertation research focused on early adopters of online honors education. In her capacity with Honors, Johnson teaches, advises, coaches, and develops programming for high-potential students. She served as the chair of the NACADA Advising High Achieving Students Commission from 2014 to 2016, is a member of the NACADA Academic Advising Consultant and Speaker Service and an editorial board member for several journals including the *NACADA Journal*. She is also a 2016-2018 board member for the National Collegiate Honors Council. Johnson frequently presents on topics related to honors education, technology, and first-year seminars.

Tim Kirkner is a professor/counselor at Montgomery College in Rockville, Maryland. He has worked in higher education since 1992 and been at the forefront of the most significant advising initiatives at the college for the past decade, including chairing a college-wide advisory group on advising. In recent years, he has also been instrumental in the development of a new comprehensive, college-wide advising structure at Montgomery College. In addition to his counseling work, he coauthored publications for NACADA and the National Resource Center for The First-Year Experience and Students in Transition and has assisted with recommendations for updates to the Council for the Advancement of Standards in Higher Education for academic advising and transfer. He has presented on both the local and national levels on a variety of topics related to advising and career development. Kirkner is a nationally certified counselor and served as the Two-Year Commission chair for NACADA.

Julie Levinson is a nationally certified counselor and professor/counselor at Montgomery College, a community college in Maryland. She has been working in various facets of higher education since 1994 and counseling/advising specifically since 2001. She has co-authored several articles related to the field of advising for NACADA and a National Resource Center for The First-Year Experience and Students in Transition academic advising guide for first-year students. She has presented at numerous conferences on topics related to advising, technology in higher education, and career development. Most recently, she focused efforts primarily on creating a college-wide framework for developmental advising and implementing a student retention system. Levinson received the Outstanding Faculty of the Year award for this and for her work in the areas of counseling, advising, and teaching.

Marsha A. Miller taught and advised underprepared first-year students at Cloud County Community College, where she served as chair of the committee that restructured Cloud's advising program. She also served as the program's director when it received the NACADA advising award and the Noel-Levitz citation for Excellence in Student Retention. Miller has been a member of the NACADA Executive Office staff since 2002 and serves as the assistant director for resources and services assigned to the Center for Excellence and Research in Academic Advising and Student Success. Miller regularly presents at conferences and publishes. She was a co-editor of the 2016 NACADA/Jossey-Bass book *Beyond Foundations: Developing as a Master Advisor* (Grites, Miller, & Givans Voller) and the 2013 book *Academic Advising Approaches: Strategies That Teach Students to Make the Most of College* (Drake, Jordan, & Miller). She has served as managing editor for NACADA-produced books and established the NACADA Clearinghouse of Academic Advising Resources on the web. She is the NACADA director on the Board of the Council for the Advancement of Standards in Higher Education.

Susan Poch is the assistant vice provost for undergraduate education at Washington State University. In this role, she oversees academic advising and the Transfer Clearinghouse and cochairs the Common Reading program. She chairs the Advising Consultant Group, representing college and advising units, and the University Academic Advising Executive Council, which oversees advising across campus. In her career, she has worked as an advisor, director of the Central Advising Unit, and as an advising administrator. Poch has presented at national and regional conferences, twice served on the editorial board for the *NACADA Journal*, and in 2013 received the Outstanding Advising Administrator Award both locally and nationally. She is currently a mentor in the NACADA Emerging Leaders Program.

Melissa Rakes is the dean of student affairs at Delaware Technical Community College, Jack F. Owens Campus. As dean, Rakes supervises all aspects of student affairs for the campus, including the academic advising center that delivers initial academic advising to every incoming student. She also co-chairs the college-wide Academic Advising Committee, which provides strategic direction and continuous improvement for advising across the multicampus institution. Before assuming the position of dean, Rakes worked as an academic counselor and was influential in establishing a new academic advising model at the college. She holds a doctorate in Education from the University of Delaware and received the 2015 NACADA Region 2 Outstanding Advising Award in the advising administrator category.

Maura Reynolds is retired from Hope College in Holland, Michigan, where she served as associate professor of Latin and director of academic advising. At Hope, she directed a faculty-only advising system, taught beginning Latin, and taught in and coordinated Hope's First-Year Seminar Program. She has been a frequent presenter at advising conferences and webinars, written for NACADA publications, served on the faculty of the NACADA Administrators' and Summer Institutes, and is a consultant/program reviewer, keynote speaker, and workshop facilitator.

Leigh S. Shaffer received BA and MA degrees in Psychology from Wichita State University in 1969 and 1971 and a PhD in Social Psychology from The Pennsylvania State University in 1974. He is professor emeritus of Sociology, Department of Anthropology and Sociology, West Chester University. He is now retired and living in Columbia, Missouri. He has served as co-editor of the *NACADA Journal* since 2009. He has authored or co-authored several articles on academic and career advising from a human capital approach.

Ryan Tomasiewicz is the director of the Health Sciences Collegiate Academy at Lake-Sumter State College in Leesburg, Florida. Previously, he was the assistant director for honors in the Division of General Studies at the University of Illinois at Urbana-Champaign. Tomasiewicz holds a doctorate in Education from the University of Illinois Urbana–Champaign, where he researched strengths-based approaches in University 101 courses. His scholarly interests and research agenda examine the integration of strengths-based approaches in higher education. Tomasiewicz has received an Advising Technology Innovation award and is a NACADA research grant recipient. He is active with the NACADA Research Committee for which he served as chair from 2014 to 2016.

Jacqueline Zalewski, PhD, has maintained ongoing research and teaching interests in work, especially changes in jobs and organizations and the growth of precarious employment. She has published on the outsourcing of professional work in information technologies and human resources. Zalewski is currently working on a book manuscript tentatively titled *Chewed Up by Two Masters: Interaction, Work, and Professional Lives with In-house Outsourcing*. She has published with Leigh Shaffer on a series of *NACADA Journal* articles on academic and career advising. Zalewski is also collaboratively conducting research on the jobs, ongoing education, and professional careers of sociology majors from West Chester University with colleague Miguel Ceballos and students in her Sociology of Organizations and Sociology of Work courses. She also collaborated with her graduate school advisor, Lauren Langman, on a book chapter on cyberactivism.